The Sun Danced
at Fatima

D0063981

The Sun Danced at Fatima

NEWLY REVISED AND EXPANDED

Joseph A. Pelletier, A.A.

IMAGE BOOKS
A DIVISION OF DOUBLEDAY & COMPANY, INC.
GARDEN CITY, NEW YORK

Image Book edition published October 1983
by special arrangement with the author

ACKNOWLEDGMENTS

The chapters entitled "The Conversion of Russia and Peace," "Obtaining the Consecration of Russia," and "At Last on May 13, 1982" contain material from chapters 13 and 14 of *Fátima, Hope of the World* and from chapters 1, 3, 4, and 5 of *Exciting Fátima News* and completely new updated material. The chapter entitled "The Secret of Fátima" is taken mainly from Father Alonso's book *The Truth About the Secret of Fátima—La Verdad Sobre el Secreto de Fátima*.

The extracts from *Era uma Senhora Mais Brilhante que o Sol*, third edition, by the Reverend João M. de Marchi, are reprinted by permission of P. J. Kenedy & Sons, who have published an American adaptation of this book entitled *The Crusade of Fátima*.

The extracts from *Vision of Fátima*, first edition, by the Reverend Thomas McGlynn, O.P., are reprinted by permission of Little, Brown & Company.

All photos courtesy of the author unless otherwise specified.

ISBN: 0-385-18965-6
Library of Congress Catalog Card Number: 83-45046

Library of Congress Cataloging in Publication Data

Pelletier, Joseph Albert, 1912–
The sun danced at Fátima.

1. Fátima, Nossa Senhora da. I. Title.
BT660.F3P4   1983   232.91'7'0946945

To
The Immaculate Heart of Mary
special refuge of mankind
in these perilous times

Contents

PART TWO

Preface

BY THE MOST REVEREND
JOHN J. WRIGHT, D.D.

Father Pelletier has worked long and hard to bring together in this book all the known facts concerning the wonders at Fátima. He has also aspired to present these facts in a narrative easily read and readily understood. His readers will be grateful to him for the competence with which he has achieved these objectives in the content and manner of his book.

Great love has inspired Father Pelletier's scholarship in writing his first book. I shall not soon forget the priestly fervor with which he first spoke to me about his plans to revisit Fátima. I could not help feeling that it takes a man of spirited zeal, quite as much as objective scholarship, to tell the story of Fátima as it should be told. The book herewith presented proves the point.

Interest in Fátima is widespread and intense. How could it fail to be both? The issues which center about the Fátima incidents are those which most intimately concern mankind and most urgently stir the human heart: the conditions of salvation or loss, the path to heaven or hell, the prospects of peace or war, the problems of time and eternity; all these alternatives are bound up with the Fátima story. These are the master knots of human fate; interest in all that sheds light on them is natural—and supernatural.

And yet, one puts down most books about Fátima still unsatisfied. Some books are too colored by the author's personal ideas or purely individual devotion. Some devote too much space and time to accounts of the author's efforts personally to unravel the mystery of Fátima. Herein they disappoint one who seeks the truth about Fátima; the reason why they do is easily seen.

Even private revelations, at least when they touch on issues so universal as those involved in the Fátima story, are not permitted by God merely for the edification or consolation of individuals alone. They have their inevitable relation to the good of the Church, of the whole Body of Christ. There is little or nothing purely personal in them. Indeed, the healthy instinct of the Church, and of authentic seers themselves, always suggests that persons privileged to serve as channels of such revelations withdraw into obscurity and even anonymity. Hence the history of Bernadette Soubirous and now of Lúcia dos Santos. It is perhaps symbolic that the very bones of one of the Fátima seers have eluded discovery, as recent attempts to identify them would appear to indicate.

Accordingly, those who write or speak of these mysteries in terms of their personal part in the unraveling of them seem to miss the point. On the other hand, some books on Fátima are too impersonal, too matter of fact. This story must be told with great personal affection and piety. The scientific spirit and the methods of strict theology have their place in the study of these phenomena; the supreme importance of that place is underscored in a recent pronouncement by Monsignor Ottaviani. But we do not merely pardon, we warmly welcome enthusiastic fervor in the telling of a story which an author has taken careful pains to check.

And so his readers will be grateful to Father Pelletier for his studies on the message and meaning of Fátima. They will be grateful, too, for the engaging manner in which he transmits to us the fruits of these studies. He has done mighty work in preparing this book, but he has worked in the spirit that lightens labor. It was the great Augustine, whose name Father Pelletier's religious order bears, who said, "Where there is love, there is no labor; and if there be labor, the labor is loved."

Here is a work on Fátima by a priest who loves his work!

+ John Wright

Bishop of Worcester

Author's Foreword

The author recalls a conversation with a friend who has done much to promote the cause of Fátima. The gist of his remarks was this: it is time that authors get together and discuss the facts concerning Fátima. There is so much diversity in the various books and pamphlets that it has created considerable confusion in people's minds. It is urgent that the facts be sifted, that the wheat be separated from the chaff.

It is hoped that this book will please our friend and others who, like him, have been pained by the variants they have encountered in different works on Fátima. We have attempted to write an authoritative and critical story of the apparitions based on authentic documents and sources, both old and new, a story that is not afraid to differ from the so-called standard works when the facts demand it.

To satisfy the exacting reader and allow him to judge for himself, the author has frequently quoted (in notes placed at the back of the book) important source material that is not generally available. He has even frequently cited the Portuguese text of certain important documents, such as Sister Lúcia's *Memoirs*. Those knowing Latin or the languages derived from it will usually experience little difficulty in grasping the meaning directly from the Portuguese, though translations have also been added.

What are these authentic documents and sources upon which the present story is based?

Two of the most important documents concerning the Fátima apparitions are Sister Lúcia's *Memoirs* and the reports of the two early canonical investigations. The *Memoirs* were written at different moments from 1935 to 1941 at the request of the Bishop of Leiria, in whose diocese Fátima lies, and the canonical interrogations were conducted in 1923 and 1924.

Another valuable document is the report made by the pastor of Fátima, Father Manuel Marquês Ferreira, at the demand of Archbishop João de Lima Vidal, Vicar General of the patriarchate of Lisbon (which then included Fátima in its territory) and its administrator in the absence of the exiled Cardinal Patriarch Mendés Belo. This report was concluded by the pastor in April 1919.

The author visited Fátima in 1948 and in 1950. Both times he led pilgrimages, truly modern pilgrimages that flew the Atlantic in four-motor TWA Constellation planes. But in 1950 he preceded his pilgrims to Portugal by two weeks with the purpose of doing some final research work on Fátima.

One of those two unforgettable weeks was spent at the residence of His Excellency José Alves Correia da Silva, Bishop of Leiria. His Excellency was extremely kind to the author. He not only provided him with two rooms, one in which to sleep and the other in which to do his research work, but also admitted him daily to his table and gave him a place immediately at his right. In this way the author was able to converse freely—in French— with the Bishop, and he learned many interesting things about Fátima from him.

His Excellency also granted the author the privilege of consulting Sister Lúcia's *Memoirs*, the two canonical interrogations, and the pastor's report, in their original handwritten text. The author was told that few have been granted this favor.

Reading Sister Lúcia's *Memoirs* in her own clear handwriting was almost like speaking with her. It was like an interview in which she gave her answers in writing.

Of course, the author had entertained some hope of obtaining a real interview with the Sister. But he was not able to do so. The Archbishop of Coimbra, who has become Sister Lúcia's ecclesiastical superior since she joined the Coimbra Carmel in March 1948, did not grant the desired permission. In all fairness to the

Archbishop it must be admitted that his reasons were quite valid: Sister Lúcia joined the cloistered Carmelites to get away from interviews; His Excellency had refused other authors and felt he could not give to one what he did not give to others.

However, the author has incorporated in his book excellent material gathered by priests who questioned Sister Lúcia before she left the Congregation of Saint Dorothy to which she formerly belonged. He has utilized information obtained by the Reverend H. Jongen, S.M.M., who saw the Sister four times in 1946, and by the Reverend Thomas McGlynn, O.P., who spent a week in her convent of Sardão near O Porto, in 1947.

Other new facts worked into the story were acquired by the author himself in conversations with Francisco's and Jacinta's mother, with Lúcia's sisters, with the Civil Administrator who kidnapped the seers in August 1917, with Canon José Galamba de Oliveira, formerly secretary to the Bishop of Leiria and author of two books on Fátima, and finally with the Bishop of Leiria.

The title of this book was suggested by the expression the Portuguese people used to describe the extraordinary movements of the sun during the great October 13 miracle. In fact, the great liberal daily of Lisbon, *O Século,* carried the following front-page headline on October 15, 1917: *Coisas espantosas! Como o sol bailou ao meio dia em Fátima.* "Bewildering happenings! How the sun danced at midday at Fátima."

Briefly, it can be said that Fátima enjoys the same approval as Lourdes. Two facts especially are worthy of note: the Bishop of Leiria approved the Fátima apparitions in a pastoral letter issued on October 13, 1930; His Holiness Pope Pius XII publicly manifested his belief in these same events in October 1942 by consecrating the world and Russia to the Immaculate Heart of Mary in response to Our Lady's Fátima requests.

The significance of Fátima becomes more obvious each day. It is heaven's answer to the actual world crisis of which Communism is but one manifestation. The message of Fátima is the only answer to this crisis and until we have finally realized this fact we shall continue to live in anguish as one deluded hope of peace succeeds another.

The author wishes to convey his sincere gratitude to those who so considerately aided in typing the manuscript at its various stages of progress, for it underwent several revisions over a span of six years. In particular, a special acknowledgment is due to the Reverend Louis F. Dion, A.A., for his steady encouragement and aid throughout the entire period devoted to the preparation of the text.

Of Fátima in these trying days, as of Our Lady at all times, it can be said: *nunquam satis,* "never enough." May this book, dedicated to the Immaculate Heart of Mary that revealed itself so startlingly at Fátima in an effort to save the world, do its part in leading souls to that loving Heart.

ABOUT THIS 1983 EDITION

The original 1951 edition of *The Sun Danced at Fátima* is being reproduced with only minor changes. Added to that edition is another section drawn substantially from two other books written by the author, *Fátima, Hope of the World,* a sequel to *The Sun Danced at Fátima* now out of print, and *Exciting Fátima News,* and from new material which updates things until the middle of 1983.

JOSEPH A. PELLETIER, A.A.

PART ONE

1

An Angel to Prepare the Way

It is 1915.[1] Lúcia dos Santos,[2] a robust lass of eight from the parish of Fátima and the hamlet of Aljustrel, is tending sheep on Mount Cabeço. With her are three young friends from Casa Velha, Maria Rosa Matias, her sister Teresa, and Maria Justino. The four girls finish their lunch and, faithful to the Marian traditions of the Fátima region, begin to recite the *terço*—the beads, namely, the third part of the rosary.

It is then that they see a strange cloud, whiter than snow, hovering above the trees of the valley lying at their feet. The mysterious object is transparent and has a human form. Neither Lúcia nor her companions can make it out clearly.

When Lúcia's mother, Maria Rosa, finally learns of the affair, she quickly dismisses it with: "Foolish girl's nonsense!" And her daughters, sharing this unbelief, taunt their sister about the vision.

Yet, some time later, Lúcia witnesses the strange phenomenon a second time, at the same place, in the same way. Then again, still later that year, the same thing happens again a third time.

The key to the mystery of the strange cloud is given to Lúcia in 1916, when she is visited three times by an angel who clearly manifests himself to her.

The first apparition occurs in the spring. Lúcia and two of her cousins, Jacinta and Francisco Marto,[3] are tending their family flocks at Chousa Velha, a field east of Mount Cabeço and the property of Lúcia's parents.

In the middle of the morning a very fine mist begins to fall. Seeking a place of shelter among the boulders, the children scamper up the side of Mount Cabeço until they come to a large roofless stone niche, a few feet deep, hidden behind an olive grove belonging to Lúcia's godfather Anastácio.[4] Though they have never entered this niche before, they now go in. Its ragged walls, rising at points to six and seven feet, offer protection from the driving mist. So much, in fact, is it to their liking that later in the morning, when the rain stops and the sun comes out again, they remain there to play. And there too it is that the angel appears to them.

They have taken their lunch and said their beads and are playing pebbles at the niche's entrance when they see him. Only a few minutes have they been playing their game when they hear the rumble of a powerful wind. The olive trees below them sway and creak. As the day has been calm and serene, they are perplexed and look up. Their initial surprise quickly gives way to stupefaction and awe.

There, in the air, at a certain distance from them, shines a most unusual light. Whiter than snow, the light comes moving toward them. Silently it glides through the valley above the tops of the trees that extend below the children toward the east. In the center of this extraordinary light the little shepherds can distinguish the form of a young man. He, too, is whiter than snow and transparent, gleaming most brilliantly, like a crystal of great beauty through which the sun's rays glisten. Lúcia recognizes him as the same mysterious visitor she has seen three times before. As the shining crystalline figure comes nearer and nearer, the little shepherds are able to discern the young man's features and age. He appears like a youth of fourteen or fifteen years. And his beauty surpasses anything they have ever seen.

Though entranced by the haloed visitor's dazzling splendor, the children are frightened and dare not speak. It is he who breaks the silence, as finally he comes to a stop very close to them at the entrance of the niche. His first words are to reassure them:

"Do not fear. I am the Angel of Peace. Pray with me."

Then kneeling, he prostrates himself until his forehead touches the ground. Moved by a supernatural impulse, Lúcia and Jacinta imitate the angel and repeat these words which they hear him pronounce:

"My God, I believe, I adore, I hope, and I love You. I implore Your pardon for those who do not believe, do not adore, do not hope, and do not love You." Three times the angel recites this prayer,[5] after which he rises and says: "Pray that way. The Hearts of Jesus and Mary are attentive[6] to the voice of your supplications."

Then he disappears.

This apparition of the Angel of Peace is so intensely supernatural and gripping that for a long while Lúcia and her little cousins practically lose consciousness of their existence. They remain in the same prostrate position they were in at the time of the angel's departure and Lúcia and Jacinta keep repeating and repeating his prayer until nearly exhausted.

Even if the beautiful youth had not said that he was an angel the children would have had no difficulty in surmising that he came from heaven. For they felt themselves possessed as it were by God during his visit. This presence of God is something undefinable yet unmistakably real. It has penetrated to the very depths of their souls and has absorbed their whole beings. This is so true that they dare not speak even among themselves, and for the remainder of this unforgettable day and the whole of the next they remain under the influence of their ecstatic feeling, which only gradually and slowly disappears.

This experience has been so intimate and so manifestly sacred that none of them ever thinks of revealing it, or even the smallest part of it, to anyone else. It is obviously a favor to be kept for themselves. Of that they are absolutely and instinctively persuaded. Only among themselves do they ever speak of the happy events of that memorable day, and then only with the greatest reserve.

Jacinta, Francisco, and Lúcia are playing quietly by the well at the bottom of the sloping field behind the dos Santos house. It is a blazing hot midsummer's day in that year 1916, one of those scorching days on which they are wont to bring their flock home from the middle of the morning until late in the afternoon in order to protect the sheep from the oppressive midday heat. The hour is that of the siesta, the early part of the afternoon.

Suddenly, without a warning of any kind, the three inseparable playmates find themselves confronted by the Angel of Peace, the angel of Cabeço.

"What are you doing?" he queries. "Pray! Pray a great deal! The Hearts of Jesus and Mary have designs of mercy on you.[7] Offer prayers and sacrifices continually to the Most High."

Lúcia is perplexed by the angel's final request.

"How are we to offer sacrifices?" she promptly asks.

"Make a sacrifice of everything that you can, and offer it to the Lord as an act of reparation for the sins by which He is offended and of supplication for the conversion of sinners.[8] In this way draw peace upon our country. I am its guardian angel, the Angel of Portugal.[9] Above all, accept and bear with submission the suffering that the Lord will send you."

Then, as abruptly as he came, the angel departs.

Again the children are completely gripped and paralyzed, as it were, by the intense overpowering supernaturalness of the apparition.

It is Francisco who, in a way, first makes Lúcia fully conscious of just how absorbed and physically exhausted she is. The lad, for some strange reason, has only seen the angel and has not heard his voice. Indeed, this is true of both apparitions he has witnessed. Later, on that same day of the angel's second visit, toward evening, as the first effects of the apparition begin to wear off and they start to play again, he asks Lúcia what the angel has said. She feels an inexplicable disinclination to speak of the matter and tells her young cousin that he will have to wait until the next day or question his sister. This latter course he follows without further ado. But Jacinta is quite as much under the compelling spell of the supernatural as Lúcia and she too replies: "I will tell you tomorrow morning. Today I just cannot talk." So poor Francisco is obliged to wait.

When, on the morrow, he encounters Lúcia, he immediately questions her: "Did you sleep last night? I was thinking all the time about the angel and about what he might have said to you." It is only then that she tells him everything that the angel has said during the two apparitions.

Francisco finds much of the angel's message beyond his eight years and questions Lúcia: "Who is the Most High?" . . . "What is the meaning of 'The Hearts of Jesus and Mary are attentive to the voice of your supplications'?" Lúcia answers to the best of her ability but does not fully satisfy her cousin and he soon returns to her with further questions. Lúcia's mind, still under the influence of the supernatural, is not at all free. Feeling unable to speak, she asks Francisco to wait for his answer until the following day. Little Jacinta shares Lúcia's sentiments, and when Francisco comes back with still more questions, she raises her voice in protest: "Be careful, these are things that should not be spoken about much!"

The children are at a complete loss to explain their feelings after the visit of the angel. "I don't know what is happening to me," Jacinta says. "I cannot speak, nor play, nor sing, and I haven't the strength to do anything." And Francisco adds: "Neither have I. But what difference does it make? The angel is more than all that. Let's think of him."

And how they love to think of the angel, and to meditate upon his words! Those words of the second apparition! They are as a light illuminating their minds and making them understand Who God is, how much He loves them and wants to be loved, the value of sacrifice and how pleasing it is to Him, and how, because of it, He converts sinners. This is so true that, from that moment, they start to offer to the Lord everything that mortifies them. They make no attempt, however, to invent mortifications or penances. They simply accept the crosses God sends them. The only self-chosen penance they inflict upon themselves is the one the angel has taught them during his first visit, the recitation, in a prostrated position, of that invocation that they have come to love so much: "My God, I believe, I adore, I hope, and I love You. I implore Your pardon for those who do not believe, do not adore, do not hope, and do not love You." Frequently they spend hour after hour with their foreheads to the ground repeating that beautiful prayer and stopping only when their backs are breaking with pain.

On his next and last visit the angel teaches them another prayer that henceforth they usually join to the former and recite along with it. It is much longer than the first but they never experience the slightest difficulty in remembering it for the angel's words always possess an intense and overpowering quality that indelibly impresses everything he says upon their memories.

This third and most extraordinary apparition takes place in the fall of the same year, 1916. It is again the niche of Cabeço which is the scene of this last mystical adventure. The three little shepherds have recited their beads and the prayer that the angel taught them during the first apparition. Then suddenly the heavenly messenger appears before them at the niche. This time the beauty of his youthful countenance absorbs them much less than on his former visits. Indeed, the angel is carrying something that arrests their attention. In his hand is a chalice, and above it he is holding a host. From the host drops of blood fall into the chalice.[10] Leaving chalice and host suspended in the air, the angel prostrates himself on the ground and repeats the following prayer three times:

"Most Holy Trinity, Father, Son, Holy Spirit, I adore You profoundly and offer You the most precious Body, Blood, Soul, and Divinity of Jesus Christ, present in all the tabernacles of the earth, in reparation for the outrages, sacrileges, and indifference by which He Himself is offended. And by the infinite merits of His Most Sacred Heart and those of the Immaculate Heart of Mary,[11] I beg of You the conversion of poor sinners."

Then, rising, he takes the chalice and host again and places the host on Lúcia's tongue.[12] To Jacinta and Francisco he gives to drink of the contents of the chalice. As he distributes the Sacred Species to the trio he says:

"Take and drink the Body and the Blood of Jesus Christ, horribly outraged by ungrateful men. Make reparation for their sins and console your God."

Once again he prostrates himself on the ground and repeats three more times with the children his initial prayer:

"Most Holy Trinity . . ."

His mission on earth then accomplished, the angel disappears. It is the last time the children ever see him.

On this occasion, as on the previous two, Francisco has not been granted the grace of hearing the angel's voice. Also, he continues to have some difficulty in comprehending the full meaning of the things experienced. In fact, he asks his cousin a rather surprising question:

"Lúcia, the angel gave you Holy Communion, but what was it that he gave to me and Jacinta?"

Even little Jacinta is astonished at her brother's lack of understanding and before Lúcia can reply she gives the answer:

"It was the same thing, Holy Communion. Didn't you see that it was the blood that dripped from the host."

His sister's explanation satisfies him fully, for it gives him the clue to a problem that had mystified him considerably.

"Now I understand," he says. "I did feel that God was in me, but I did not know how."

Then he kneels on the ground with his little sister and remains there a long time repeating the latest prayer that the angel has taught them.

The supernatural power that prompts the children to imitate what the angel has done, to prostrate themselves as he has done and repeat the prayers that he has said, is something sweet and compelling. It is so intense that it absorbs and almost completely annihilates them. It practically deprives them of the use of their bodily senses. In the days following the apparition they perform their physical actions as though led and impelled by that same supernatural power. They enjoy peace and happiness, but these sentiments are, so to speak, purely interior. While their souls are almost rapturously concentrated in God, their bodies are subject to a mysterious depressing force that prostrates them. They experience a certain physical apathy, an annihilation in the Divine Presence, and even a difficulty in speaking.[13]

2

A Lady All of Light

This sunshiny Sunday of May 13, 1917, is destined to be a memorable day hereafter in the religious history of Portugal.

Having finished the beads, Lúcia and her two cousins, Jacinta and Francisco, lead their flocks up the northern slope of the Cova da Iria, which is a pasture belonging to Lúcia's father. Once the sheep are grazing peacefully on the summit of the hill the children's thoughts turn spontaneously to play. Jacinta's extreme fondness for games and fun prompts her to speak first.

"What are we going to play today?" she asks.

"Forfeit," suggests Lúcia.

"No," replies the willful Jacinta with a crisp tone of finality.

"Let's play tag then," ventures Francisco.

"No, not that either," retorts Jacinta again. "Let's build a wall around that bush over there. Lúcia and I will fetch the stones and you can make the wall."

Francisco is delighted and affirms his approval. Lúcia, long acquainted with the futility and danger of opposing her young cousin's choice of games, also agrees. Soon a small wall begins to rise around the bush. As the children work with great zest and earnest, little do they realize that exactly eleven years later to the day, three hundred thousand persons will be assembled at the Cova da Iria watching a representative of the Catholic Church bless, on the very spot where they are building today, the cornerstone of one of the largest of all the churches in Portugal.

Suddenly a bright flash of light illuminates the Cova and causes the children to stop their work. They look questioningly at each other.

"What was that, Lúcia?" asks Francisco.

"It must be lightning," she replies. "Yet it is funny that there are no clouds in the sky. Even so, there must be a storm beyond the hills and we had better get our sheep together and leave for home."

Ever responsive to the suggestions and leadership of their older cousin, Jacinta and Francisco indicate their willingness and immediately begin rounding up the sheep. Soon the flock is headed southwestward in the general direction of Aljustrel.

The sheep have been driven about halfway down the northwestern slope of the Cova and near a large holm oak (still standing today) when another bright flash, even more brilliant than the first, lights the sky and surrounding country and causes the three little shepherds to blink their eyes. Their hearts begin to pound rapidly within their heaving breasts and they prod their flock along at an even faster pace.

As they are approaching the center of the great hollow from the right they suddenly come to a complete halt, for there at a distance of about twenty-five yards from the large oak tree they find themselves caught in a glowing light that almost blinds them. Following a common inspiration, the three youngsters raise their heads and look straight ahead. Their little hearts almost stop beating at the sight that greets their eyes.

Just a few feet before them, above the top branches of a sturdy four-foot carrasqueira or holm oak, stands a lovely maiden. She is in the very center of a glowing light that radiates out from herself just far enough to reach and envelop the three of them.

Conscious of the children's fear of a storm and of their desire to rush quickly home, "the Lady"[1] sets about to reassure and detain them, for she has come with a message of vital importance.

"Do not be afraid," she says. "I will not harm you."

Tranquilized as much by the maternal tone of the Lady's voice and the gentleness of her manner as by her words, the children gaze in silent ecstasy and fill their souls with the heavenly beauty that shines before them.

The lovely youthful Lady is clothed in white or, more exactly, in white light. For she is all of light and radiates a light that is clearer and brighter than a cup of crystal filled with purest water and penetrated by the most sparkling rays of the sun. In a word, she is more brilliant than the sun itself and her face is so dazzling that it causes the children to occasionally blink and lower their enraptured eyes.

Perfect in every way, though taller than average height, the Lady is too beautiful, too heavenly to be appropriately described by man-made words. Even less can she be compared with other earthly creatures. The children have never seen any person or picture that so much as approaches their celestial visitor in grace and in charm.

The Lady's countenance with its exquisitely refined features of ineffable loveliness bears a look of maternal sweetness tempered by graveness and seriousness that borders on sadness.[2] Her head and shoulders are slightly inclined toward the children at her feet.

Her graceful hands are joined at the height of her breast in a pious posture of prayer. A precious rosary with white crucifix and white beads that resemble pearls, hangs between the closed palms and over the back of the right hand.

She is dressed in a simple luminous white tunic that has neither collar nor cuffs and that falls to her feet. Though gathered in at the waist, the tunic bears no belt or sash. A mantle—also of white light and finely edged along the sides and bottom with a line of gold that stands out on the background of light as if it were a ray of sunshine more brilliant than the rest—covers her head, shoulders, and body. Yet her forehead and the entire front of her tunic remain fully exposed. Two strips of cord, like two rays of sunlight of a more intense and yellow light than the tunic and mantle, hang in front from the neck. They join and end, slightly above the waist, in a little ball of the same yellow light. And lower down in the center of the tunic at about a foot from its lower edge shines a yellow star.

Her uncovered feet, which like her face and hands are as of flesh-colored light, rest lightly on the tops of the leaves of the sturdy carrasqueira tree.[3]

Such is the Lady of light who stands in the middle of light and is completely surrounded by light. Human words are indeed quite inadequate to describe her. She is all of light. This light is in waves and gives the impression that her garments are undulated. Tunic and mantle appear as different waves of light, one on top of the other. The light assumes various colors, that is, it has different tones of yellow, white, and other colors according to its greater or lesser intensity. And it is by these various intensities or tones of light that the children can distinguish the different parts of the Lady's body and garments, her face and hands, her tunic and mantle.[4]

After a few moments of rapturous contemplation, Lúcia ventures a question.

Donde é vossemecê? "Where are you from?"

Eu sou do céu. "I am from heaven," the Lady graciously replies.

"And what is it that you want of me?" the child continues.

"I have come to ask the three of you to come here for six consecutive months, on the thirteenth day, at this same hour. Then I will tell you who I am and what I want. Afterward I will return here again a seventh time."[5]

Greatly encouraged by the readiness and amiability with which this lovely Lady answers her, Lúcia pursues her questioning.

The Lady says that she comes from heaven. She must have much information concerning that wonderful place.

"Will I go to heaven?" the child expectantly inquires.

"Yes, you will."

"And Jacinta?"

"Yes."

"And Francisco?"

"He too will go, but he must say many beads."[6]

Two girls from Aljustrel have died recently. Though they were both considerably older than Lúcia, she had known them quite well, for they had been in the habit of coming to her home to learn weaving from her sister. Maybe the kind Lady will be so good as to tell her something about these two friends.

"Is Maria das Neves in heaven?" she asks.

"Yes," comes the reply.

"And Amelia?"

"She will be in purgatory until the end of the world."[7]

After answering all of Lúcia's questions, the Lady makes a very important request:

"Are you willing to offer yourselves to God and bear all the suffering He wishes to send you, as an act of reparation for the sins by which He is offended and of supplication for the conversion of sinners?"[8]

Lúcia recognizes in these words a request very similar to the one which the angel made during his second visit last year. Knowing that her two cousins agree perfectly with her on this point, she answers without hesitation:

Sim, queremos! "Yes, we are willing!"

But little does the child realize how much she and her young friends will soon have to endure. Indeed, the future holds such suffering for the youngsters that Our Lady, imitating in this the conduct of her divine Son toward His chosen disciples, announces that trials and tribulations await them and gives them assurance of heavenly assistance.

"Then you will have much to suffer," she continues, "but the grace of God will be your comfort."

As she speaks these words, the Lady opens her hands much after the fashion of the priest at the *Dominus Vobiscum* of the Mass and communicates a very intense light to the little shepherds. The light is like a reflection emanating from her glowing hands. It penetrates the children's breasts and the most intimate recesses of their souls, "making them see themselves in God, Who was that light, more clearly than in the best of mirrors."[9]

Moved by an inner impulse, they throw themselves upon their knees and repeat with great fervor this prayer:

"O Most Holy Trinity, I adore You! My God, my God, I love You in the Most Blessed Sacrament!"

After a few moments the Lady speaks again, making a final request:

"Say the beads each day, to obtain peace for the world and the end of the war."

Her mission for the day now completed, the lovely Lady turns slowly around and rises majestically and serenely, gliding with motionless feet in the direction of the east, where she disappears into the immensity of space. She is surrounded by a vivid light that seems to open a path for her, as it were, among the stars and planets.[10]

The apparition of a Lady from heaven at the Cova da Iria is one act of a great drama, whose prologue had been the various visits by the angel who called himself the Angel of Peace and the

Guardian Angel of Portugal. Other intimately related acts of this same drama are also enacted on this thirteenth of May 1917, in other parts of the world.

As the Lady speaks to the children of Fátima about peace, the Holy Spirit descends with the plenitude of the priesthood upon a man whose name spells peace, and who has chosen for his episcopal coat of arms the dove and olive branch of peace. Yes, on this same Sunday morning of May 13, Eugenio Pacelli, who later as Pope Pius XII will do so much to spread the message of Fátima, is being consecrated Bishop in the Basilica of Saint Peter at Rome.

And on this same spring day the spirit of evil plots against the world with all the ingenuity at his command. For years he has been weaving and warping the mind of the man whom he will use as his chief instrument, the Marxist Nicholas Lenin. The scene for today's masterstroke is Moscow, the nerve center of Russia. The hour has come when the Russian Communists are about to abet the fiendish plans of Satan and his cohort of fallen angels. Lenin has ordered the horsemen, his henchmen, on their way for the first of a series of acts of violence that will eventually end in Communism's triumph in Russia.

Resolutely these madmen ride until they come to the Roman Catholic church where the helpless Maria Alexandrovitch teaches catechism to two hundred children. Through the church door and down the aisle they charge their steeds. Up over the communion rail they go. The altar is the first object of their diabolical fury. Next they turn on the statues along the side aisles and destroy them. Then to make sure that people will understand that this marks the beginning of an all-out struggle against God and religion, these heartless atheists vent their satanic hatred upon the children, charging and killing some of them.

3

The Lady Was So Pretty!

For some time after the heavenly Lady's departure, the children continue to gaze with wistful eyes at the point where she faded into space.

Hardly have the first ecstatic effects of the apparition begun to wear off, when a man comes along and addresses the children.

"Say, you youngsters. Your sheep strayed into that patch of vetches over there," he says, pointing to a plot of land owned by o Senhor José Matias. "I threw some stones at them, but they must have eaten some of the plants."[1]

Immediately the children dash over to the vetches. Already they seem to hear their parents scolding them for having neglected the flock and occasioned annoying damage to a neighbor's garden.

But as they walk through the rows of the garden and examine the plants a look of surprise comes over their faces. Then together, almost in a single voice, they exclaim: "Why, the sheep didn't eat a single vetch!"

No further comment is made, but each of the children now feels more firmly convinced than ever that the Lady whom they have been privileged to see is the Mother of God.[2]

Their minds again at ease, the three little shepherds seek the shade of a friendly oak tree where they may sit and relive the happy moments of the apparition.

After a few minutes of silent contemplation, Francisco speaks to his cousin:

"Lúcia, what did the Lady say when she was talking to you?"

"What is the matter, Francisco," abruptly interrupts Jacinta, "didn't you hear the Lady?" The child's surprise is great, for she heard every word that the celestial Visitor said and supposed that her brother had done likewise.

"No, I didn't," he replies. "But I could hear everything that Lúcia said to her."[3]

"Then I will tell you what she said," Lúcia obligingly declares. "I don't feel the way I did after the apparitions of the angel. I don't mind talking today. The Lady said she was from heaven and that Jacinta and I would go there. When I asked her if you would go too, she said yes, but added that you would have to say many beads."

"O Our Lady! I will say as many beads as you want," the lad exclaims, crossing his hands upon his breast in delight at the thought that he will be admitted to the world of the beautiful Lady for so little.

"The Lady," continues Lúcia, "wants us to return here for six months in a row, on the thirteenth of each month, and at this same hour. Then she will tell us who she is and what she wants. And she said, too, that she will come back here again a seventh time, but she did not say when.

"I asked her if Maria das Neves was in heaven and she answered she was, but she said that Amelia was still in purgatory and that she will remain there until the end of the world.

"Then the Lady asked me if we were willing to offer ourselves to God and were ready to make sacrifices and accept all the suffering that it might please Him to send us, in reparation for the sins by which He is offended, as supplication for the conversion of sinners, and in reparation for the sins committed against the Immaculate Heart of Mary. I said that we were willing. I knew that you and Jacinta would be willing because the angel had already asked us to make sacrifices and to accept the suffering the Lord would send us, in reparation for sins and for the conversion of sinners, and we have been trying hard to do what he asked.

"After that the Lady said: 'Then you will have much to suffer, but the grace of God will be your comfort.' It was at this time that she opened her hands and sent that intense light to the very bottom of our hearts.

"Her last words were: 'Say the beads every day, to obtain peace for the world and the end of the war.'"

As Lúcia ends, she notices that her two cousins are in a pensive mood. Francisco has his arms folded across his chest and is looking blankly at the horizon. Jacinta, with her elbows on her knees and her chin on the knuckles of her hands is staring with the same empty fixedness at the distant blue sky. This does not surprise Lúcia, for she herself feels strongly inclined to reflect upon the great event that has just taken place.

It is with distinct pleasure that she joins her two cousins in their silent meditation. The first thing that strikes her in her solitary musing is the great difference that exists between the way she feels now, after the Lady's visit, and the way she felt after the apparitions of the angel. To be sure, there is the same intimate joy, the same peace and happiness. But instead of the former physical apathy, she now experiences a certain expansive alacrity; instead of that annihilation in the Divine Presence, an exultation of joy; instead of that difficulty in speaking, a certain communicative enthusiasm.

Jacinta and Francisco are also vividly conscious of this remarkable difference. It is the former who finally is the first to break the contemplative silence of the group. The interior pressure of her expansive joy is too great to be contained for long.

Ai, que Senhora tão bonita! "Oh, what a pretty Lady!" she exclaims with great feeling.

"Wasn't she shining brightly," comments Francisco. "The light that came from her was so strong I had to keep lowering my eyes."

A frown of worry gradually furrows Lúcia's brow as she observes the communicative expansiveness of her two friends. She remembers only too well the heavy price she paid when one of the girls who had seen the angel with her two years ago had spoken to her mother about "a headless woman." If she or her little cousins mention this Lady they have just seen they can expect the same mockery and jeering that accompanied the last divulgation. And then there is something within her that tells her clearly that certain things which the Lady has said should not be revealed. She is on the point of cautioning Jacinta and Francisco against speaking of the Lady when the former suddenly exclaims again:

Ai, que Senhora tão bonita! "Oh, what a pretty Lady!"

"I can see," Lúcia declares disappointedly, "that you are going to tell this to somebody."

"Oh, no, I won't tell. Don't worry."

"Well, be sure that you don't."

The remainder of the afternoon flies by in sweet conversation and blissful meditation. It is only as the setting sun sends long shadows across the Cova that the children find the courage to gather their sheep together and leave the hallowed hollow that for ten fleeting minutes has given them a foretaste of the everlasting joys of heaven.

On leaving her two little cousins at their home, Lúcia issues a final warning:

"Remember, not a word to anyone! Not to anyone!"

"We'll remember," they both reply. "We won't say anything to anybody."

4

Jacinta Talks

That evening Lúcia eats supper in silence. Her soul is too filled with the sweetness and beauty of the heavenly Lady to talk of anything but her. And of her nothing must be said. After saying the night prayers and listening to her mother read a chapter of the New Testament, she goes quietly to bed with the precious secret of the day's great event safely locked in her heart.

But with little Jacinta, things are different. She waits impatiently at the left front door of her home for the return of her father and mother, who have gone to the town of Batalha at the foot of the Fátima plateau.

When they finally arrive it is late and dark, but Jacinta is still there at the door to greet them. As soon as she recognizes her mother, the child darts over to her and embraces her with great ardor. The good woman does not know what to make of this unusual welcome, for Jacinta is not at all accustomed to acting this way. But this initial surprise gives way to dismay when she hears the child's excited greeting.

"O Mamma, I saw Our Lady today at the Cova da Iria!"

"I don't believe it. You are a fine saint to be seeing Our Lady," the mother declares ironically.

Instantly the child's face falls. Her mother does not believe her! But how can she doubt her! For she did see a Lady who said she was from heaven. And there is something in her heart that firmly assures her that this lovely Lady is the Blessed Virgin.

"Mamma, please believe!" she pleads, putting in her voice all the earnestness of her childish heart.

Without answering, Olímpia passes through the door.

But Jacinta is close on her heels.

"Mamma," the child declares as soon as they have both entered the house, "I am going to say the rosary with Francisco, because that is what Our Lady asked us to do."

Glad to be rid of the child in whose story she places no belief, the mother lets her go. But her peace is short-lived. No sooner has Jacinta finished saying the rosary with her brother than she returns to the attack.

"Dear Mamma," she says, "we must say the beads every day."

"But that is not the custom. I don't have to say the beads now, do I?" the mother retorts.

"Pray, Mamma, pray," the child insists.[1]

Though Olímpia does not believe her daughter's story, her curiosity is aroused, and later during the supper she questions both Jacinta and Francisco about the apparition in the presence of the family and two relatives who happen to be in the home at the time. But these additional reports do not increase her faith in the event and she continues to attach little importance to it.[2]

There is at least one member of the family who is very seriously impressed by the children's tale and that is the father. Knowing Francisco's and Jacinta's absolute truthfulness and doubting their ability at their tender age to make up such a story, Manuel Pedro feels disposed to believe what they say. Then too, admitting that Our Lady has appeared many times in the course of history and to the distinct advantage of mankind, he can see no reason why Almighty God should not allow her to make another earthly visit. Yes, he definitely feels inclined to accept as true what the children say.[3]

Early next morning as Lúcia is dreaming blissfully of the lovely Lady from heaven under a fig tree in the sloping garden behind the house, she is accosted by Maria dos Anjos, Mary of the Angels, her oldest sister. Mary has just heard of the apparition from a neighbor, who in turn was told of it by a Senhora Marto herself. Pressed by the insistent questions of her sister, Lúcia admits that she did see a beautiful Lady from heaven who asked her and her two cousins to return six months in succession and who promised to tell them later what she wanted.

Francisco arrives on the scene shortly and confirms the terrible report that Jacinta has told everyone at her house of what happened the previous afternoon.

So Jacinta has spoken! It is just as she had feared. Now the unbelievable happiness that has been hers since yesterday and that she had hoped would last forever is seriously assailed. Waves of disappointment and sadness, even of anger, surge through Lúcia's whole being. Then suddenly she is seized with the desire to have it out with her tattletale cousin.

"Francisco," she says, "come and let's see if we can find Jacinta."

When Lúcia and Francisco come around the corner of the dusty, stony path that winds its course through Aljustrel from the dos Santos residence to the Marto home, they see Jacinta leaning upright against the front wall of the house and staring blankly at the ground. As they advance down the slope toward the house they notice that she is frowning deeply and appears fretful. In fact, she is greatly upset and worried, for she has finally come to the realization of what she has done. She has broken her word and opened the door to much trouble.

When Jacinta sees Lúcia and Francisco approaching, she furtively bows her head and lowers her eyes. A quick glance at the reproachful look on her cousin's flushed face has sufficed to tell her that she knows of her disastrous indiscretion.

"Jacinta," Lúcia unceremoniously and tartly exclaims, "what did you have to go and tell for? My sister Maria knows about the Lady, because she just spoke to me about her. Your mother told the women of the village what you told her last night, and now everybody will know. See, you did just what I thought you would! You went and told!"

Jacinta does not dare look at her cousin and listens in silence to her bitter accusation. Her whole attitude is one of profound shame and of deep contrition. When Lúcia has terminated her rebuke, the child speaks, but her voice is hardly audible and big tears start to trickle down her cheeks.

"I had something here inside of me that wouldn't let me keep silent," she declares, placing one of her little hands upon her breast.

"Don't cry anymore now," says Lúcia, touched by Jacinta's grief and sincere regret, "and don't say anything more to anybody about what the Lady told us."

"I have already said it."

"You have said what?" Lúcia inquires anxiously, fearing lest her cousin has revealed the "secret."

"I said that the Lady promised to take us to heaven."

"And right off you went and said that!" Lúcia adds reproachfully, though inwardly relieved that Jacinta has not revealed more.

"Please forgive me, Lúcia, and I won't say anything more to anyone."

5

At the Rectory

Two weeks have passed since the "apparition" and Maria Rosa has just received word that the pastor, Father Ferreira, wants her to come to the rectory with Lúcia.[1] Ashamed though the mother is to have to appear before the parish priest in these circumstances, she is nevertheless glad that he will speak to the child. Maybe he will be more successful in getting her to confess her terrible lie.

Going to the kitchen door that opens on the small fenced yard, she calls her young daughter:

"Lúcia, come here in the kitchen, I have something to tell you."

When the child has taken a stool near the open fireplace the mother begins:

"Lúcia, tomorrow I am going to take you to the rectory to see o Senhor Prior.[2] When you reach there I want you to get down on your knees and confess your lie. And you will ask forgiveness and will perform the penance he imposes."

The next morning mother and daughter leave home early, for Maria Rosa wants Lúcia to hear Mass before seeing the pastor.

Poor Lúcia! How her heart thumps as she closes the door of the house. In about an hour she will be face to face with the pastor. For, kind as she has always known him to be, she is terrified at the thought that this is no ordinary visit she is making. Silently she follows her mother along the dirty, rough road. As the couple passes by the Marto dwelling, Lúcia suddenly darts away from her mother and into the house for a word with Jacinta. She feels the need of unloading her heart and confiding in her dear cousin even if only for a fleeting moment. She finds Jacinta in bed. Rapidly, for she dares not keep her mother waiting, she describes her plight and begs the aid of the child's prayer. Then, dashing out of the house, she runs and overtakes her mother, who has continued alone along the road. She is careful to stay a slight distance behind her in the hope that she may avoid another of those frequent and tiresome tongue-lashings. Her caution, however, is of no avail. They have proceeded but a short distance from the Marto residence when Maria Rosa starts off on her usual tirade against lying. Finally, as they are approaching the church, Lúcia gets in a word:

"But, dear Mother, how can I say that I did not see the Lady, when I did see her?"

Strangely, Maria Rosa does not answer. The truth is, she does not know what to answer and so prefers to keep her peace.

Though Lúcia's heart is filled with deathly fear and apprehension all during the Mass, she is sufficiently master of herself to remember the Lady's request and to offer her suffering to God in reparation for sins and for the conversion of sinners.

The Mass is over now, much too quickly. Lúcia would have liked it to last forever. Her pulse racing madly, she follows her mother out of the church. Together they cross the dusty square and advance toward the parish house that lies to the right. As they are mounting the stairs that lead to the veranda, Maria Rosa turns abruptly on Lúcia.

"Don't torment me any longer," she says impatiently. "Tell o Senhor Prior now that you have lied so that on Sunday in church he may say that it was a lie and in this way put an end to the whole affair. Do you think this can keep on, all these people running to the Cova da Iria to pray in front of a carrasqueira tree?"

Maria Rosa has now reached the veranda. She knocks on the door and is admitted into the rectory by the pastor's sister. As the priest is still in the church making his thanksgiving, Maria Rosa and Lúcia are given a bench and asked to wait.

Advised by his sister that the dos Santos are awaiting him, the Reverend Manuel Marquês Ferreira makes a last hurried appraisal of the situation before leaving the church. He has been anxious for this visit, since he feels that it is his duty to get to the bottom of this story of an apparition. The various reports that have come to his ears have not been identical, but he has heard enough of them to be able to form a fairly clear idea of what the children claim has taken place. Yes, "what the children *claim* has taken place," for personally he is far from conceding that their story is true. He is frankly perplexed and has no clear-cut opinion concerning the reality of the so-called apparition.

His uncertainty is accompanied by serious anxiety and embarrassment. Everyone wants to know what he, the official religious leader of the locality, thinks about the affair. How he wishes that he could make up his own mind! Then he would be delivered of those atrocious doubts that persistently torture his soul. Yes, then he would at least enjoy interior peace, a thing which has been sadly lacking since he first heard of the so-called apparitions at the Cova.

Once again, for at least the hundredth time, he reviews in his mind what he considers the five possible explanations of the Cova affair.

It may be a true apparition. In reality, Our Lady may be honoring Portugal with a visit as she did France at Lourdes in 1858. In that case, what a blessing this would be for his parish and for his country! A thrill of pure joy runs through his massive frame as he considers the possibility of the vision being authentic. But this happiness is short-lived, for deep in his heart he considers it most highly improbable that Our Lady actually appeared at the Cova da Iria.

If the apparition is not true, which would seem to be the case, there still remain at least four alternatives. It may simply be a lie, a story invented by the children in order to give themselves importance. This supposition he quickly rejects, for, though he has been at Fátima but four years, he knows the three children involved too well to believe them capable of such a falsehood.

It could possibly be a machination of the parents devised

through a motive of vainglory or for reasons of financial exploitation. What an honor for a family to have a seer! And what possibilities of pecuniary return if such an affair were properly handled! But again, the reputation of both the Marto and dos Santos families, notwithstanding Antônio dos Santos' propensity for wine, obliges him to disregard any such possibility. Also, it is common knowledge that a Senhora Maria Rosa vehemently declares she does not believe in the Lady and continually persecutes her daughter, whom she accuses of lying.

Hallucination is another possibility. The Lady may be a fiction of childish and pathological imaginations. The supposed seers may be the sincere victims of their own sickly minds, which are unable to distinguish between their subjective creations and reality. Yet these children come from families free from the taint of any mental abnormality, and they themselves have never been known to manifest any sign of mental trouble. Nor do they seem to have any tendency or disposition to the same. They are strong and healthy, and they spend their days out in the open air and sunshine. There seems to be, then, no reason for admitting this supposition.

It is the final possibility which has so tormented the pious and zealous pastor. The affair may be the result of diabolical intervention. He shudders every time he considers this possibility. God preserve these dear children, their families, and the parish from such a frightful calamity! Why, oh why, does this, of all the possible explanations, have to seem the most probable to him? He detests and abhors the very thought of it. But ponder as long and as often as he may, in the final weighing of each hypothesis, this one always tips the scale.

"O Most Holy Virgin," he murmurs from the very depths of his priestly soul, "spare these good children and my good people from such a horrible fate! But, if this is the work of the devil, obtain for me the light I need that I may detect and expose the father of lies and deception."

Sighing heavily, he rises from his prie-dieu, genuflects, and casts a last imploring glance at the tabernacle. Then gravely, with the air of a man deeply preoccupied, he departs from the church and goes to the rectory.

As the door opens and Father Ferreira's heavy-set figure fills the frame of the door, Lúcia's heart jumps. The man possesses a powerful physique—big, broad shoulders and large square face crowned with bushy black hair. But there is nothing harsh or forbidding in his appearance. To the contrary, he has a gentle air about him and seems almost timid, and this morning a particularly kind smile lights his face as he greets the two visitors. Lúcia immediately feels more at ease. With a courteous gesture, the priest invites her and her mother to enter his office. Offering a bench to a Senhora Maria Rosa and seating himself at his desk he calls Lúcia to his side. Noticing that the child is nervous and embarrassed, he deliberately questions her with great kindness and amiability. Accustomed by now to severe and harsh treatment, Lúcia is struck by the priest's extreme graciousness. The interrogation proceeds for some time in an atmosphere of both seriousness and delicate kindness. Question after question is leveled at the child. Many are captious and adroitly conceived to trap Lúcia should she be lying. But she replies with utter candor, and there is not the slightest contradiction nor disparity in any of her statements. The pastor does not find her very communicative, but at least he must admit that she is not deliberately lying.

This, however, is a point on which Maria Rosa still differs in opinion. Seeing that the pastor appears quite well impressed with Lúcia, she voices a protest.

"O Senhor Prior," she exclaims, "what the child says is not true. It is all a lie. I have tried to get her to admit it, but my efforts have been in vain."

Then addressing her daughter directly, she continues:

"Now, Lúcia, admit to the pastor that this is all a lie."

"But I can't say that it is a lie if it isn't," is the child's candid reply.

"See how obstinate she is, o Senhor Prior. I have menaced her with all kinds of things if she continues to lie and say that she saw Our Lady, but I get absolutely nowhere with her."

"Come, come, my good woman," says the pastor, trying to calm the woman, who has become agitated. "If what Lúcia has said is true, it is a great honor for her and for her family."

"Ah, yes, if it is true," quickly snaps a Senhora Maria Rosa. "But suppose that it is a lie, suppose that it is a lie?"

"Well, until it is proved to be a lie, I want you to treat your daughter as you were accustomed to doing before all this occurred."

And with this the pastor dismisses the mother and her child.

6

A Heart Pierced with Thorns

Lúcia, flanked by Jacinta and Francisco, advances up the Cova toward the carrasqueira tree of the May apparition. When about ten feet from the tree she stops and scans the horizon in the direction of the east, which is that of the town of Fátima. It must be approaching noon and it is quite possible that the Lady is on her way.

But the child is interrupted in her silent gazing by a pious and ailing woman from nearby Moita, Maria Carreira. Devoutedly interested in anything that concerns the Blessed Virgin and having put herself to much trouble to come to the Cova this morning, the sickly woman wants to be fully prepared for the apparition when it takes place.

"My child," she inquires, "which is the carrasqueira tree where Our Lady appeared?"

"See, this is where she stood," Lúcia obligingly replies, advancing as she speaks and placing her hand over the top of the straight leafy branches of the vigorous and stubby tree of the apparition.

Then she raises her head again and scrutinizes the sky with expectant eyes. And once more she lowers them without having seen the ardently desired Lady from heaven. It cannot be as near noon as she had suspected, so she motions to her two young cousins and together they go to sit and wait at the foot of a large shady holm oak which stands at fifty paces from the tree of the apparition.

The visitors, who total about fifty in number, have come from distant towns and villages. Not knowing how much longer they may have to wait before the heavenly Lady arrives, they open the food baskets that they have taken along with them. Some offer to share their frugal fare with the seers. But the most each will accept is an orange.

Other children who are present start to eat and play and it is not long before the little seers have joined them. Lúcia, however, soon loses her taste for games. She becomes pensive and finally asks Jacinta to stop playing, for she has a presentiment that the Lady is about to appear.

A girl from Boleiros has a prayer book with her and begins to read aloud from it.

It is quite close to noon now and the midday June sun is very hot. The ailing Maria Carreira's strength is waning and she begins to feel very weak. She fears that she is at the end of her endurance.

"Lúcia," she inquires anxiously, "will Our Lady be much longer in coming?"

"No, Senhora," the child replies assuringly, "she will not be long in coming."

And once again she studies the sky for some sign of the heavenly Visitor.

As the Lady is still not visible, the children and people recite the beads together while waiting. When that is finished, the girl from Boleiros wants to start the recitation of the Litany, but Lúcia stops her.

"There is not time for that now," she cries.

Then rising quickly to her feet and arranging her shawl and white kerchief, she exclaims excitedly:

"Jacinta, there comes Our Lady now! The flash of light just came!"

Immediately the three seers run to the little carrasqueira tree. They are promptly followed by the breathless bystanders. When the youngsters stop and kneel at a few feet from the tree the people fall to their knees also.

Once again the happy children find themselves carried, as it were, into another world. The Lady that they contemplate is exactly as she was on her first visit. She stands on the top branches of the evergreen oak tree and is as beautiful and brilliant as on the former occasion.

The children spend the first few moments in silent, ecstatic rapture.

Then Lúcia, looking intently at a spot above the carrasqueira tree and with her hands folded as though praying, speaks to the Lady.

O *que me quer vossemecê?* "What do you want of me?" she inquires.

Hearing Lúcia speak, Maria Carreira strains her ears for a reply. She cannot distinguish any words but she does hear something that sounds like a very faint voice or the buzzing of a bee. Others, too, detect the same sound.

The spectators cannot understand what the Lady says, nor can they see her. But, as they scrutinize the expression on the children's faces it becomes manifest to them that these fortunate youngsters are contemplating something very extraordinary and very delightful. They are clearly absorbed by the vision, though they also seem conscious of what is going on about them.

When Lúcia questions the apparition about the purpose of her coming, Francisco hears every word she says. Expectantly he leans forward for the Lady's reply. The answer comes forth in measured terms but, as in May, he alone of the trio is denied the joy of hearing it.

"I want you to come here on the thirteenth of the coming month, and I want you to recite the beads[1] every day,"[2] the heavenly Visitor says.

"I desire," she continues in the same pleasing tone, "that you learn[3] to read. Later I will tell you what I want."

Lúcia remembers a petition she has been asked to transmit to the apparition.

"There is a cripple who has asked that you cure him," she says.

"Tell him that if he converts himself he will be cured within a year."

Enheartened by this first favorable reply, Lúcia now attempts a request for herself and her little friends.

"I would like to ask you to take us to heaven," she pleads, her heartbeat quickening as she awaits the reply.

"Yes," comes the answer. "I will take Jacinta and Francisco

within a short while, but you are to remain here on earth for some time longer.[4] Jesus wants to use you to make me known and loved. He wants to establish in the world the devotion to my Immaculate Heart. To those who embrace it, I promise salvation. These souls will be loved by God like flowers placed by me to adorn His throne."[5]

"You are to remain here for some time longer." These words plunge like a dagger into Lúcia's young and affectionate heart. Can it be that she has rightly understood?

"I am to remain here alone?" she inquires.

"No, my daughter," the apparition answers with reassuring tenderness. "Does this cause you to suffer much? Don't be discouraged. I will never abandon you. My Immaculate Heart will be your refuge and the way that will lead you to God."

As the Lady pronounces these last words, she opens her hands as she did on the previous visit and for the second time transmits to the seers the reflection of the immense light that envelops her. They see themselves in this light as though submerged in God. Jacinta and Francisco seem to be in that part of the light which rises up toward heaven, and Lúcia in that which spreads itself over the earth.

Their eyes ever feasting on the Lady, the children notice that she holds out the rosary on her opened and slightly raised right hand, as though entreating them to take it and grasp it to their hearts. Then their gaze is attracted to a heart which is vertically encircled by large thorns that pierce it on all sides. The thorns alone, of the entire apparition, are not made of light. They look burnt-out, brown, and natural in quality.[6] The heart stands out from the body at the left side of the Lady's breast. It is several inches above the left hand, which is held close to the body at the waist with the open palm and fingers pointing downward.[7]

Their minds interiorly enlightened by divine grace, the children understand that they are contemplating the Immaculate Heart of Mary outraged by the sins of humanity and that this Heart is seeking reparation. The beams of light that stream out from the Lady's graceful hands seem to pour into their souls a special knowledge and love of the Immaculate Heart of their heavenly Visitor, in the same way that in May the rays which emanated from her hands had infused into their minds and hearts an un-

usual knowledge and love of God and of the mystery of the
Blessed Trinity. Kneeling there, bathed in this light, they feel as
though their little breasts will burst, so great is the love that wells
up within them for the Immaculate Heart of Mary.

And it is with utmost regret that they now see the lovely Lady
with the sorrowful Heart suddenly rise and glide in a blazing trail
of light toward the east.

Getting up from her knees very quickly, Lúcia raises her arm in
the direction of the departing apparition and cries:

"Look! If you want to see her, there she goes! There she goes!"

Excited by the child's cry, the spectators strain their eyes expectantly in the hope of catching at least a fleeting glimpse of the
Lady. But their efforts are in vain. However, some of them hear
an explosion, like that of underground thunder, coming from the
tree of the apparition. To Maria Carreira this noise seems more
like the sound of a rocket taking off. She and others observe a
small light cloud, like smoke, rise from the tree of the apparition.
It ascends very high and very far in the direction toward which
Lúcia points, until it finally disappears from sight.[8]

The three children gaze longingly at the Lady as she rides majestically through the sky. Finally Lúcia calls out again:

"There! Now you can't see her anymore. Now she has entered
heaven. Now the doors are closed!"

And, indeed, the Lady has once again faded away into the invisible recesses of her celestial abode.

Sure now that the apparition has ended, the people close in
quickly on the three little shepherds. In fact, several people seem
more concerned about the tree of the apparition than the seers
themselves. Foremost among these is the sickly Maria Carreira,
who for the moment is so surprised that she has forgotten her
weakened condition. The more closely does she scrutinize the top
branches of the stubby little tree, the greater does her astonishment become. For she observes that the top center shoots, vigorous and very erect before the apparition, are now bent toward the
east, as though the Lady's clothes had tilted them in that direction.[9]

It is not long before some of the spectators begin to break off
twigs and remove leaves from the top of the tree of the appari-

tion. Noticing this, Lúcia protests and asks the people to respect the part of the tree where the Lady rested her feet and to confine their souvenir-collecting to the lower branches.

Naturally curious to know what has taken place during the ten minutes of motionless gazing, the people begin plaguing the children with questions.

"Was it really Our Lady? What did she look like? What did she wear? What did she say?"

The seers' answers, given mostly by Lúcia, are brief and carefully worded. "Our Lady said to recite the beads. She told us to return here on the thirteenth day of next month. She wants us to learn to read."

Not a word do the children whisper of the vision of the Immaculate Heart and all that the Lady said about it. Nor do they mention the predictions made concerning their future. Indeed, though the apparition did not explicitly request that they keep this a secret, they experience an unmistakable inner conviction that such is God's wish.

When some of the more inquisitive spectators press them and inquire if during all the time she spoke the Lady did not have more than that to say, they evasively reply: "Yes, but it is a secret."

Finally, the people say the Litany and depart for Fátima singing and reciting the beads with the children along the way.

Later that afternoon, when the three happy little shepherds finally find themselves alone under the trees near the well in Lúcia's garden, Francisco, who has been waiting impatiently for this moment, eagerly bursts into questions.

"Lúcia," he asks, "what did the Lady say? Did she mention me?"

After Lúcia has given a detailed account of the Lady's every word, Francisco becomes very pensive and remains silent for some time. Then looking up at his cousin, he puts a question to her that explains his perplexed look:

"Why did Our Lady with a heart over her hand spread that very great light, which is God,[10] over the earth? You, Lúcia, were with Our Lady in the light that went down to earth, while Jacinta and I were in the light that went up to heaven."

"That," replies the cousin, "is because you and Jacinta will soon go to heaven, while I will remain on earth with the Immaculate Heart of Mary for some time longer."

"How many years will you stay here?"

"I don't know exactly. But quite a few anyway."

"Was it Our Lady who told you so?"

"Yes. I saw it in that light which she put in our hearts."[11]

"Yes, that's right," adds Jacinta. "I saw that too."

Silence now falls over the trio as they ponder in their hearts the full meaning of the momentous message that the Lady from heaven has delivered this day. Francisco and Jacinta, soon to leave this world for the heavenly abode of the lovely Lady; Lúcia, to remain alone on earth for some years because Jesus has a mission for her, that of spreading knowledge and love of the Immaculate Heart of Mary throughout the world.

7

A Last-Minute Change of Mind

The spectators present at the June apparition have not been idle. They have told the story of the sensational happenings of that day to their friends and acquaintances. As a result, an ever-increasing number of people now believe in the children's story of a lovely Lady from heaven.

The press, always so eager for the sensational, has seized upon the Cova events. Many of the newspapers are anticlerical, and though they have no intention of promoting the cause of religion and do not actually write their articles in a way that begets respect and belief, they do, by the simple fact that they mention the apparitions, spread their news far and wide.

This ever-widening publicity explains why, on this afternoon of July 12, people can be seen coming into Fátima and Aljustrel in considerable numbers. From the nearby towns and villages and from distant places, pious believers, curious unbelievers, and inquiring skeptics are arriving at this land of wonders. They prefer to be a day ahead than an hour late.

So the Cova is a very busy place on this eve of the Lady's third rendezvous. Once there, newcomers experience little difficulty in finding the exact spot of the Lady's manifestations. For on arriving, their attention is quickly drawn toward the center of the immense natural amphitheater by the presence of persons praying near two rustic monuments.

Both of these simple monuments owe their existence to the

Carreira family from Moita. The first, which is visible even above
the throng crowded in about it, is a wooden arch. It stands immediately in front of the carrasqueira of the apparitions. Simple as
the faith that inspired it, it consists of two roughly hewn twelve-
foot poles driven into the ground at a distance eight feet apart
and joined on top by a somewhat smaller piece of wood. A broad
flat board runs from pole to pole at a height of about six feet
above the ground and serves to strengthen this none-too-solid
structure. About halfway between this middle board and the
ground are two smaller movable horizontal poles that serve as a
fence to keep the people away from the tree of the apparitions.
Two small supports placed opposite each other about midway on
each vertical post and extending down to the ground at an angle
give the arch a fair degree of solidity. The top horizontal connect-
ing beam is surmounted by a peculiar sort of wooden cross. Beneath this same bar, and some twelve inches inside each vertical
pole, hang two lanterns that burn night and day in honor of the
Lady from heaven.

The second monument, even simpler than the first, consists of a
rectangular wall of dry stones two feet high built around the little
evergreen oak of the apparitions. In the center of the front part of
the wall, which touches both vertical posts of the rustic arch, is a
small opening permitting direct access to the tree. The lower movable poles of the arch serve as a fence to close this entrance.

Friday, July 13, 1917, turns out to be a splendid summer day.
But the bright clear rays of the sun fail to pierce the heavy black
cloud that envelops Lúcia's heart. She feels dull and listless. The
world could come to an abrupt end and it would not matter to
her. She would even rather welcome this, for it would bring relief
to her inner misery and suffering.

As she watches the numerous persons, isolated and in groups of
varying numbers, plod their way toward the Cova da Iria, a feeling of pity for them comes over her. Poor people, they are falling
into a trap set by the devil and do not realize it!

How excited some seem, talking rapidly and gesticulating pro-
fusely as they walk along. Others, more recollected, appear absorbed in serious meditation. Many are publicly reciting the beads
or singing hymns. All are visibly living in anticipation of some-

thing great and extraordinary. And all seem so happy! How this contrasts with her own dreary, gloomy self. Life has lost all its meaning for her now that there is no longer any lovely Lady from heaven. For a full month she had lived under the spell of the vision's compelling charm. Each hour of each day had been gilded by the ever-present souvenir of her celestial beauty and her ineffable graciousness. Then had come the second apparition, with all its joy and unforgettable heavenly bliss. And then! Yes, and then had followed the second visit to the rectory and the fatal monition by o Senhor Prior that the Cova affair might be a trick of the devil! After that the cold creeping tentacles of doubt had gradually entwined her soul and choked her joy. And finally she had decided not to return to the Cova for the Lady's next rendezvous.

Suddenly a tremor runs through Lúcia's sturdy body. Though her eyes remain fixed on the world without her, her mind is no longer busy with the broken string of visitors that continues to wind its way toward the Cova. Her mind is now completely focused on an inner image that has spontaneously surged up from the secret hold of her memory. This all-absorbing image is that of the Lady from heaven.

But why should the Lady's memory and mental picture be so vivid this morning? It is as though she were back again at the Cova in the Lady's very presence. She clearly perceives that indefinable beauty wherein the charm of youth and the dignity of motherhood are so perfectly blended. And how clearly all the details of the apparition stand out in her mind: the dress of white light, the dazzling line of gold along the front and lower edges of the white mantle, the pearly rosary and the white cross. Even the feeling of sweetest rapture that has accompanied each vision seems to be taking possession of her again.

Why, oh why, does the Lady have to come back and haunt her on this day! For there simply is no Lady from heaven! It is all a deception of the devil. Jacinta and Francisco can go to the Cova today if they wish. But they will only be fooled again as she was twice fooled in the past. Yes, they will be fooled again. Most certainly they will be fooled.

Suddenly Lúcia stops her interior arguing with herself. She is astonished. An incomprehensible change is coming over her. Indeed, there is within her an almost irresistible force compelling her to go to the Cova. And, strangely, she feels no desire to resist this powerful inner impulse.[1]

Quickly she snatches her shawl from a stool and dashes out of the house toward the Marto home.

There is her uncle's house. Now, are Jacinta and Francisco still there, or have they already departed for the Cova? She had better not take a chance. It would be wiser to stop and see. She bursts through the outer door and into the living room, where she comes to an abrupt stop. What is that sobbing she hears? It must be Jacinta, for the sound comes from her room. She rushes into the child's bedroom and finds her little cousin kneeling with her brother beside the bed. The two of them are crying bitterly.

Both parties remain spellbound for a moment. Then Lúcia speaks with a husky voice.

"Well, aren't you going to the Cova?"

"We don't dare go without you. But come on, Lúcia, come with us!"

"Sure, that is where I am going," she replies to their great astonishment.

Instantly the two children jump to their feet, ready to depart.

"Lúcia," Francisco exclaims, "I am so glad you are going to the Cova. I didn't sleep at all last night. I spent the whole time crying and praying that Our Lady would make you go."

8

Hell, War, and the
Immaculate Heart of Mary

Both Manuel Pedro and Olímpia decide to go to the Cova da Iria. Olímpia gets there first and is already standing near the tree of the apparitions when her husband arrives. The three little seers are there also and the crowd is so thick around them that two thoughtful men, one from Ramila and the other from the parish of Fátima, have appointed themselves guards to keep them from being crushed.

Lúcia's mother has not come because the pastor advised her to stay away.[1]

Among those waiting most anxiously and closest to the carrasqueira tree are a Senhora Maria Carreira and the various members of her family. Her seventeen-year-old crippled son, João, is seated on a stone near the seers. She asked Lúcia to allow him to remain close to her and her cousins, for she is a firm believer in the Lady and hopes, through Lúcia's intercession, to obtain the cure of her son.

A crowd of some four or five thousand persons, spread all over the vast terrain of the Cova but concentrated mainly in the vicinity of the tree of the apparitions and behind the three little seers, waits impatiently for the hour of noon, the announced hour of the Lady's arrival.

The seers await the Lady's arrival impatiently too. And as they wait, Lúcia attempts to recall the numerous petitions that people have asked her to transmit to the apparition. Even this morning as she and her two cousins had wormed their way through the closely knit crowd, several persons had tugged at them, asking questions and submitting requests to be relayed to the Lady.

Finally, Lúcia kneels down a little in advance of the others. She removes her rosary from her skirt pocket and immediately Francisco and Jacinta take theirs in their hands. Word of this spreads quickly through the packed gathering, and in a matter almost of seconds the beads appear on all sides, between dainty manicured fingers, in rough cracked hands, and in hard calloused fists.

Then Lúcia's clear voice rends the air: "Hail, Mary, full of grace . . ." And thousands of hearts unite in public reply: "Pray for us sinners . . ." Many long years have slipped by since some of these lips have moved in prayer. And some of the eyes now moist or glistening with tears are those of men whose hearts were thought forever closed to any emotion. Few are they who remain untouched by the communicative fervor of this praying multitude.

Hardly are the beads said, when Lúcia leaps to her feet. She turns toward the east, whence the Lady usually comes, and scans the skies. Almost immediately she is blinded by the intense flash of light that so far has always heralded the heavenly Visitor.

"Close your umbrellas! Close your umbrellas!" she cries to those who are shading themselves from the midday sun, "the Lady is already coming there!"

Lúcia and her two cousins watch the blinding light. It is not lightning but simply a reflection of the very brilliant light that surrounds the Lady at all times. They observe it advancing from the east until it rests over the carrasqueira tree. Finally, in the center of it they behold the Lady.

She is every bit as lovely this day as on her two former visits, and as unbelievably brilliant and glowing.

Once again it is the exclusive privilege of the three children to contemplate the Lady. Yet the spectators nearest the seers can see her presence reflected on their countenances. It is visible in their very bearing, for they are in ecstasy and something of an otherworldly happiness is seen mirrored in their persons.

As Lúcia looks and looks, filling her eyes and heart with the Lady's loveliness and sweetness, a feeling of shame creeps over her. Little more than an hour ago she had in fact doubted the very reality of this Lady. She had thought it might be the devil.

And, of course, the Lady knows all this. How can she ever hope to speak to her again? Already she is presumptuous in daring even to look at her after what she has done.

But as Lúcia continues to gaze rapturously and yet apprehensively, she can detect nothing in the Lady's features or attitude which bespeaks reproach. Her face is indeed serious, so serious that it is almost sad. But so likewise was it during the first two apparitions.

Enheartened by the Lady's gracious attitude, Lúcia finally speaks:

O que é que vossemecê me quer hoje? "What do you want of me today?"

"I want you to return here on the thirteenth of the coming month and to continue to say *o terço*, the beads, every day in honor of Our Lady of the Rosary to obtain peace for the world and the end of the war, for she alone can succor you."[2]

How gracious the Lady is. She has said nothing of Lúcia's doubt, and has not uttered a single word of reproach. She is going to come back each month until October, as though nothing had ever happened. If only now she would be kind enough to tell her name and perform a miracle in proof of the reality of her visits, how wonderful that would be! O Senhor Prior would no longer be inclined to believe the apparitions are a trick of the devil. Her mother and father and sisters and everyone would be convinced of the truth of their story and would cease persecuting her and her two cousins.

So much is at stake and the Lady is so kind! Timidly, yet hopefully, Lúcia gives voice to her thoughts:

"I would like to ask you to tell us who you are. And would you perform a miracle so that everyone will believe that you are appearing to us."

The Lady might answer that on June 13 she had already given definite proof of her presence. She could recall the buzzing sound heard during the apparition; the loud noise and the small moving cloud observed as she departed. She could also call Lúcia's attention to the bent shoots of the carrasqueira tree that had so impressed Maria Carreira.

But since people have not yet been sufficiently convinced that she is really appearing, she will give additional proof. She has come to bring a vital message to her erring and unhappy spiritual children of the world and is prepared to authenticate this message with overwhelming evidence. Lúcia asks for a miracle that will convince men that she is really appearing at the Cova da Iria. Well, she will perform just such a miracle, a sensational miracle that will leave no room for doubt in the minds of those who witness it.

And, what is more, she will reveal in advance the time and place of this great wonder. Here is a thing she has never done before. She has wrought miracles in proof of her appearances, and even upon request, as in Mexico, where she made roses bloom in mid December on a barren rocky hill and where she left an exquisitely painted picture of herself on the coarse tilma of her humble Indian servant Juan Diego. But never before has she performed a public miracle at an appointed hour and spot. In fact, not since her divine Son predicted His resurrection on the third day, as a predetermined sign of His divinity and messianic mission, has anything of this kind been wrought.

Briefly she announces her momentous decision:

"Continue to come here every month. In October I will tell you who I am and what I want. And I shall perform a miracle which all shall see, in order that they may believe."

Delighted at receiving such complete satisfaction and encouraged by the Lady's benevolence, Lúcia now pleads the cause of the needy and hopeful souls, of the blind, crippled, and dumb persons, who have confided their petitions to her. She asks for the cure of Maria Carreira's crippled son, João, the speedy taking to heaven of a man from Atouguia, the conversion of a family at Fátima, and other favors of a like nature.

With loving condescension, the Lady of light answers that she will cure some within a year if they say their beads. As to João Carreira, she will either cure him or furnish him the means of gaining his livelihood. And he too is told to always say the beads in honor of Our Lady with his family.[3] Finally the man from Atouguia should not be in a hurry to die: she knows best when to come for him.

Of much greater value to the world than the promised miracle, than the cure and other favors which the Lady from heaven so willingly concedes, is the spiritual message of salvation that she has come to impart to mankind through the children. Indeed, she grants the former mainly to assure the acceptance of the latter.

Sacrifice and devotion to the Immaculate Heart of Mary are essential parts of this message. They are things that Lúcia had once well understood and generously put into her daily life. But since her month-long agony of fear and doubt, her ardor for them has died. It is important that their flame be rekindled in her heart. And this the Lady now takes upon herself to do.

First, she speaks: "Sacrifice yourselves for sinners, and repeat often, especially whenever you make a sacrifice for them: 'O Jesus, it is for love of You, for the conversion of sinners and in reparation for the sins committed against the Immaculate Heart of Mary.' "[4]

Then, as she utters these last words, she opens her graceful hands in that same gesture that recalls the *Dominus vobiscum* of the Mass. Almost immediately Lúcia utters a cry of horror. Only the spectators nearest her detect the sound. But all those who are in a position to observe the seers' faces notice at this moment a sudden change in their expression. The serenity of their features, their appearance of complete satisfaction and sublime contentment, give way to a look, first of supreme terror, then of great sorrow.

For, as the Lady parts her hands, beams of reflected light radiate from them and seem to penetrate the earth. And the abyss of hell is unveiled before the children's horrified eyes.

They observe an immense sea of fire which appears to be under the earth. Immersed in the fire are the devils or fallen angels and the souls of damned human beings. The two categories of individuals are easily distinguishable. The souls have a human form whereas the demons appear in the terrifying and loathsome forms of horrible, unknown animals. But both the devils and the souls are transparent and black or bronze-colored, like live embers. Floating and tossed about in the conflagration by the flames which issue from them with clouds of smoke, they fall about on all sides without weight or balance, as sparks do in a great fire. All the while they emit shrieks and groans of pain and despair which horrify the children and cause them to tremble with fear.

It is fortunate that this vision lasts but a moment and that the Lady has prepared the children for it by her promise to take them to heaven, for otherwise Lúcia believes they would have died of fright.[5]

Shaken to the utmost depths of their beings, the seers raise their eyes beseechingly. The Lady reads their silent question and there is much tenderness and sorrow in her voice as she replies:

"You have seen hell where the souls of poor sinners go. To save them God wants to establish in the world the devotion to my Immaculate Heart.

"If people will do what I shall tell you, many souls will be saved and there will be peace.

"The war is going to end, but if people do not stop offending God another and worse one will begin during the reign of Pius XI.[6] When you see a night illuminated by an unknown light, know that this is the great sign that God is giving you that He is going to punish the world for its crimes by means of war, famine, and persecution of the Church and of the Holy Father.

"To prevent this I shall come[7] to ask for the consecration of Russia[8] to my Immaculate Heart and for Communions of reparation on the first Saturdays.[9]

"If they heed my requests, Russia will be converted and there will be peace. If not, she will spread her errors throughout the world, promoting wars and persecution[10] of the Church, the good will be martyred, the Holy Father will have much to suffer, various nations will be annihilated.[11]

"In the end[12] my Immaculate Heart will triumph. The Holy Father will consecrate Russia to me and she will be converted, and a certain period of peace[13] will be granted to the world.

"In Portugal the dogma of Faith will always be preserved."[14]

For reasons that she does not divulge, the Lady wants the terrifying vision of hell and the appalling prophecy of worldwide calamity kept secret. She now advises the children of this fact:

"Don't tell this to anyone.[15] But, of course, you can tell it to Francisco."

The Lady pauses a moment then continues:

"When you recite the beads, say after each mystery: 'O my Jesus, forgive us; save us from the fire of hell; lead all souls to heaven, especially those in greatest need [in greatest danger of damnation].'"[16]

Again she pauses, and this time for so long that Lúcia, feeling the Lady has fulfilled her mission, inquires of her:

"Isn't there anything else that you want of me?"

"No," comes the reply. "Today I want nothing further of you."

So the Lady's third visit has come to an end. And, today again, as on the two former occasions, she rises gracefully toward the east until she finally fades into the immensity of space.

As she leaves, a loud noise is heard, and Lúcia, rising from her knees and spinning quickly around, points to the sky and exclaims:

"There she goes! There she goes! . . . Now you can't see her anymore!"

Soon many of the curious spectators gather around the seers and storm them with all sorts of questions.

"What did she look like?"

"What did she wear?"

"What was it the Lady said that frightened you and made you cry out *ai!?*" someone asks of Lúcia.

The child is taken aback by this last question, and pauses a moment before replying.

"That is a secret," she finally states tersely, mindful of the Lady's parting admonition not to reveal the terrifying vision of hell.[17]

A secret! A secret! The word passes through the electrified crowd like wildfire. Their imaginations fired with curiosity, the excited spectators close in more tightly about the seers. Manuel Pedro Marto becomes concerned lest the children be crushed or suffocated. He surges forward and forces his way to Jacinta's side. Then, with beads of perspiration rolling down his cheeks, he picks her up in his arms and carries her safely through the throng.

Various extraordinary phenomena have again been observed by the spectators at the Cova da Iria during the Lady's visit. A buzzing or humming sound, a decrease in the sun's glow and heat, a small whitish cloud about the tree of the apparitions, and a loud noise at the Lady's departure are the things noticed today. Those who have been privileged to experience them carry home a strong conviction that what the children say is true.[18]

The secret revealed by the Lady from heaven becomes the object of much speculation. Everyone wonders what it contains.

One day some peasants stop the three little shepherds and question them.

"Would people be sad if they knew this secret?" they inquire.

"Yes," answers Jacinta.

Hopefully the people turn inquiring eyes toward the other two children. Maybe they will add some information to this terse reply. But Francisco simply nods his head affirmatively in corroboration of his sister's brief answer and Lúcia remains silent and stolid, refusing to reveal her thoughts by either word or gesture.

9

Strange Happenings

The children always regret the moment when they must leave the
meadows. This means abandoning their quiet prayer and their delightful reminiscing about the beautiful Lady and her messages.
And it also means resuming the torture of endless questioning.
When they arrive home they are almost certain to find inquisitive
people waiting there for them. Rich and poor, neighbors from
nearby villages and travelers from distant cities, all have unending questions to ask.

Curiously, the most trying visitors are the members of the
clergy. Because of their trained minds and their habit of making
fine distinctions, they ask subtle and often captious questions. Yet
it is not so much the exacting nature of the priests' questioning
which annoys the children as the air of incredulity, which at times
borders on antagonism and hostility, that many of them manifest.
Indeed, several priests have shown a definite lack of tact and re-
straint. And there have been some who have leveled ridicule at
the children's guileless replies. As a result of this, the seers come to
fear the very sight of a clergyman and attempt to hide whenever
they see one coming down the road toward their homes.

But not all the priests are troublesome. Some are very kind and
even helpful. One day two such charitable and zealous priests
speak to the children about the Pope and his great need for
prayers. Jacinta's generous heart is quickly inflamed with love for
the Vicar of Christ, and from that day onward she never fails to

add the words "and for the Holy Father" to the prayer which she and her two playmates recite when offering a sacrifice, prayer which the Lady recommended during the last apparition. And at the end of each rosary she adopts the practice of saying three special Hail Marys for the Pope's intentions.

Jacinta is seated on one of the massive stone slabs that cover the dos Santos well. Everything is quiet, for the well is hidden away near the bottom of the slope at a considerable distance from the house, and Lúcia and Francisco are busy looking for wild honey among the bushes that grow on a nearby banking. The child appears pensive.

Some minutes pass. Suddenly she calls out to her cousin:

"Lúcia, didn't you see the Holy Father?"

"No," replies Lúcia with considerable surprise.

"I don't know how it was," continues Jacinta, "but I saw the Holy Father in a very large house. He was kneeling by a table with his face in his hands and he was crying. Outside the house were many people. Some of them were throwing stones at him, others were cursing him and saying many ugly words at him.

"Poor Holy Father," she concludes sadly, "we must pray for him a great deal."[1]

In the hallowed niche of Cabeço the children are prostrate with their foreheads touching the ground. In that position now so familiar to them, they recite the prayers taught by the Angel during his two visits at this very place.

After some time Jacinta gets up and calls her cousin:

"Lúcia, don't you see many highways, many roads and fields filled with people who are weeping with hunger and who don't have anything to eat? And the Holy Father in a church praying before the Immaculate Heart of Mary? And many people praying with him?"[2]

Several days later Jacinta questions Lúcia:

"Can I tell that I saw the Holy Father and all those people?"

"No," she replies. "Can't you see that is a part of the secret, and that if you did that, it would become known almost immediately?"

"All right. Then I won't say anything."

Today the children have led their flock to a spot called Pedreira. Once the sheep are busy browsing, the youngsters engage in one of their favorite games. They run from boulder to boulder shouting at the top of their voices and listening to the echoes that come back from the mass of stone.

But Francisco, as is his wont, soon withdraws alone to an opening among the rocks. A considerable lapse of time goes by. Suddenly Lúcia and Jacinta hear cries of distress:

"*Ai! Ai!* Lúcia, Jacinta, *Nossa Senhora!*"

Worried by Francisco's unusual cries, the two girls set out instantly to find him.

"Where are you, Francisco?" they call as they turn and look in every direction.

"Here, here," comes the reply.

Unable to locate Francisco's voice immediately, Lúcia and Jacinta take some time to find him. When they finally do come upon him, he is still on his knees trembling with fear and his affliction is so great that he is unable to rise.

"What is the matter with you? What has happened?" the two girls anxiously inquire.

His voice choked with fear, Francisco replies: "It was one of those big beasts that we saw in hell. It was here sending off light."[3]

10

Summoned by o Senhor Administrador

According to the standards of the world, o Senhor Artur de Oliveira Santos has a great future ahead of him. He is handsome and
unscrupulous. Gazing at the regular features of his oval face and
at his well-groomed hair and narrow, neatly trimmed mustache,
one has the feeling that the man is an aristocrat, but one soon de-
tects that there is more arrogance than nobility in his makeup.
There is a hard, cold gleam in his dark eyes that is somewhat surprising in a person of thirty-three.

That hard look has been acquired during the course of a
unique career. Son of the local blacksmith, Artur de Oliveira
Santos has enjoyed but a primary school education and has em-
braced the profession of tinsmith, whence his nickname o *latoeiro*,
"the Tinsmith." But from youth he has also been vividly interested in political and religious questions and their dissemination
through the press. Though a baptized Catholic, he was won over
as a young man to the anticlerical ideas that were spreading
through his country. He quickly developed into a militant free-
thinker and anticlerical. His interest in journalism led him to become director of a local newspaper, *O Ouriense*, which gives him
an outlet for his antimonarchistic and antireligious spleen.

When in 1910 the freethinkers and anticlericals overthrew the
Catholic monarchy and seized power, establishing what they
chose to call a republic, they quite naturally turned to Artur de
Oliveira Santos, though he was only twenty-six years of age, as

their agent of regional civil government for the area of Vila Nova de Ourém.

Notwithstanding the man's meager education, youth, and open hostility to the Catholic majority of the region, the anticlerical Republican government named him Administrator of the Vila Nova de Ourém district, president of the Municipal Council, and deputy district judge. This accumulation of power, joined with the strength that came from publishing a local newspaper, made of the Tinsmith the most influential and feared man in the district. And, indeed, he exerted a virtual dictatorship over the entire locality, including Fátima, which was within the Vila Nova de Ourém district.

Artur de Oliveira Santos is in a particularly vicious mood on this Friday, tenth day of August. He has heard recently of the Cova da Iria events and is greatly upset. He has finally decided to call the children to Vila Nova de Ourém and question them. In fact, he has just sent a man to summon the youngsters and their fathers to appear before him tomorrow.

This Fátima affair is one of the nastiest pieces of business he has had to handle as Administrator of the Vila Nova de Ourém district. He and his fellow anticlericals have been fighting the Catholic Church ever since the October Revolution, that is, for seven years. They have even declared that the law of separation between Church and State would destroy Catholicism in two or three generations.

Their plans seemed to be working out so well. It looked as though the Church would soon be a forgotten relic. But now, unexpectedly, the clergy has devised this story of heavenly apparitions to revive interest in religion. And the worst is that it is succeeding, it is taking hold. It has seized upon the imagination of the ignorant masses in an incredible way. He heard that in June there was but a handful of people at the Cova da Iria, whereas in July there were between four and five thousand persons. And there are to be three more apparitions! What will it be like in October?

Well, he will see to it that there will be nothing going on at the Cova on October 13. He will put a stop to this business, and will do so quickly. He will take care of it tomorrow when he questions the children. He has but to learn the content of the famous secret they conceal and the entire affair will crumble. Yes, the secret is the key to this whole thing, and he will wrench it from the children in short order.

As the Administrator's agent rides leisurely back to Vila Nova de Ourém astride his donkey, he cannot but reflect on the difference in manner in which the two fathers received the summons to appear tomorrow at Vila Nova de Ourém for a questioning.

There had been a cool gleam in o Senhor Marto's eyes as he had firmly replied that he would go alone to see the Administrator, that it was too much to expect young children to travel three leagues on foot or on a donkey's back.

But o Senhor dos Santos had answered in a completely different vein. "My daughter will go," he had said. "She can answer for herself. I don't understand anything in this sort of affair. And, if she is really lying, it is only proper that she be punished."

The next day Lúcia does go with her father and Manuel Pedro Marto to the town hall at Vila Nova de Ourém. There all three of them are submitted to an interrogation by the Administrator. But it is especially Lúcia who is the object of the crafty government agent's questions. He tries by every means to get her to reveal the Lady's secret, but nothing, not even the threat of death, can get her to unlock her heart and betray her heavenly friend.

11

Unlucky Thirteenth

August 13, though a Monday and therefore a day of work, sees streams of people passing through Vila Nova de Ourém in the direction of Fátima. People traveling in every imaginable way: on foot, on horses and donkeys, in carts and carriages, in automobiles, on bicycles. And everyone heading for Fátima.

The Administrator's carriage advances very slowly through the maze that blurs the road to Aljustrel. Is Portugal going crazy, he reflects. He knows that if this road is so loaded with people, the other routes and paths leading to Fátima must also be filled with travelers. Why, there must be thousands and thousands coming in from all directions. Fools that they are! Allowing themselves to be deceived by ignorant children!

How glad he is that he too is traveling to Aljustrel. He must make a supreme attempt to stop this folly and save the people from this recurrence of medieval superstition. Yes, he will make one final effort to get the children to reveal the secret and to promise not to go to the Cova. If that fails! Well then he will have no other course left but to execute the plan which he has carefully worked out and decided to use as a last resort.

But he must hurry. He had not anticipated such a crowd. It is slow business weaving his carriage in and out of the numerous obstacles that block his path. He curses the fools that give him all this trouble. And fools they truly are. Leaving their homes and their fields for one, two, three and possibly more days; walking mile upon mile over hot and dusty mountain roads and trails; living out of a basket that many carry on their heads; sleeping under the stars or at the most under a tent cover at night. Surely these people must be fanatical fools to do such things. They almost deserve to be left to steep in their ignorance and superstition. They seem so happy in it. Their bare feet are bruised and burning, their legs and backs are weary, their lips are parched and parted in thirst, and yet they seem so contented as they walk along reciting the rosary and singing hymns in honor of the Virgin Mary.

Ah, at last! There is the low, tile-roofed, whitewashed Marto home with its two doors opening on the sloping street. But how will he ever get there? The road does not go as far as the house.[1] He has no choice. He must leave his carriage and make the remainder of the distance to the Marto residence on foot. And he must hurry, for it is nearing ten o'clock.

Working his way through the crowd that is milling around the house, he finally succeeds in entering and asks a Senhora Olímpia if he can see the children. She invites him to sit down in the front room and, after talking with him for a while, sends for her husband, who has gone to the garden to get some corn.

Manuel Pedro arrives in a few minutes. After washing his hands in the kitchen, he enters the front room.

With feigned nonchalance, the Administrator addresses him: "Well, Senhor Marto, why do you suppose that I have come here today? It is because I want to go to the Cova da Iria. I want to see the miracle." He pauses just an instant, and then, hypocritically calling on his lost Catholic heritage, he invokes Holy Scripture: "Yes, I am like Saint Thomas. I want to see and believe."

"You do well, *Senhor Administrador,*" Manuel Pedro replies, though in his heart he still distrusts this man who only two days ago threatened Lúcia with death and ridiculed his own belief in the apparitions.

As o Senhor Marto watches the Tinsmith he notices that he is nervous and fidgety and that his eyes dart anxiously around as though in search of something. In fact, the Administrator has not seen the children and wonders where they are. He fears they may upset his plans by going to the Cova da Iria before he has a chance to talk with them. It is not long before he inquires:

"Where are the children? I would like to take them to the

Cova da Iria with me in my carriage. It is getting late and I think we had better send someone for them."

"No, that is not necessary," Manuel Pedro replies. "They know enough to bring their flock back in time to get ready for the Cova. However, I will tell my wife to call them."

But Olímpia's messenger serves no real purpose, for the children are already on their way home, where they soon appear.

Lúcia also arrives at the Marto residence very shortly after her two cousins. It had been difficult to break away from the swarms of people who tugged at her and pushed her around like a plaything, asking her questions and submitting requests to be presented to the heavenly Lady. But finally she had succeeded in getting out of her house, and now, led by her father, she enters her cousins' home to find the two of them seated in the presence of the terrible Tinsmith.

A final attempt is made by the Administrator to get the children to reveal the all-important secret and to promise not to return to the Cova da Iria. But he fails. The children prefer death itself to betrayal of the Lady's secret or to failure to keep their Cova da Iria midday appointment.

The man is now desperate. If he fails in stopping these religious manifestations, what will become of him in government circles? He will be ridiculed, to be sure. But worse than that, he may be demoted. He may lose one or all of the various positions that have made of him THE MAN of the district. And most certainly any ideas he may have of further advancement will be doomed.

It is clear that further pleading with the children to tell their secret or to stop going to the Cova will fail. Now is the time to press forward with the plan that he has come prepared to put into effect in just such an eventuality.

"Well, children," he says, "if you insist on going to the Cova da Iria, I shall go too. And we might as well all go together. You can come with me in my carriage."

"No, we prefer to walk," they reply, horrified at the thought of riding with this terrible man whom they fear so much.

"Come, come, now, children," the Tinsmith insists. "Riding with me will be much quicker, and you won't be bothered by people along the road."

"No," they stubbornly persist, "we prefer to go by ourselves."

"Don't worry about them, Senhor Administrador," quickly adds o Senhor Marto, in support of the children, with whom he completely sympathizes. "They are quite capable of getting to the Cova by themselves."

Cold sweat breaks out on the Administrator's brow. Things are not proceeding according to plan. Is he going to be foiled by these youngsters? He must get them in his carriage at all costs. His mind races feverishly with that peculiar agility so common in times of stress. Then suddenly a sly smile lights his face. He has thought of a way. It involves a certain danger, but at this point he has little choice left. He will ask the children and their parents to go to the rectory on the pretext of a questioning in the presence of the pastor. This may quiet their fears and render them more amenable to a ride in his carriage once the interview is over.

"Senhor Marto and Senhor dos Santos," he says, "will you please take your children to Fátima, to the rectory, for I would like to question them there in the presence of the pastor. Since the children do not care to ride with me, they can go by themselves. I will take my carriage and meet you there."

When the two fathers arrive at the rectory with their children, the Tinsmith is not yet there, so they all wait for him on the veranda. But he arrives shortly and immediately enters the parish house. In a few moments he returns to the veranda.

"Tell the first one to come here!" he calls.

"The first one? Whom do you mean?" inquires o Senhor Marto.

"Lúcia!" the man replies.

"Go ahead, Lúcia," Manuel Pedro says, though he has a premonition that something sinister will come of all this.

Lúcia enters the house with the Administrator. The pastor is waiting for them in his office. As soon as the group is seated, the Tinsmith speaks:

"Senhor Prior, will you please question this child about these supposed apparitions. I have not been able to obtain any satisfaction from her or from the other two children."

"Gladly," replies the pastor, happy at this opportunity to show a high government official that he is not linked with these events in any way.

Looking sternly at the child and speaking gruffly, he begins:

"Who taught you to say those things that you go about saying?"

"That Lady whom I saw at the Cova da Iria," the child calmly answers.

"Anyone who goes around spreading such lies, which do so much harm, like the lie you are telling, will be judged, and will go to hell if what they say is found to be really a lie. This is all the more true in your case since so many people go to the Cova da Iria because they have been deceived by you."

This terrible sentence pronounced by a man for whom she has the greatest veneration and respect does not trouble the child in the least. Her answer is direct and carries a strong ring of conviction and sincerity:

"If a person who lies goes to hell, then I will not go to hell, because I do not lie. I simply tell that which I have seen and that which the Lady has said to me. In regards to the people who go to the Cova da Iria, they go there solely because they want to. We don't tell anybody to go."

Taken aback by Lúcia's fearless attitude and her almost fiery tone, the pastor shifts the conversation:

"Is is true that that Lady confided a secret to you?"

Sim, "Yes, but I can't tell it. Yet, if your reverence wants to know it, I shall ask the Lady, and if she gives me permission, I will tell it to you."

The Administrator, seeing that he is deriving no benefit from the interview and that it is turning in Lúcia's favor, suddenly interrupts the questioning and brings it to an abrupt end.

"Those are supernatural matters," he says. "Come, let us go."

And, without waiting any longer, he rises and makes his way out of the room with Lúcia. When he reaches the veranda, Jacinta and Francisco, fearing that it is their turn to be questioned, look apprehensively at the Administrator. They are happily surprised to find that they will be spared this ordeal.

"There is no use spending any more time here," he declares. "The children may go now if they want to. Or, rather, let us all go to the Cova together, for it is getting late. My carriage is right here."

Knowing the children's dislike for the Tinsmith, o Senhor dos Santos speaks out in their favor:

"Thank you, but the children will go by foot."

As the seers remain immobile on the veranda and show no inclination to accept the offered ride, the Administrator silently motions the driver of his carriage to advance the vehicle close to the steps that lead from the veranda to the church square.

When the carriage reaches the steps, the Tinsmith turns toward the seers.

"See here," he cries, "you children had better come and get in the carriage with me, otherwise you will be bothered by people all along the way to the Cova da Iria."

Then quickly descending the stairs he gets in the carriage and beckons the children to follow him.

"Go ahead, Lúcia, get in," orders the weak-willed Antônio.[2]

The child obeys immediately. She steps into the rear of the carriage and is followed by Jacinta. Francisco jumps in too and sits down in front. This is all done so quickly that before o Senhor Marto has time to realize what is taking place the horse is off at a trot. At first, when he sees the carriage cross the square in the direction of the Cova da Iria, he sighs with relief. But this feeling of assurance is short-lived, for, when the vehicle nears the road to the Cova, at the southwestern corner of the square, it swerves suddenly to the right. Then, at a snap of the whip, the horse breaks into a gallop and heads for Vila Nova de Ourém.

The helpless father shakes his head ruefully. His vague misgivings were only too well founded! This affair is ending tragically. The Administrator is kidnapping the children. His threat that he would stop at nothing to prevent their going to the Cova da Iria was not an idle one.

But the coup is carried out with such cunning that o Senhor Marto cannot help muttering: "What a beauty that was!"

"This is not the right direction!" cries Lúcia as soon as she sees the carriage dart off toward Vila Nova de Ourém.

"I know it," replies the Administrator. "I am taking you to Ourém to see the pastor. But don't worry. I will get you to the Cova da Iria in time. I will take you there by automobile."

It is not long before some of the many pilgrims who are walking in the direction of the Cova da Iria recognize the Administrator and the children. A man gathers stones from the road and begins to throw them at the highly detested government agent. But the resourceful Administrator is not to be intimidated and robbed so easily of his prizes. He throws a blanket over the children and, with them thus hidden, rides along without further disturbance.

"Here we are," the Administrator shouts, as he stops the carriage at the entrance to the enclosed yard before his modest home.

"But this is not the right place," exclaims Lúcia. "Take us to the rectory to see o Senhor Prior, as you said you would."

"I will take you there later, but first you must eat," replies the crafty Tinsmith. "Come with me," he adds, as he jumps from the carriage and enters the small courtyard before the house. When the seers have joined him, he leads them up the stairs onto the narrow, second-story veranda that runs along the front of the residence. Then he enters the house with the children and quickly huddles them into an isolated room. It is only then that he reveals his hand to them.

"I told you that I would win out, didn't I?" he says. "Well, you are now my prisoners. And you are going to stay locked up in this room until you reveal the secret."

Left to themselves, the youngsters look at one another with consternation. All three faces mirror the same keen disappointment and fear. No one utters a word. A few moments pass in this way as the horrifying realization of their plight and all its implications slowly dawn upon them.

They are soon drawn from their depressing thoughts by a soft rap and slow squeaking of the door. Instinctively the children turn in the direction of the sound and find a kind, motherly woman smiling sweetly at them. It is a Senhora Adelina dos Santos, wife of the terrible Tinsmith.

"Come, my children," she says in a reassuring voice. "And don't be afraid. You must be very hungry. I will give you a good little lunch and then you will feel better. And when you are through eating you can play with my children and look through some picture books I have."

12

The People Are Not Left Forgotten

It is close to noon and the crowd at the Cova da Iria is impatient. Most of the eighteen thousand people, standing, sitting, or kneeling, have been waiting for hours, reciting the rosary and singing hymns in honor of the Blessed Virgin. When, at eleven o'clock, Maria dos Anjos, Lúcia's oldest sister, had arrived at the now leafless and branchless tree of the apparitions with some candles that she intended to light when the Lady appeared, a tremor of expectation had run through the throng. But this had died down quickly as Lúcia and her two cousins had failed to follow her.

Even the pious Maria Carreira, who has been sitting beside the despoiled holm oak since early morning, is becoming worried. She has come to the Cova da Iria in spite of the fact that many people have tried to dissuade her with a terrifying rumor that has been circulating throughout the region. It has been whispered that it is the devil who is appearing at the Cova and that he plans to attract large numbers there and then open the bowels of the earth and swallow up everyone. She had scoffed at the suggestion that there could be anything evil in the apparitions since there was so much praying done at the Cova. And she has given additional evidence of her belief in the Lady by placing a table with flowers before the hallowed carrasqueira tree.

Suddenly, above the hum of the crowd comes the sound of the Angelus ringing out from the village church. Meant as an invitation to prayer in honor of Our Saviour and His Blessed Mother, the peal of bells today serves only to remind the people that it is noon, the hour of the heavenly Lady's rendezvous. From all sides the same anxious cry is heard:

"Where are the children? Where are the children?"

A man on a bicycle who has just arrived from Fátima announces that the Administrator has kidnapped the three seers. Like wildfire the news spreads from one corner of the Cova to the other. Impatience gives way to indignation and the crowd quickly becomes a rumbling sea of seething anger. Just as the more conservative are becoming apprehensive lest the mounting resentment may soon express itself in some form of violence, a formidable clap of thunder is heard. The people tremble with fright, and, fearing that their end is near, emit great cries that are heard as far as Aljustrel. Thinking that bombs have been placed near the tree of the apparitions, they begin to run away from it. But suddenly a bright flash of light near the hallowed carrasqueira commands their attention. The sun loses its brilliance and the atmosphere becomes hazy. But the pilgrims hardly notice this because they are almost immediately attracted by another more striking development.

"Look, look!" some of the people cry as, fascinated, they observe a small whitish cloud form around the trunk of the tree of the apparitions. It is very light, like mist or smoke, and very beautiful. For several minutes it hovers about the carrasqueira tree, then it rises into the air and melts away.[1]

But this is not the last of today's wonderful signs. Indeed, the most spectacular one is just beginning. The clouds in the sky have turned crimson red. And now quickly they change color and become rose, yellow, blue. In rapid succession they assume all the colors of the rainbow. The people appear tinted with these same hues. And so do the trees and stones. The Cova da Iria becomes a vast and fantastic fairyland, with every leaf looking like a flower and every object magically alive with color.[2]

Then, just as mysteriously as it had all occurred, everything returns to normal. The colors disappear, the sun shines with its usual intensity and the air regains its customary appearance. But the spectators have been profoundly impressed and they quickly draw their own conclusions.

"It is a miracle performed by the Blessed Virgin."

"The Lady has given proof that she has come."

The first movement of the throng, so deeply stirred by these signs, is to pray. But once the initial impression of amazement and awe has worn off, everyone's thoughts revert to the children. The Lady has come but the seers were not here to greet her. What a shame! No, what a crime, since they were willfully impeded by the Administrator. By the Administrator, and by others too! For the story speedily spreads that the youngsters were seen with the Tinsmith at the parish house shortly before their abduction. The pastor, who in recent weeks has affirmed his disbelief in the apparitions to more than one person, must therefore be involved in the kidnapping of the children. And doubtless the *regedor*—the mayor —has also had a share of responsibility in this despicable act. They must all be made to answer for this. On to Fátima and to Ourém!

And so the peaceful and well-intentioned pilgrims, who at the cost of considerable sacrifice have come to the Cova da Iria to observe the children and to pray, are transformed by the brutal kidnapping of the little seers into an infuriated and dangerous mob. A wave of violent anger sweeps over them and the light of reason gives way to the blind impulses of passion. Shouts rend the air:

"Let's punish the guilty people!"

"Let's go to Vila Nova de Ourém and complain to the Administrator about this kidnapping!"

"And let's go to Fátima and see the pastor. He's guilty too!"

"And don't forget the *regedor*. We'll settle with him too!"

O Senhor Marto thinks that the Administrator, the pastor, and the *regedor* are all guilty, but he does not share the mob's desire to take justice into its own hands. Fearful of its mounting fury and desiring to avert a calamity, he courageously intervenes:

"Come on, calm down! Let's not hurt anyone. Let the Almighty settle this account. He will see to it that those who deserve punishment get it. This whole affair is in His hands."

But the vengeful throng is in no mood to listen to the dispassionate voice of reason. It sets out in the direction of Fátima, unaccompanied, however, by o Senhor Marto, who departs for his home.[3]

In some inexplicable way, the anger of the Cova da Iria mob

spends itself before it gets to Fátima, and its various threats are never carried out.

Though not one of the spectators claims to have seen the Lady, the great majority of them are convinced that she has kept her promise to the children and has come again to the little carrasqueira tree.[4] What else could be the meaning of the spectacular things they have just seen and heard. Why, the phenomena witnessed today were more striking and varied than they were in July!

If the Lady is producing such miracles—and miracles the people definitely believe these things are—then she must have some very important message to authenticate. What a shame that the children were not there today to hear what she had to say. Maybe in September she will tell them the things she had intended to tell them today.

Though the irate Cova da Iria throng finally disperses before committing any acts of violence, news of its seething agitation and ominous threats quickly reaches the ears of the pastor and he is greatly disturbed. He deems it necessary to justify himself, and so he pens the following letter, which is published in local newspapers and even in one Lisbon daily.

Dear Editor:

I beg you to grant me the great honor of publishing the following in a prominent place:

To believers and nonbelievers:

With all the reluctance of a Catholic priest's heart, I wish to make an open statement and a declaration to all those who already know about or may come to learn about a rumor which is all the more defaming and repulsive because it endangers my existence and jeopardizes my priestly dignity. This rumor claims that I was an accomplice to the brutal kidnapping of the children who claim to see Our Lady in our parish . . .

I wish to deny this calumny, which is as unjust as it is insidious, and I wish to proclaim to the entire world that I had no part, no matter how small it may be, either directly or indirectly, in this heinous and sacrilegious act.

The Administrator did not confide the secret of his intentions to me.

And if it was providential—which it was—that the authority took the children away furtively and without any opportunity for resistance, no less providential was the calming of spirits excited by this diabolical rumor. Otherwise, today this parish would be mourning the death of its pastor as an accomplice.

But, if once again the snare laid by the devil did not succeed in bringing about the desired death, it was certainly due to the Virgin Mother.

After a lengthy questioning of the children in their homes, the authority had them brought to my house under the guise of obtaining information, but in reality in order to have them reveal to him a secret which they had disclosed to no one. From there, at a favorable moment, he commanded them to get into a carriage, and telling the parents and other persons present that he was going to take them to the place of the apparitions, he left at full speed for Vila Nova de Ourém.

What were his intentions in coming to my house?

Avoid the consequences that his act was going to provoke?

Get the people roused, as they became roused against me—as accomplice?

Or . . . some other aim?

I don't know. The only thing I know is that I reject all the responsibility involved in such a way of acting. God always watches over His own.

No one can obstruct the works of God.

Thousands of witnesses say that the presence of the children was not necessary for the Queen of Angels to reveal her power. They will indeed testify to the extraordinary events and to the phenomena which they observed and which strengthened their faith even more.

Now it is not an affair of three children—of nine to eleven years of age—but of thousands of people of every age, class, and condition, and from various parts of the country.

If, as pastor, my absence from the place of the apparitions is felt by the believers, so too would my presence be equally felt by the unbelievers, to the detriment of the truth of the facts.

The Virgin Mother does not need the pastor's presence to manifest her goodness. Moreover, the enemies of religion should not be given the opportunity of tarnishing the luster of her benevolence by attributing the belief of the people to the presence or counsel of the pastor. Indeed, faith is a gift of God and not of priests. There you have the real motive of my absence and apparent indifference regarding such a sublime and marvelous affair. And that is why I have never stated my frank opinion [*o meu claro parecer*] to the thousands of persons who have questioned me or written to me.[5]

The enemy does not slumber. He roars like a lion.

The Apostles were not the first to announce the Resurrection of the Virgin's Son.

I abstain from narrating the phenomena that occurred at the place of the apparitions because this letter is already lengthy, for which I beg pardon, and because by this time the press must certainly have mentioned these things.

Please accept this expression of my deep gratitude . . .

P.e MANUEL MARQUÊS FERREIRA

13

Prison and Boiling Oil

As the afternoon wears on, the children tire of playing and looking at pictures. A feeling of loneliness and abandonment creeps over them. Jacinta, especially, feels keenly the absence of her dear mother.

But they must not complain. No, they must endure their lot in patience and offer their sacrifice and suffering to Jesus, for love of Him, for sinners and in reparation for the offenses committed against the Immaculate Heart of Mary, as the Lady requested during her last visit. And they must recite their rosary, asking the Lady for the strength to keep her secret faithfully.

When the first rays of dawn end their restless night the children attempt to brace themselves for the ordeal that they believe lies ahead. And, indeed, it is not long before they hear a key turning in the door. They fear that it is the Tinsmith who is coming to question them again. But to their surprise and relief they see an old lady enter the room. With all the art and cunning she can muster, the old woman attempts to pry the secret from them. Her efforts, however, like those of all the others who have tried before her, are in vain. When she closes the door behind her the secret is still safely locked in the youngsters' hearts.

Toward ten o'clock the children are taken from the Tinsmith's residence to the offices of the administration in the town hall. Providence is kind to them, for on their way they encounter a priest they have never met before, the Reverend Luís de Andrade e Silva. He proves to be friendly and listens sympathetically as Lúcia describes all that transpired the preceding day. He is the first person in whom they have dared to confide, and they derive great consolation in unloading their heavily burdened hearts to him. His comforting words and kindness give them new courage.

And they need great courage, for the Tinsmith is in a nasty mood as he begins to question them. He is determined to extract the secret from them at all costs. First, he has recourse to insidious questions, by which he attempts to trick them into revealing the all-important secret. As this fails, he then turns to the use of threats and menaces. But again he is unsuccessful. Finally, he decides to try a new bit of strategy. He plunges his hand into his pocket and brings forth several glittering gold pieces. These he jingles temptingly before their eyes, tossing them about in the palm of his hand. Then, leaning forward over his desk, he speaks softly and suavely:

"These pretty pieces of gold will be yours if you will but talk."

It is little Jacinta who replies, and her answer is short and decisive: "You can keep your gold. Even if you gave us all the world we wouldn't tell the secret."

As Lúcia and Francisco vigorously nod their assent to what Jacinta says, the Tinsmith is forced to admit his defeat and decides to let matters rest for a while. Noting that it is almost time for lunch, he sends the children back to his home.

The kind attention of the Administrator's wife helps the youngsters forget somewhat the morning's unpleasant experience. But this respite is brief, for in the course of the afternoon the heartless magistrate submits them to another torturing third-degree. The same grim determination and flat refusal to reveal the Lady's secret greets these new efforts.

Vexed beyond measure, the Administrator now attempts to terrorize the youngsters by locking them in the public jail and threatening to leave them there if they do not tell the secret.

Hardly has the key turned in the jail door lock when the seers find themselves addressed by the other inmates of their new and unattractive abode:

"Well, well, look what we have with us. What on earth could you children have done to be thrown into jail?"

"We saw a Lady from heaven at the Cova da Iria. She gave us a secret that she does not want us to tell, but o Senhor Administrador insists that we must reveal it to him," Lúcia replies. "He said that we will have to stay in jail until we tell the secret, and that they will even fry us in oil if we don't tell it."

Reminded of her plight, Jacinta starts to feel homesick. Tears come to her eyes. Lúcia quickly notices this and goes over to console her little cousin.

"Jacinta," she says with great tenderness, "what is the matter? Why are you crying?"

"Neither your parents nor mine have come to see us. They do not care for us anymore."[1]

Francisco, who is a brave little man, comes over now to his sister's side and saves the day by recalling the heavenly Lady's request.

"Don't cry," he says. "If we don't return to see our mother, let's be patient and offer it to Jesus for the conversion of sinners. The worst would be if Our Lady did not come back. That is what bothers me most. But I offer that too for the conversion of sinners!"

Then raising his eyes and his folded hands toward heaven, he makes the offering: "O Jesus, it is for love of You and for the conversion of sinners."

Jacinta is greatly strengthened by her brother's courageous example, and, though her tears are still flowing, she completes the sacrificial formula which Francisco has only partially recited. "And also for the Holy Father and in reparation for the sins committed against the Immaculate Heart of Mary," she adds.

The prisoners gaze in wonderment at this scene. Finally, one of them speaks:

"Now my dear children, don't be so upset. All you have to do is tell o Senhor Administrador your secret and he will set you free."

"Yes," adds another, "go ahead and tell the secret. What difference does it make to you if the Lady doesn't want you to reveal it?"

"That! Never!" Jacinta cries, and with such vivacity that all are taken aback. "I would rather die than do that!"

"Well," one of the prisoners rejoins, "if you are decided not to tell the secret, that means you will be staying with us for a while. We don't want you to cry anymore. Crying won't do you any good anyway. How about singing for a while, fellows? Maybe that will cheer these youngsters up a bit."

"Good idea," they all reply.

So the men begin to sing merrily. And, as one of the men has an accordion, it soon adds its gay note to the entertainment. The children are delighted and soon forget their troubles. Jacinta's tears dry quickly. Her slight little body begins to sway to the lively rhythm of the music and singing.

One of the men with a liking for dancing notices the graceful swinging of Jacinta's head and shoulders.

"Do you children know how to dance?" he hopefully inquires.

"Yes, we know the fandango," Jacinta replies, her eyes sparkling with anticipation, for dancing is her favorite form of amusement.

"Well, let's go then," he immediately suggests.

And without waiting, he snatches Jacinta's hand and off they go in a merry twirl. In a moment the drab prison is transformed into a cheerful room of spinning figures and smiling faces. But Jacinta is the happiest of all. She is so small that her big partner has picked her off the floor and to her great delight is whirling her through space like a little doll.

When the dancing and fun-making have finally subsided, Francisco becomes very serious and voices his thoughts:

"Don't you think it is time we said the *terço?*"

The two girls agree. And Jacinta, who, since the apparitions, is as earnest in prayer as she ever was in play, takes a medal from around her neck and asks a prisoner to hang it on a nail in the wall. A bit embarrassed, though edified by the child's simplicity and fervor, he complies with her wish and suspends the medal from the nail.

The children remove their rosaries from their pockets and kneel reverently before their newly improvised shrine. Oblivious of the others, Lúcia leads the prayer, and her cousins reply. First one, then another, and another of the prisoners gets down on his knees. And, profoundly stirred by these extraordinary children, they soon begin to mumble the prayers of the rosary, accompanying the seers as best they can. One of the prisoners who is wearing a beret even removes it at Francisco's request.

Once the *terço* is over, Jacinta's thoughts revert to her dear mother. Leaving the other two, she goes over to the window. There the weight of her loneliness again proves too much for her and she begins to cry. Lúcia, ever alert, is the first to observe her cousin's distress.

"Jacinta," she says, "what is the matter? Don't you want to offer this sacrifice to Our Lord?"

"Yes, I do," comes the sobbing reply. "But when I think of my mother I can't help crying."

An idea comes to Lúcia, which she hastens to impart to her little friends.

"When we offer prayers and sacrifices now, we always do it for three intentions. But how about each choosing one intention? One could offer his prayers and sacrifices for sinners, another for the Holy Father, and another in reparation for the sins against the Immaculate Heart of Mary."

"Fine," says Jacinta.

"Sure," adds Francisco.

"All right, since we all agree, you choose first, Jacinta," says Lúcia, who has acquired the habit of giving her once-capricious cousin the first choice in everything. "Which intention do you pick?"

"I will offer mine for all the intentions, because I like them all so much," the child unhesitatingly replies.

The moment of the great ordeal has arrived. The Tinsmith has resolved to play his trump card. Short heavy steps and the jingling of keys are heard. The cell door swings open and the prison guard walks in.

"Come with me," he says to the children. And he beckons them with a motion of his arm.

Apprehensive, the seers follow him across the hall to the Administrator's office. Artur de Oliveira Santos is seated at his desk, and never has he looked so terrifying. Without waiting a second he snaps at them:

"Are you going to tell the secret?"

"No," comes the quick and unswerving answer.

"Well, I am through fooling with you. If you don't tell me the secret, I am going to roast the three of you in boiling oil."

Then nodding to the guard, he says: "Go into the next room and prepare a kettle of boiling oil."

After the man departs, there follows a long period of complete silence. The Administrator waits for his threat to work upon the impressionable imaginations of the youngsters. But, though the children are firmly convinced that the man will carry out his abominable threat and that their last hour has really come, no one makes a move to reveal the secret.

Seeing that this first stratagem does not succeed, the Tinsmith goes to the door through which his henchman departed. He opens it, peers out into the hallway, and then, with the door still open, calls Jacinta:

"Come here. The oil is boiling. If you don't tell the secret, you will be the first to be scalded."

Without a word, without even saying farewell to Francisco or Lúcia, the child departs immediately. Though her heart seems to have left her and her knees tremble, there is not a tear in her eyes. As she prepares for death she makes what she believes is her last offering: "O Jesus, it is for love of You . . ."

When the door has closed behind her, Francisco turns to Lúcia. "They say they are going to kill us. If they really do we shall soon be in heaven. Isn't that wonderful!" he declares, manifesting such enthusiasm and serenity of soul that Lúcia is surprised.[2]

After a few moments, a look of concern comes over the brave boy's face and he speaks again:

"I hope that Jacinta doesn't get scared. I guess I had better say a Hail Mary for her."

And removing his hat and joining his hands he begins the prayer immediately.

It is not long before the door swings open and the Administrator reappears. Looking at Francisco, he says:

"We've fried the first one. Now, it is your turn, unless you reveal the secret!"

"I can't tell the secret to anyone," the lad replies without the least trace of fear in his voice.

"Oh, you can't. We shall see if you can't," the Tinsmith sarcastically retorts. And, seizing the boy by the arm, he pulls him out of the room.

Lúcia now finds herself completely alone. The minutes drag by and seem as long as centuries. She is firmly convinced that death awaits her in the other room. But strangely she is not afraid. She recommends herself to the Blessed Virgin and calmly awaits the opening of the door.

When her turn finally comes, she is told that her companions have been scalded and that she will share their fate if she does not reveal the secret. As she refuses, she is taken to a room of the jail where, to her great surprise, she finds her two dear playmates very much alive and talking to each other.

"What, you are not dead?" she exclaims. "Didn't they boil you in oil?"

"No. The Administrator questioned us and tried to make us tell the secret, but he didn't hurt us."

The children have just had time to thank the Lady for her maternal protection when the door opens and the prison guard again menaces them:

"Don't think you are safe. The three of you are going to be put in boiling oil very soon."

Not much time elapses before Jacinta withdraws from the company of her brother and cousin and goes over to a window that looks out on the cattle market.[3] At first Lúcia pays no attention to her, thinking she has gone there to distract herself. But soon she sees that Jacinta is not interested in what is going on outside. She has gone to be alone with her grief and to cry.

Going over to the sobbing child and gently drawing her to her side, Lúcia inquires:

"Jacinta, why are you crying again?"

"Because we are going to die without returning to see either our fathers or our mothers." And, amid a veritable torrent of tears, she adds: "I wanted at least to see my mother."

"Then you don't want to offer this sacrifice for the conversion of sinners?"

"I do! I do!"

At the mention of the Lady's message and request for sacrifices, Jacinta, forgetful of the tears that are still streaming down her cheeks, raises her hands and eyes heavenward and makes the habitual offering: "O Jesus, it is for love of You, for the conversion of sinners, for the Holy Father, and in reparation for the sins committed against the Immaculate Heart of Mary."

Having failed once with the trick of the boiling oil, the Tin-smith knows very well that he will never succeed again with that same threat. So he sends the children back to his home, where they spend the night once again in the same room.

However, the man has not given up. He simply must find out what the secret is. Too much depends on that. Therefore, the next morning finds him again questioning the children in his office at the town hall. But promises and threats continue to prove futile.

Finally the Administrator realizes that he is utterly defeated. He could question the children until doomsday and still they would not disobey their so-called Lady from heaven. No power on earth could wrench their secret from them.

There is only one thing left to do: send the youngsters home. So the humiliated magistrate orders his carriage and announces to the seers that he is about to take them back to Fátima.

On the road home from Vila Nova de Ourém the Administrator cannot resist making a final threat: "I am taking you children home now, but if you ever return to the Cova da Iria, I will go and get you and bring you back to Ourém."[4]

14

The Heavenly Lady Won't Be Denied

Four days have passed since the children's happy homecoming. They are their old carefree selves again. So far, this Sunday has been a particularly agreeable one for the youngsters. Mass, the rosary together at the Cova da Iria, and the pleasant diversion of a noonday meal with Lúcia's married sister Teresa! Now Lúcia and Francisco and his oldest brother João are enjoying the afternoon breeze under an olive tree at nearby os Valinhos, a pasture belonging to one of Lúcia's uncles and situated between Aljustrel and Mount Cabeço. They are tending sheep. Jacinta is not present because she has been retained at home by her mother.

Toward four in the afternoon as Lúcia's sister Teresa and her husband are walking along the road at the entrance to the village of Fátima they notice a sudden lowering of the temperature. At the same time the sun becomes yellowish. Then it begins tinting the countryside and objects with various colors as it had done at the Cova da Iria on the thirteenth of the month. Teresa is mystified. However, when the couple arrives at the parish church the phenomena cease.

At this same hour, Lúcia and Francisco become very concerned. They feel something supernatural approaching and enveloping them. There is the paling of the sun and the cooling of the air. Suspecting that Our Lady is coming and not wanting Jacinta to miss seeing her, they turn to her brother João. As usual, Lúcia takes the initiative: "João," she says, "the Lady is coming and Jacinta is not here. Won't you go and get her?"

As João does not want to go, Lúcia tries to lure him: "I will give you two vintens* if you go, one now and the other when you get back." Lúcia has found the right argument. He takes the coin and dashes off for his sister.

On reaching home, João discovers that Jacinta is not there. She is at her grandmother's, he is told. So, off he goes again. This time he is successful and finds his sister. As soon as she discovers what is happening, she departs in haste for os Valinhos with João at her side.

As João and Jacinta are approaching Lúcia and Francisco, the latter two see a flash of light, that reflection of the brilliant light which surrounds Our Lady.

Hardly has Jacinta joined Lúcia and Francisco when the three of them blink their eyes and start gazing fixedly above the top of a carrasqueira tree, which stands close to them at the very edge of a rustic road. A glowing light has come to settle about this holm oak, which is similar to, though considerably taller, than the one on which the Lady always stands at the Cova da Iria. As the children stare at the dazzling light they soon perceive, standing in its center and above the top branches of the tree, their heavenly friend. She is clothed as usual in white and gold and is as beautiful and gracious as she ever was at the Cova. They fall on their knees in the road and feast their souls in rapture.[1] When Lúcia has recovered from the initial shock of all this light and beauty, she addresses the celestial Visitor:

O que é que vossemecê me quer? "What do you want of me?"

"I want you to continue to go to the Cova da Iria on the thirteenth of the month and to keep on reciting the beads every day."

Our Lady knows that the children, and especially Lúcia, have had much to suffer. And she is aware that the torment endured at Ourém still weighs heavily upon them. To restore their peace of mind and heart, she repeats the promise she made on July 13:

"In the last month, I will perform a miracle so that all may believe."

Unfortunately, she must add a qualifying statement: "If they

*About four cents.

had not taken you to the town,† the miracle would be better known."[2]

However, she ends this part of her message on a happy note. There will be other good things happening on October 13: "The Child Jesus will come with Saint Joseph to bless the world.[3] And Our Lord will come to give peace to the world."[4]

Lúcia then remembers that Maria Carreira has asked her to question the apparition about the money she is holding in deposit.

"What should be done with the money the people leave at the Cova da Iria?" she inquires.

"Two biers should be made for the feast of Our Lady of the Rosary. You and Jacinta and two other girls, dressed in white, carry one; Francisco and three other boys carry the other. The money on the biers should be used for the feast of Our Lady of the Rosary."[5]

Lúcia now submits other requests that had been made to her.

"Several sick people have asked me to implore you to cure them."

"Yes, I will cure some of them within a year,"[6] comes the Lady's reply.

Many people are concerned about the health of their bodies, fewer about the welfare of their souls. The Lady from heaven is concerned about the body, as she has proved by her willingness to grant cures at Lúcia's request, but she is especially anxious about the eternal salvation of souls, and this she impresses upon the seers in a supreme recommendation.

"Pray, pray very much," she says, as her beautiful features take on a look of great sadness, "and make sacrifices for sinners, for many souls go to hell because they have no one to make sacrifices and to pray for them."

Then the children's rapture of ten minutes comes to an end as the Lady of light glides silently and majestically toward the east.

"Look, Jacinta, there she goes!" Lúcia cries.

João, who had hoped that he too would share the others' joy in seeing the Lady, has strained his eyes and ears in vain during the entire time that his more fortunate playmates were in ecstasy. But

---

† *aldeia*, the popular designation for Vila Nova de Ourém.

as Lúcia announces the Lady's departure, he hears a noise like the roar of a rocket.

As the three seers rise to their feet, João bursts into questions: "What happened, Lúcia? What was that noise? Who were you talking to all that time?"

"We saw the Lady from heaven again," she replies.

Francisco, as on the previous visits, has not heard the Lady. He is curious to know what she has said.

"Lúcia, what did the Lady say?" he asks.

Patiently and faithfully, not forgetting a word, Lúcia tells her cousin everything the celestial Visitor said. The boy remains pensive for a few moments. Then he joins Jacinta and Lúcia when he hears them discussing whether they should break off the two-pronged branch upon which the Lady rested her bare feet. Though the children have strongly disapproved of the removal of the branches of the Cova carrasqueira tree by relic seekers and have even complained about it, today they have no scruples about doing the same thing themselves, and they decide to break off the hallowed bough on which the Lady stood. And, of course, it is Jacinta who claims the prized object once it is removed from the tree.

Jacinta would like to stay and spend the remainder of the afternoon near the tree where the lovely Lady has deigned to appear, but practical-minded Francisco, reminding her that her mother had not permitted her to come with the flock today, tells her she should go home. And to persuade her more effectively, he starts off in the direction of Aljustrel.

As the two happy children enter the hamlet, they see Maria Rosa, Maria dos Anjos, and other people standing at the door of the dos Santos home. Exuberant little Jacinta loses no time in divulging the great news.

O tia, "O Auntie," she cries exultantly, "we have just seen Our Lady again! We saw her at os Valinhos!"

"Jacinta!" Maria Rosa says angrily. "Will you children ever stop telling me lies? Are you trying to make believe that Our Lady is going to appear to you now wherever you go?"

"But, Auntie, we did see her!" Jacinta insists.

Then, extending her arm toward Maria Rosa, she waves the

carrasqueira bough jubilantly and speaks, pointing successively to each of the two prongs of the branch:

"Look, Auntie, Our Lady put one foot on this part of the branch and the other foot on that part."

"Give me that branch, you little liar!" Maria Rosa snaps at her. Snatching the branch which Jacinta holds out to her, the good but irascible woman raises it to her nose. For a moment she stands spellbound, and her eyes open wide in wonder.

"But what is this I smell?" she finally exclaims with a trace of emotion in her voice. Then, still sniffing at the branch: "Why, this odor is very nice. But I can't make it out. It's not perfume, it's not incense, it smells almost like roses, yet it is not that either. Anyway, it is very nice."

Their curiosity aroused, Maria dos Anjos and the others close in quickly around Maria Rosa, and each takes a turn in smelling the mysterious branch. No one can identify the aroma, but all agree that it is extremely pleasant.

Finally Maria Rosa places the branch on a table and says: "We shall see later if anyone can recognize that odor."

Then she leaves the room to go about her work. She is glad to be alone, for she is disturbed. Persistent and soul-shaking questions keep shooting through her mind. What was that odor? But, especially, how explain it? Where did it come from? Wasn't it the Blessed Virgin who was responsible for it? Yes, wasn't it the Blessed Virgin who was trying to make her believe in what the children said? She wondered . . . she wondered . . .[7]

Later that afternoon a friend drops into the dos Santos home to speak with Maria Rosa. It is Lúcia's godmother, another one of the neighbors who is skeptical about the Cova da Iria apparitions. She is accompanied by her sister. When a Senhora dos Santos sees the two women she loses no time in imparting the latest bit of news to them.

"Have you heard about Jacinta?" she says. "She was here not long ago and she said that Our Lady appeared again."

Lúcia's godmother pales and a queer look comes over her face.

"What is the matter?" inquires Maria Rosa. "Are you sick?"

"No," answers the upset relative. "But you do not know what has just happened to my sister and me. We were walking back from the fields where we had been working when we saw all kinds of colored lights. I said to my sister: 'There are those same lights that the people talked about on the thirteenth. If this were the thirteenth they would claim that it is an apparition of Our Lady!' "[8]

Still later that day, toward sunset, Jacinta, who has regained possession of the odoriferous carrasqueira branch, goes to her home. She finds her father alone in the kitchen, sitting on a stool, chin in hand. A friend has just told him of the unexpected apparition and he is pondering this very important news. On hearing the child approach, he looks up and notices that she is carrying a branch and that she is very happy. Before he has an opportunity to say a word she speaks:

"Oh, Daddy! Our Lady came back and appeared to us again at os Valinhos."

But o Senhor Marto hardly notices what the child is saying. His attention has been caught by a most exquisite aroma that he detected as soon as Jacinta entered the room. He is completely mystified by this very extraordinary odor. It seems to emanate from the little bough that Jacinta carries so triumphantly.

"What is that you are carrying?" he inquires.

"It is the branch on which Our Lady stood."

Jacinta then hands him the branch and he quickly raises it to his nostrils. His eyebrows arch in surprise. But what is this? The fragrant aroma that he so clearly perceived but a second ago has now disappeared!

The intervening days between August 19 and September 13 are days of increasing penance for the little seers. There are the usual vexations, such as the interminable interrogations by an ever-increasing number of curious visitors, and the continued persecution of Lúcia within her home. This latter trial, however, has decreased somewhat because of the episode of the odoriferous branch. Not only is the mother shaken in her disbelief in the apparitions, but the father's attitude changes. When fun is made of Lúcia at home, he comes to her defense and says: "Let her alone! Maybe what she tells us is true."

But there is much more than that. Moved by the desire to fulfill the heavenly Lady's latest request to pray and to do penance for the numerous souls menaced by the flaming sea of hell, the youngsters pray continually and perform many acts of mortification. There springs up among them a holy rivalry for discovering new forms of self-denial and self-punishment. They repeatedly devise fresh schemes for crucifying their flesh or their spirit. Almost everything they encounter during the course of a day becomes the occasion of a penance to offer to Jesus and the Lady for sinners, especially for those for whom no one prays or makes sacrifices. Refreshing grapes, luscious fresh figs are sacrificed at the precise moment when they are most ardently desired. When prickly nettles are encountered in the fields, the children occasionally pluck them and beat their bare legs with them. They suddenly interrupt their play to pray, because of the sacrifice this involves. These and other penances, joined to the rosaries recited before the Cova carrasqueira tree and to the long hours spent prostrate in the niche of Cabeço reciting the angel's prayers, make of their lives a perpetual holocaust.

It is little Jacinta, the youngest of the group, who is the most active in discovering and suggesting sacrifices, though all three seers are truly devoured by this saintly zeal. Lúcia is greatly impressed by her young cousin's ardor for penance and it seems to her that she is the one of the trio to whom the heavenly Lady communicates the greatest abundance of grace. For this spoiled child, who formerly thought only of herself, has truly become a heroine of self-sacrifice. Now her sole preoccupation is to save souls from falling into the unending fire of hell.

But Lúcia herself is not devoid of fervor in regard to penance, nor is she lacking ingenuity. One day she finds a piece of heavy rope lying in the road. Playingly she picks it up and ties it around her arm. She fastens it so tightly that it cuts into her skin and pains her.

"My, that hurts," she remarks to her two inseparable friends. Then a moment later she adds: "You know what? . . . We could tie this around our waists and offer the penance to God."

Jacinta and Francisco, who never have to be asked twice when a suggestion of this type is made, agree immediately. So, with the aid of a sharp stone, the rope is cut into three parts and made into penitential belts with which the delighted youngsters joyously girdle their bodies.

Tied firmly against the flesh and worn continuously day and night, the coarse rope chafes and pinches and occasionally causes intense suffering. At times Jacinta's pain is so great that she cannot hold back her tears. When on these occasions Lúcia suggests that she remove her instrument of penance, the youngster's answer is invariably the same:

"No, I want to offer this sacrifice to Our Lord in reparation for sins and for the conversion of sinners."

15

Thirty Thousand Strong

Had the Tinsmith sought to find a means of building up faith in the Cova da Iria apparitions he could not have devised a better one than the kidnapping of the three seers. This brutal and inhuman act convinced people of the children's good faith and absolute sincerity and thereby transformed a great number of hesitant persons into firm believers. The Tinsmith was too clever: he promoted the very cause that he sought to destroy.

And so it is that, once again, on the day preceding the Lady's rendezvous, people are flocking to Fátima.

To come to the Cova da Iria for September 13 implies considerable sacrifice for many of the pilgrims. Indeed, for most of them it means losing three full working days. And this is late summer, a season when every day in the field counts so much for these weather-beaten peasants with the calloused hands. Yet, the roads and paths are black with them and they seem not the least concerned about the material things of this world. Not only are they oblivious of their cattle, their farms and vineyards, but they appear to have forgotten the very weight of life itself. Feet, sore and swollen after miles of plodding over rocky mountain trails or stony country roads; arms, heavy and weary from the load of bundles or the weight of the young and the sick; necks, stiff under the burden of heavily laden baskets; backs, aching from the constant jolting of rustic carts or donkeys' backs; dust, that rises in clouds and clings to sweaty faces and chokes parched throats—none of these things seems to count. At least, no one seems bothered by them, for hymns in honor of Our Lady and the public recitation of the rosary echo from the hills. The country for miles around is alive with sound, the sound of human voices rising heavenward in choruses of faith and hope.

Vainly have government troops attempted to block the roads to the Cova da Iria and vainly have they tried to drive the people away, pursuing them through the fields. At ten o'clock on Thursday, September 13, the huge bowl of the Cova is a moving sea of thirty thousand pilgrims, and the roads and lanes leading to it are filled with vehicles of every kind.

The people present at the Cova today are, for the most part, prayerful believers. The few who have come out of simple curiosity soon find themselves gripped by the ardent faith that radiates from almost every face. There is a supernatural current that flows incessantly through the crowd and electrifies even the most indifferent. Men are hatless, and both they and the womenfolk spend long moments on their knees in devout prayer. Rosaries hang from most hands. Fingers that are worn by hard work or withered with age and that in recent years have rarely counted beads are now busy and active, seemingly making up for lost time as Hail Mary follows Hail Mary. There is no distinction here between rich and poor, city dweller or mountaineer. All spectators mingle equally in their common quality of adopted children of God and spiritual children of Mary, no less than in their common expectation of momentous happenings.

Most of the vast throng are packed in tightly around what is left of the tree of the apparitions. Everyone wants to be as close to this blessed spot and to the three seers as possible. There are, however, two exceptions. Two men, dressed in black suits and wearing the distinctive Roman collar, stand at some hundred yards from the main body of the closely knit group. They remain aloof this way, for they hope to go unobserved as much as possible. The place they have chosen is a high spot that dominates the vast amphitheater of the Cova da Iria. From this vantage point they can observe all that is going on. Since their arrival an hour ago, they have been watching things closely, and with a decidedly critical eye. Members of the local clergy, Father João Quaresma and his friend the Reverend Manuel do Carmo Gois have heard so much in favor of the apparitions, and so much against them, that they decided to come and see for themselves. They are not ardent believers in the Lady. Like the majority of the clergy at the moment, they are skeptical and rather prejudiced against the apparitions.

As they rode along in their creeping horse-drawn carriage that beautiful morning, it had seemed that they would never complete the journey from Leiria to the Cova da Iria in time for the apparitions. Yet they arrived considerably in advance of noon, and each succeeding minute has made them more and more pleased that they endured the hardships of their journey. The spectacle they have been contemplating is well worth the price of patience and aching backs.

There is something undeniably exceptional in the spirit of faith, in the constant and intensely religious prayer of the thousands of souls who wait so eagerly and so hopefully for the Lady's arrival. In all their years of experience as priests they have never witnessed anything like it before. Father Quaresma is visibly moved. His companion seems less affected, but even he does not totally escape the mysteriously enchanting influence of this unusual scene. At this moment, Father Carmo Gois's attention is caught by a familiar face.

"Say, João," he asks, "do you see who is over there? Isn't that man standing by himself in the road, about two hundred yards from the tree of the apparitions, the Reverend Doctor Manuel Nunes Formigão, professor at the seminary and the lyceum of Santarém?"

"I believe you are right, Manuel. Well, there is nothing to be surprised about in that. He was given the mission, at least unofficially, by Archbishop Lima Vidal of Lisboa, to investigate and supervise events here at the Cova."

"So the Administrator of the patriarchate has judged these happenings important enough to send an investigator, has he!" remarks Father Gois. "I wonder if there are any other priests here today? Let's see if we can find any. O yes, look over by that tree. Do you see those two men? You recognize them, don't you? One is the Prior of Santa Catarina, and the other is Father Manuel Pereira da Silva."

"I have noticed many seminarians here this morning," says Fa-

ther Quaresma. "There is one group of four or five who have been
running all over the place and having a grand time. But I have
also remarked some twenty or twenty-five others who are considerably more sedate."

Suddenly the conversation of the two priests is interrupted by a
movement of the crowd toward one of the paths leading into the
Cova. The three children are arriving, but it is only with great
difficulty that they are able to advance at all. They are slowed
down continuously by anxious pilgrims who press them with questions and requests of every sort. And the nearer they get to the
tree of the apparitions the more they are impeded and harassed by
these overzealous but well-meaning people.

"Say, João," Father Carmo Gois calls to his friend, "look at
those people. See how they elbow and fight their way through the
crowd to get near the children. Some of those energetic men and
women are quite evidently people of considerable means and social standing. Look at them, will you? Throwing themselves at the
children and kneeling at their feet. I wonder what Dr. Formigão
thinks of that?"

"Come, Manuel, be fair to these good people. They believe in
the Lady and have favors to ask of her and are requesting the children to intercede for them. After all, although we do not believe
in these apparitions, we must not forget that the Church has not
yet condemned them."

Numerous persons, in fact, are desperately seeking to approach
the seers with the intention of pleading with them to transmit
their requests to the heavenly Lady. Only a few are actually able
to reach the children. Many of the less-fortunate souls, who struggle in vain to break through to the children, send their pleas over
the heads of the crowd, hoping against hope that their cries will
be heard. The more intrepid climb trees so as to be better seen or
at least better heard. From all sides come the same ardent, heart-
rending supplications: "For the love of God, pray the Blessed Virgin to cure my crippled son! . . . Ask her to cure my blind
child! . . . My deaf youngster! . . . Plead with her to send my
husband back from the front . . . to send my son back . . . Pray
her to convert a sinner who is dear to me . . . Ask her to rid me
of my tuberculosis and to restore my health."

The whole gamut of human misery is, in this way, recom-

mended again and again to the children as they fight their way
along as best they can, aided by a few gentlemen who open a path
for them through the crowd. While advancing, they answer as
many people as possible, promising to present their prayers and
requests to the heavenly Lady. Deeply touched and even disturbed
by the sight of people kneeling at their feet, they quickly offer
their hand to them in an attempt to get them to rise.[1]

Worn and weary, the children finally arrive at what is left of
the tree of the apparitions. They sense a deep feeling of liberation
on arriving there. Since the first hours of the morning, their
homes have been so packed with people that it has been practically impossible to move from one room to another, and of course
it is they who have been the object of all this undesired attention.
The tiresome tugging and questioning and the incessant recommendation of intentions which began at that time have not
ceased for a moment. But now, at last, they are free. Yes, at last
they can lift their hearts to God in prayer and prepare their distraught souls for the visit of their sweet and beautiful Lady.

With an assurance and calm self-possession most unusual in a
child of ten, Lúcia turns to the crowd and asks the people to say
the rosary. Then, taking the lead herself, she starts to recite it
aloud in a clear, unshaking voice. Her request is transmitted
throughout the place as though by magic, and those who are not
already on their knees quickly kneel. In a matter of seconds the
Cova becomes a solid, throbbing mass of supplicant souls who
humbly rejoice in being led in prayer by this simple mountain
lass.

It is now exactly noon and a glowing sun burns brightly in the
cloudless sky. The peals of the Angelus ring out softly from the
parish belfry. The bells of Saint Anthony's are inviting the faithful to prayerfully remember the Annunciation and the Incarna-
tion of the Son of God, but today nature itself seems to have
heard their plea, for, as their first melodious accents reach the
Cova da Iria, the sun loses its customary glow, the atmosphere as-
suming the same golden tint seen on previous occasions. The people gaze in silent wonder as the sun grows dimmer and dimmer,
fading to such a degree that some actually see the moon and the
stars.[2]

Abruptly Lúcia interrupts the rosary, and, her face glowing with a joy that earthly words can never describe, exclaims: "There she is! I see her!"

Lúcia's jubilant cry is drowned in a roar of shouts that rise at this very same moment from thousands of throats. With arms raised and fingers indicating a definite point in the sky, delighted pilgrims excitedly beckon from every side: "Look! There she is . . . There she is, down there . . . Can't you see her? I can . . . Oh, isn't it beautiful!"

What these gesticulating and thrilled spectators are actually seeing is not the Lady herself but a globe of light which advances from east to west, gliding slowly and gracefully down the valley. As it floats majestically along, this globe shines brightly with a most pleasing light.

Hearing the cries of the throng and observing the thousands of arms pointed skyward, Father Quaresma spontaneously raises his eyes and begins to scan the heavens, hoping that he too may be able to see what so many others are contemplating. His friend, noticing the movement of his head and eyes, arches his eyebrows and maliciously remarks: "So, you too are beginning to look!"

Father Quaresma hardly hears his companion, so absorbed is he in what he sees. Finally he replies, his voice husky with emotion and his eyes still glued to the sky: "Yes, I clearly see a globe of light. It is moving slowly down the valley toward the children. There, look!" he says, pointing with his hand toward the east.

"Oh, I too see it now!" exclaims Father Carmo Gois.

Then suddenly the radiant globe disappears from the sight of the two priests. They conclude that the phenomenon has ended, but a voice, that of a little girl of Lúcia's age, cries joyously: "I still see it . . . I still see it . . . Now it is going down toward the bottom of the hollow!"

Indeed, the luminous globe has come to rest on the tree of the apparitions. As the people gaze in awe and astonishment, they see a lovely white cloud form about the tree and the three children, and out of the cloudless sky a shower of mysterious shiny white petals commences to fall.

This mysterious downpour of what at first seem like brilliant petals or flowers is something quite unique. These white glistening balls, for that is what they are in reality, come down from above in the midst of a great jet of light. And this big beam of light, which has its origin high in the skies, sends down rays that broaden as they approach the amazed throng. As the people stare at this strange sight they soon notice that the falling, glistening globules, contrary to the laws of perspective, grow smaller and smaller as they near them, and when they reach out their hands and hats to catch them, they find that they have somehow melted away.

While the people witness these unusual phenomena, the children are lost in another sight, the vision of their lovely Lady. For, when the luminous globe comes to settle over the mutilated carrasqueira tree, Lúcia, Jacinta, and Francisco see the Lady from heaven. The brightly glowing light has once again suddenly and mysteriously revealed the brilliant Lady in its very center.

And she is as poignantly charming as ever. Neither smiling nor sad, her countenance is marked as usual by a serious and grave look.

Since she remains silent, Lúcia starts the conversation with her usual question:

"What do you want of me?" *O que é que vossemecê me quer?*

"Continue to say the beads so as to bring about the end of the war," she replies. Then she adds: "In October, Our Lord will come, and so will Our Lady of Sorrows and Our Lady of Mount Carmel. Saint Joseph will also come with the Child Jesus to bless the world."[3]

Here the Lady pauses, and the lines of her face soften. There is great tenderness in her voice as she continues: "God is pleased with your sacrifice, but He does not want you to sleep with the rope. Wear it only during the day."

Lúcia, who had lowered her eyes during the Lady's flattering remark, now raises them and speaks: "The people have implored me to ask you many things. There is a deaf-mute who wants to be cured. And there are requests for conversions . . . and requests for all kinds of cures."

"I will cure some of them within a year, but not the others."

Recalling that a Senhora Maria Carreira and certain other pious persons are anxious that a chapel be constructed on the site of the apparitions, and that they have asked her to inquire of the Lady whether she would consent to some of the Cova offerings being used for this purpose, Lúcia says:

"Would you like a little chapel built here with the money the people have left?"

"Yes, I would like a little chapel built here in honor of Our Lady of the Rosary. But tell the people to use only half of the money for the new chapel. The other half should be used for the cult and feast of Our Lady of the Rosary. Two processional biers should be purchased with the money and the remainder of it carried on these biers to the parish church during the festivities in honor of Our Lady of the Rosary. You and Jacinta and two other girls carry one; Francisco and three other boys carry the other."[4]

Satisfied on this point, Lúcia now turns to a very acute personal problem: "There are many who say that I am an impostor and that I deserve to be hanged and burned. Please perform a miracle so that all will believe!"

Obligingly, the Lady repeats her promise: "Yes, in October I will perform a miracle so that all may believe."

And with these words she departs for her celestial abode in the same manner as in the past.

Seeing the Lady rise, Lúcia cries to the throng, pointing to the east as she does: "If you want to see her, look there!"

Avidly the people stare in the indicated direction. Many are granted the sight of the same phenomenon that was witnessed as the Lady arrived. They see the same radiant globe return down the valley and gradually rise until it disappears into the light of the sun. Father Quaresma and his friend strain their eyes to the fullest but can see nothing. The little girl who stands near them, and who had continued to see the globe after they had lost sight of it at the start of the apparition, is again more fortunate than they. "Now she is going up!" the youngster gleefully cries, and with her outstretched hand she follows the globe across the sky until it fades into the sun.

The departure of the glowing globe marks the end of the other phenomena. The lovely white cloud that envelops the children and the tree disappears, the mysterious petals cease to fall, and the sun regains its natural brilliance and color.

If nature has regained its normal serenity, not so the crowd, which is now in a state of considerable agitation. Gesticulating hands and arms cleave the air in support of excited voices and everybody speaks at once and attempts to outshout his neighbor. After the first moment of excitement has abated, there follows a rush of spectators toward the three children. No one saw or heard the Lady and everyone is anxious to know what she looked like, what she wore, and especially what she said. A thousand questions are fired from all sides at the weary youngsters, especially at Lúcia, since she alone spoke to the Lady. But it is impossible for her even to attempt to answer. Because of the pushing and shouting of the people around her she can neither distinguish nor understand those who fling queries at her.

As the attempt at questioning the seers goes on, Father Quaresma and his friend exchange their impressions.

"What do you think of that globe, Manuel?" asks Father Quaresma, once he has sufficiently recovered from the spell produced by what he has seen and heard.

"I think it was the Blessed Virgin," the priest instantly replies, the speed of his answer underlining the firmness of his belief.

Father Quaresma smiles. He is not in the least surprised by this emphatic answer—though his friend was far from possessing such sentiments but ten short minutes ago—for Father Carmo Gois's countenance and entire person simply radiate enthusiasm, an enthusiasm that has grown steadily since he first caught a glimpse of the glistening globe.

"I agree with you, Manuel," he says, "and our conviction is evidently shared by this vast throng, if we are to judge from the cries of joy and shouting in honor of Our Lady that come to our ears from all sides. And yet everyone has not seen the globe.[5] Just look at that poor woman over there crying bitterly and bewailing the fact that she has seen nothing."

"Well, I feel sorry for the lady," declares Father Carmo Gois. "I myself am so happy. That woman undoubtedly deserved to see more than I, for you will not have any difficulty in recalling the mental attitude with which I came here this morning. Let us go and question the people. I would like to know exactly how much everyone saw and how they feel about everything . . . even at the risk of being recognized," he adds, smiling slyly.

"Fine idea, Manuel," agrees Father Quaresma, with an acknowledging grin. "And I, like you, pity those who did not see the globe. It was so beautiful. It was a heavenly vehicle that carried the Mother of God from her throne above to this forbidding wasteland of the Serra de Aire."

The two jubilant priests go from group to group questioning people of all types and from all classes of society. It is the enthusiastic Father Carmo Gois who does most of the talking. The answers obtained are practically all the same. Everyone affirms with like certainty the reality of the phenomena which they themselves have witnessed.

Both clerics finally depart from the hallowed pasture more than satisfied and firmly resolved to return there again on the thirteenth of the next month to witness the great miracle that has been promised. There is no doubt in their minds that the miracle will occur, since they both firmly believe that it was Our Lady who made the promise.[6]

But Dr. Formigão is not as enthusiastic as these two priests. The only thing he has observed is the decrease in the sun's light. He has witnessed none of the other prodigies that have impressed so many of the spectators.

The Lady has promised a great miracle for October 13, a miracle that will be capable of convincing every soul of good will. But she has not waited until that day to give proof that she is really appearing over the little carrasqueira tree as the three seers claim. Many feel convinced that the extraordinary phenomena observed today and on preceding visits are miraculous and fully authenticate the little shepherds' story.[7]

16

The Last Visit over the Carrasqueira Tree

For days people have been trekking the roads and even sailing the sea lanes from the islands toward Fátima, the geographical center —now fast becoming the religious center—of Portugal. And since last evening thousands upon thousands of persons have been praying and singing hymns at the Cova da Iria while an endless stream of visitors has continued to flow in all during the night and morning. The certainty of biting October winds, the threat of chilling rain, terrifying rumors of a bomb that will be exploded near the tree as the children talk to the apparition, these and other hazards have not been able to deter the seventy thousand people who have set out to witness the great miracle announced for noon today by the Lady of the carrasqueira tree.

There has been much talk of the terrible danger that menaces the seers and even their parents if the promised miracle does not occur. Yesterday morning the fretful Maria Rosa dos Santos rose early, and, waking Lúcia, suggested that they go to confession together to prepare for death. As she said to the child: "They claim that if the Blessed Virgin does not perform the promised miracle tomorrow, they will put us to death at the Cova da Iria. They will murder us." But to this Lúcia simply replied: "Mamma, you can go to confession if you want to, and I will accompany you, but it will not be because I am afraid they are going to kill me. The Lady will do tomorrow what she has promised to do."

Not one of the three little seers is the least bit afraid. A kind lady, sister of the Portuguese academician M. Marquês da Cruz, recently took Jacinta and Lúcia to her home for a few days in the nearby village of Reixida. She wanted to enjoy their company and give them a much needed rest from the importunities of curious and indiscreet visitors. But their retreat was soon discovered and people began coming to question them there. Seeing the fanaticism of some of the inquisitive folk, the good woman declared: "My dear children, if the miracle that you announce does not take place, the crowd could well burn you alive." To which the children calmly replied: "We are not afraid. The Lady never deceives us. She told us that there would be a great miracle and that everyone would be obliged to believe it."

On another occasion, when Lúcia was told that the authorities had decided to explode a bomb near her and her two cousins during the apparition, she quickly relayed the information to Jacinta and Francisco. Neither she nor they had manifested the slightest fear. They had all agreed: "Wouldn't it be wonderful if we were granted the grace of being taken directly to heaven with the Blessed Virgin."

However, the children's admirable confidence and courage have not quelled the apprehension of Lúcia's family, and the morning of October 13 finds her father, mother, and sisters in a state of great anxiety. As the minutes go by and the moment of Lúcia's departure for the Cova draws nearer and nearer, a Senhora Maria Rosa becomes terribly distressed. She is a sad sight as she goes about shaking her head and wringing her hands and casting furtive glances at her daughter, whom she feels she is seeing for the last time. The gossiping neighbors have spoken to her so often of impending calamity that she has finally come to believe in their gloomy predictions. She really fears for Lúcia's life, and that fear, having its roots in her deep affection for her child, engenders in her heart an overwhelming sadness. Finally tears of anguish gush forth, and in such abundance as to astonish Maria Rosa herself. But through all this Lúcia maintains such perfect possession of her soul that she is able to comfort her distraught mother.

"Don't fear, Mamma," she whispers, as she passes her hand caressingly over her mother's graying hair. "Nothing will happen to us. Our Lady will do what she has promised to do."

Lúcia's calm assurance quiets her mother somewhat, enough at least to dry her tears. The child decides to profit by this temporary lull to depart for the Cova da Iria. As it is raining hard, she takes an umbrella and then starts for the door with the intention of first going to her cousins' house before actually leaving for the Cova. But she has not yet crossed the threshold when her mother suddenly jumps to her feet and grimly declares:

"If my daughter is going to die, I want to die with her!"

"And so do I," quickly adds o Senhor Antônio, who, for all his weaknesses and faults, loves his daughter sincerely.

In a few seconds the three of them are under their umbrellas and on their way to the Marto home. Though the distance is short, it takes them a long time to get there because of the crowds that fill the narrow street. When they finally arrive they push their way through the thick throng that blocks the entrance to the house. Once inside they find little relief, for visitors are in every room, sitting on the beds and on all available furniture, and packing every foot of space.

Poor Olímpia Marto! She is greatly annoyed by the turmoil and disorder caused by this human cyclone which has swept into her home. But she is especially apprehensive about what will happen shortly to her children at the Cova da Iria. For she too has fallen victim to the sinister prophecies made by her neighbors and even by some of the visiting priests concerning bombs that will explode at the Cova, and the like. Moreover, she has never been able to bring herself to share her husband's unshakable faith in the children's Lady and in the Lady's promise of a great miracle.

How confident and completely unruffled Manuel Marto is! Why, as he stands near the fireplace calmly surveying the chaos before his eyes he seems to be enjoying himself. And that is definitely the impression he gives his wife as he bends close to her ear and says in a loud voice, so as to be heard above the din of the crowd: "My dear, don't worry. Now that the house is packed full no one else can come in."

In the living room Lúcia quickly becomes the object of much tugging and questioning and is eventually approached by a woman from the village of Pombalinho. This lady has come to fulfill a pious mission, that of offering the two girls some special clothes for this great occasion. She has with her two blue dresses and two white veils, and she also carries garlands of white paper flowers with which to adorn their heads.[1] She finally succeeds in getting the two children into a nearby bedroom, where she dresses and arranges them herself with the greatest care, for she wants them to look their very best on this day of days.

Soon the two girls, now looking as prim and trim as can be, make ready to depart for the Cova da Iria with Francisco and their parents. As Manuel Pedro is leaving the house, a well-intentioned neighbor seizes him by the arm and pulls him aside for a word of warning.

"Marto," he says discreetly in his ear, "if I were you I wouldn't go to the Cova. You might get hurt. The children are young and small and no one will harm them. But you run a risk of getting hurt if things don't go right."

"Thanks, friend," Manuel Pedro politely replies, "but I think I'll go just the same. I am really not the least bit afraid for myself and I have no fear about the outcome of this affair."

Then, just before he goes through the door, he turns and glances at his wife. She is clearly worried. There are deep lines across her brow and at the corners of her eyes. And what is more, he can discern the movement of her lips as they move earnestly in prayer. Indeed, as she leaves her home with a fear worse than death in her heart, Olímpia's last act is to recommend herself to the Blessed Virgin.

Heavy rain splashes down upon the seers and their parents as they pass through the door and down the single stone stair that leads to the street. And when they stop in the road to open their large black umbrellas their feet sink into the mud. Yet, neither rain nor mud can dampen the fervor of several women, including a few fine ladies, who, on seeing Lúcia and her two cousins, fall reverently to their knees. The seers and o Senhor Marto do not find this to their liking and the latter tells these well-meaning but ill-advised pilgrims to cease their excessive demonstration of veneration.

After considerable struggling and many forced stops along the way, the group of parents and seers finally arrives at the Cova da Iria where seventy thousand[2] anxious and, for the most part, fervently praying souls await their coming.

What a crowd this is that waits so heroically beneath umbrellas in the pouring rain for three simple mountain children from the unknown hamlet of Aljustrel! Never has Portugal in all the long centuries of its existence witnessed anything quite like it.

The explanation for this astonishing gathering lies in the fact that the news of the promised miracle has been carried on the wings of gossip almost as fast and as far as by the press. And how active the press has been! Liberal newspapers with a wide circulation have frequently spoken of the Cova da Iria and the seers, even though their articles have generally sought to discredit the apparitions. Indeed, the important publications of the country have, directly or indirectly, intentionally or more often unintentionally, given considerable publicity to the Cova events. And many of them, like *O Século*, the great liberal paper of Lisboa, and *Ordem*, the only Catholic daily of that same city, have their own correspondents on hand for the promised prodigy. Some have even sent their men out in advance so as to have eyewitness reports of the marching throngs that for days have sung and prayed their way through the meadows and over the hills and mountains and that have slept under the open sky or in makeshift tents with biting October winds chilling their tired bodies.

The ever-enlarging throng, made up of all professions and classes, and of all shades of opinion, belief and unbelief, is packed so tightly from the entrance of the Cova to the tree of the apparitions that it is practically impossible for the seers to advance. Seeing their desperate plight, a chauffeur picks little Jacinta up in his arms and, pushing vigorously forward, slowly opens a path toward the rustic arch with its cross and lanterns. "Make way for the children who have seen Our Lady," he shouts repeatedly, as he elbows and shoulders his way forward.

O Senhor Marto follows close in the children's wake but he is less fortunate than they. Seeing him pressed and pushed by the milling crowd, Jacinta becomes worried and shouts: "Don't crush my father! Don't crush my father!"

Finally the tree of the apparitions is reached without serious incident. The tree, which is now but a branchless trunk, was decorated last night with flowers and silk ribbons by a Senhora Maria Carreira, the self-appointed caretaker of this primitive, growing shrine. Having arrived very early this morning, the good woman now stands very close to the carrasqueira tree, where she eagerly awaits the Lady's coming and her long-promised miracle.

On reaching the spot of the apparitions, the chauffeur sets Jacinta down on the muddy ground. The pressure and excitement of the crowd at the sight of the seers is such that the youngster becomes frightened and begins to cry. But her tears are not of long duration. She quickly regains her calm and composure when Lúcia and Francisco protect her by placing her between them.

Moved by an inner impulsion,[3] Lúcia asks the people to close their umbrellas and to recite the beads with her and her two cousins. This they gladly do, happy at the opportunity to pray with those who have seen Our Lady.

Among the people standing near the hallowed tree of the apparitions are Jacinta and Francisco's father and mother and Lúcia's mother. A priest who has spent the night near the rustic arch is also nearby. When the awaited hour of noon finally arrives, and the crowd gradually calms down, the priest engages the seers in conversation.

"When is the Lady supposed to appear?" he asks.

"At noon," Lúcia replies.

"Look," the priest declares, as he takes out his watch and glances at it, "it is already noon. Our Lady doesn't tell lies! Something seems wrong here. We shall soon find out."

As time goes by without any sign of the Lady from heaven, the priest becomes impatient. He removes his watch again and looks at it.

"It is well past noon," he cries, whatever faith he had in the apparitions now gone. "This whole affair is an illusion! Let everyone get out of here."

But Lúcia, whose faith in the lovely Lady remains inflexible, refuses to move. Whereupon the priest, firmly convinced that the apparitions are pure fictions of the seers' imaginations and therefore a serious menace to the spiritual welfare of the thousands of expectant souls who stand breathlessly by, tries to push the three children away from the spot where they so confidently stand. Lúcia, whose respect for the clergy is very great, is disturbed and saddened by the priest's aggressiveness and determination, but she by no means shares his views, and she quickly voices her protest:

"Whoever wants to go away may do so. But I am not going. This land belongs to my father and I have a right to stay here.

Our Lady said that she was coming. She came before and she will come again this time."[4]

Then she glances expectantly toward the east whence the bright light and the beautiful Lady have always come. Instantly a smile of exultation brightens her face, and she and her young cousins simultaneously exclaim: "*Ai!*"

Raising her head so that her voice will carry farther, Lúcia shouts: "Silence! Silence! Our Lady is coming! We have just seen the flash of light!"

It is exactly noon by the sun, though close to one-thirty according to the official government time.

The bright light that Lúcia and her two cousins see in the east advances rapidly toward the decorated stump of the carrasqueira tree, where it finally comes to rest.

Once again the lovely Lady of light stands in all her brilliant splendor before the blinking eyes of the enraptured seers. And again they find themselves engulfed in the glowing light that emanates from the Lady and that envelops her person and the mutilated tree upon which she rests her feet.

Slowly but quite visibly the expression on the three children's faces changes and becomes more spiritual and ethereal as the ecstatic power and the ineffable beauty of the vision gradually pervade their bodies and souls.

But it is not the transformed beauty of Lúcia and of the other two seers that attracts a Senhora Maria Rosa's attention at this moment. At the very instant when Lúcia shouted that the Lady was coming, the good woman began to smell, and she actually continues to smell, the same fragrance that she perceived on Sunday, August 19, when she took from Jacinta's hand the branch upon which the child claimed that the Lady stood at os Valinhos. That first experience made quite an impression upon her but it was as nothing compared to the tremendous upheaval that this second one produces within her. This repetition of exactly the same sweet, yet strange, unknown odor on two days of supposed visits by the children's Lady is too much to be attributed to mere coincidence. Yes, why should she notice this wonderful, undefinable aroma on two occasions linked with these so-called apparitions, and only on such occasions. It would be pure obstinacy on her part to attribute that solely to chance. In all honesty, she must admit a supernatural intervention. This phenomenon must be the work of the children's Lady. It must be the Blessed Virgin attempting, in a supreme and loving effort, to dissipate from before her unseeing eyes the black clouds of doubt and unbelief that have caused her so much suffering.

And so the tender roots of faith in the Cova Lady, which sprouted on August 19, today grow a little deeper in the still stubborn soil of Maria Rosa's soul.[5]

Lúcia and her two companions are now completely absorbed in the resplendent Lady, who today is more brilliant than ever. She shines with such fierce intensity that the light emanating from her, though not actually hurting the seers' eyes, does cause them to occasionally blink and lower them. Except for her added brilliance, the Lady is exactly as she was on the other days. She is draped in the same clothes of white light, her hands are again folded with the rosary hanging between them and over the back of the right hand, and her beauty is still such that it fills the children's souls with an indescribable joy, a foretaste of heaven.

As Lúcia is so completely lost in blissful contemplation that she does not speak, Jacinta nudges her with her elbow and says:

"Lúcia, talk to Our Lady! She is already there waiting."

Thus abruptly recalled, Lúcia sighs heavily[6] and then finally addresses the heavenly Visitor.

O que é que vossemecê me quer? "What do you want of me?" she asks.

"I want a chapel built here in honor of the Lady of the Rosary. Continue without fail to say the beads every day.[7] The war is going to end and the soldiers will soon return to their homes."[8]

Since the Lady has promised to say who she is on this day, Lúcia now inquires of her:

"Will you tell me what your name is?"

"I am the Lady of the Rosary," comes the reply.

Recalling the numerous requests that have been confided to her for this occasion, Lúcia speaks again:

"I have many favors to ask. Many people seek cures and conversions."

"I will grant some of the requests but not all of them. They must amend their lives and ask forgiveness for their sins," the Lady answers.

Jacinta, Francisco, Lúcia. This picture appeared in the daily O *Seculo* of Lisbon, on October 15, 1917.

Where Lúcia dos Santos was born and spent her childhood. Her sister Maria dos Anjos stands at the doorway.

Where Jacinta and Francisco Marto were born and lived. Their brother João stands near the doorway.

O MILAGRE DE FÁTIMA

Varios aspectos do povo ajoelhado e orando no momento de descobrir o sol e de se dar o fenomeno que tanto impressionou a multidão.

no vagalhão colossal d'aquele povo que ali se juntou a 13 de outubro. O teu racionalismo sofreu um formidavel embate e queres estabelecer uma opinião segura socorrendo-te de depoimentos insuspeitos como o meu, pois que estive lá apenas no desempenho de uma missão bem dificil, tal a de relatar imparcia'mente para um grande diario, O Seculo, os fact os que diante de mim se desenrolassem e tudo quanto de curioso e de elucidativo a eles se prendesse. Não ficará por satisfazer o teu desejo, mas decerto que os nossos olhos e os nossos ouvidos não viram nem ouviram coisas diversas, e que raros foram os que ficaram insensiveis á grandeza de semelhante espectáculo, unico entre nós e de todo o ponto digno de meditação e de estudo ..

[Carta a alguem que pede um testemunho insuspeito].

Quebrando um silencio de mais de vinte anos e com a invocação dos longinquos e saudosos tempos em que convivemos n'uma fraternal camaradagem, iluminada então pela fé comum e fortalecida por identicos propositos, escreves-me para que te diga, sincera e minuciosamente, o que vi e ouvi na charneca de Fátima, quando a fama de celestes aparições congregou n'aquele desolado ermo dezenas de milhares de pessoas mais sedentas, segundo creio, de sobrenatural do que impelidas por mera curiosidade ou receosas de um logro... Estão os catolicos em desacordo sobre a importancia e a significação do que presenciaram. Uns convenceram-se de que se tinham cumprido prometimentos do Alto; outros acham-se ainda longe de acreditar na incontroversa realidade de um milagre. Foste um crente na tua juventude e deixaste de sel-o. Pessoas de familia arrastaram-te a Fátima,

O que ouvi e me levou a Fátima? Que a Virgem Maria, depois da festa da Ascenção, aparecera a tres crianças que apascentavam gado, duas mocinhas e um zagalete, recomendando-lhes que orassem e prometendo-lhes aparecer ali, sobre uma azinheira, no dia 13 de cada mez, até que em outubro lhes daria qualquer sinal do poder de Deus e faria revelações. Espalhou-se a nova por muitas leguas em redondeza; voou, de terra em terra, até os confins de Portugal, e a roma-

The famed (first) Thedim statue taken from the capelinha and placed on a column at the spot where the tree of apparitions formerly stood.

Niche in boulders on Mount Cabeço where an angel appeared for the first and third times in 1916 and gave the three children Communion.

The well behind Lúcia's house where the second apparition of the angel took place. A secluded spot, it became their favorite place for saying prayers taught by the angel.

Town Hall in Ourém where children were placed in prison and the "boiling oil" incident occurred during the August 13–15 kidnapping.

Os Valinhos, where Our Lady appeared on August 19, 1917, because of the kidnapping of children on August 13.

Vision experienced by Sister Lúcia at the Dorothean convent chapel at Tuy in 1929. It represents in picture form the entire Fátima message. On that same occasion, Our Lady gave the Sister the "collegial" formula for the consecration of Russia to the Immaculate Heart of Mary.

His Excellency, the Most Reverend José Alves Correia da Silva (left), first Bishop of Leiria who approved the apparitions and began building the shrine. Photo taken on May 13, 1949, eight years before his death.

His Holiness, Pope Paul VI, with Bishop João P. Venancio, successor to Bishop Da Silva, and Sister Lúcia at the Fiftieth Anniversary celebration on May 13, 1967.

On May 12, 1982, Pope John Paul II prays at the capelinha before the statue marking the spot of the apparitions. (Photo courtesy of Blue Army)

May 13, 1982. At the end of the Mass, the Pope, in spiritual union with the bishops of the world, consecrated the world and Russia to the Immaculate Heart of Mary. (Photo courtesy of Blue Army)

Pope John Paul II converses with Sister Lúcia at Fátima on the occasion of his recent visit. The Sister has said that the Pope's consecration of the world and Russia on May 13 was "the first and most important phase of the collegial consecration of Russia" requested by Our Lady in 1929. (Photo courtesy of Blue Army)

Then, with a look of great sadness that deeply moves the children, she adds:

"People must not offend Our Lord anymore, for He is already greatly offended."

These grave words, which impress the seers far more than anything else the vision has said,[9] are her parting request and mark the end of her visit over the carrasqueira tree.

17

The Sun Dances

Though the Lady from heaven has pronounced her last words over the mutilated Cova tree, the epic of Fátima is not ended. Indeed, its most dramatic episode is about to begin.

As the celestial Visitor takes her leave, turning toward the east and gliding slowly upward in that direction, Lúcia looks at the sun and, although she is unconscious of the fact, she emits a loud cry: "Look at the sun!"

Though Lúcia is as unaware of her shout as she is of the presence of the crowd around her, there is a good reason for her sudden exclamation. For, as the Lady ascends in the direction of the east, she opens her hands and turns her palms upward toward the center of the sky. At this precise moment the rain stops and the heavy gray clouds suddenly burst asunder, dashing to the sides in broken, transparent strips and puffs. From the Lady's upturned palms rays of light are reflected upon the sun, which can be seen without discomfort by the naked eye as a spinning disc of brilliantly glowing silver.

Yet, strangely, it is not the fast spinning plate of brightly shining silver that absorbs the attention of the three seers. Their gaze is riveted on something else. Though they remark the rotating silvery sun, they also observe beside it something else that the other people do not see. They see the Lady of the Rosary. She, who a moment ago was rising with motionless feet toward the east and into the clouds where she finally disappeared, now stands to the right of the sun, whose light is paled by her brilliance. She is still all of light and is clothed in a dress of glowing white, just as she always was over the stubby carrasqueira tree. However, this time she wears a mantle of blue.

And, what is more important, she is not alone. She promised that she would come in October with Saint Joseph and the Child Jesus, and that she herself would appear as Our Lady of Sorrows and as Our Lady of Mount Carmel. Now that promise is being fulfilled. In addition to the Lady the children see Saint Joseph with the Child Jesus standing at his right side. Both the Child Jesus and Saint Joseph are dressed in red, and both are blessing the world.[1] All three persons are close to the base of the sun, with Our Lady on its right and the other two on its left.

This apparition of the Holy Family does not last long and is immediately followed by changes of light and a vision of Our Lord and Our Lady which Lúcia, alone of the trio, is privileged to enjoy. She sees the bust of Our Blessed Saviour, from waist to head, clothed in red and at the right side of the sun. As she gazes lovingly at Him, she notices that He is making signs of the cross with His hand over the people.[2] At the left of the sun, dressed in purple, she sees Our Lady of Sorrows, yet with this particularity: there is no sword piercing her heart.

Then again, while Our Lady remains on the right of the sun, another change of light takes place and she appears to Lúcia clothed in strange garments that the child has difficulty in identifying. But, as she has twice promised the children to come as Our Lady of Mount Carmel, and, as there is something hanging from her right hand, Lúcia supposes that this object is a scapular and that the Lady she is contemplating is Our Lady of Mount Carmel.[3]

While Lúcia is absorbed in the apparitions of Our Lord and of the Blessed Virgin as Our Lady of Sorrows and Mount Carmel, her younger cousins are busy contemplating the sun. Together with Lúcia they had seen the sun as a whirling mass of flashing silver at the moment when the rays from the departing Lady's up-turned palms had first focused their attention upon it. But since that time it has changed in appearance and now as Lúcia is lost in contemplation of the solar tableaux, Jacinta and Francisco gaze spellbound at the sun, which they see as a weird disc that turns rapidly on its own axis and casts off beams of colored lights in all directions. Shafts of red light shoot out from the rim of the sun and color the clouds, the earth, the trees, the people; then shafts of violet, of blue, of yellow, and of other colors follow in succession and tint all these objects with the various hues of the rainbow.[4]

But Jacinta and Francisco are not the only ones to whom it is given to witness this fantastic display of heaven-made fireworks. For this grandiose spectacle is part of the great miracle that the Lady from heaven promised she would perform and which she declared would be for all abundant proof of her apparitions.

Seventy thousand amazed and tense faces are raised and pointed at the colorful spinning sun. And they have been this way ever since Lúcia unknowingly shouted: "Look at the sun!" and the clouds suddenly split apart. One of the things that strikes most of the people as they fix their marveling eyes upon the sun is the fact that they can look at it without pain or harm.

How describe this stupendous sight at which Jacinta, Francisco, and the astonished crowd stare with wonder while Lúcia pursues her solitary contemplation of the changing vision beside the sun? Never has anyone seen the luminary of the skies as it now appears among the broken clouds. Both its appearance and its movements are novel and intriguing.

Though the color of the whirling mass resembles the moon, in that it is closer to white or silver than to gold, its shape differs markedly from the spheric form of that planet. It is more like a disc or flat plate than a solid ball. Yet there are some who wonder whether its flatness is not simply an impression or an optical illusion attributable to the terrific speed at which it rotates upon itself.

But even in color the spinning disc differs considerably from the moon, for its silvery tone is not in the least dull or lusterless. To the contrary, it is very bright and shiny and glows with an intense and rich brilliancy, although for some strange reason it does not blind or hurt the naked eye. And, if this were not enough to convince everyone that it is not the moon they are looking at, the intense heat that radiates from the rotating object would be more than sufficient to prove the point.

One of the most fascinating things about this whirling silvery disc is the rim of color, which can clearly be seen to surround it. At first this rim is red and the contrast of the red on the silver is so great that the sun looks like a hoop or crown of fire, empty in the center. But this outer border of flaming red changes color; from red it goes to violet, then to blue, then to yellow, and on down through all the delightful hues of the spectrum. And the spinning sun appears alive with color, for all the constantly changing hues of the border are sent off in great beams of tinted light that transforms the clouds, the Cova da Iria, and the surrounding countryside into a veritable fairyland of colored wonder and give to the sun the appearance of a gigantic spinwheel.

When the sun first becomes visible through the rent rain clouds its motion is one of extreme rapid rotation upon its own axis. It spins and casts off colored rays for two or three minutes. Then it ceases its rotating and play of lights and begins to tremble and roam within the opening in the clouds, occasionally passing behind a transparent strip or puff. Shortly it begins to whirl again, painting everything with great shafts of red, violet, blue, yellow, and other colored light. After some three minutes of this it again ceases its whirling and splashing of color to move and wander about anew within the break in the clouds.

And finally now, as Lúcia gazes intently at the last of the solar apparitions, that of Our Lady of Mount Carmel, the electrified throng sees the sun begin its exotic dance for a third time. It starts again to turn at terrific speed, casting off the same changing, gorgeously colored rays.

Then it ceases its dizzy spinning and spraying of colored light. And once again it trembles and moves. But this time it does not advance horizontally across the sky. It seems to have shaken itself loose from its moorings by its gyrations and unusual movements and to be falling from the sky. Indeed, it plunges in zigzag fashion toward the earth and the horrified spectators, who stare with faces white as death. Closer and closer it comes in its grotesque reeling descent. Terror that in many cases borders on panic strikes into most hearts as this soulless monster of scorching heat staggers implacably downward, getting bigger and warmer as it nears the earth. Surely, think those whose minds are not completely paralyzed by fear, this is the end of the world and everyone will be either crushed or burned to death by this hurtling molten mass.

Cries of horror and anguish rise from all sides as the majority of the multitude fall to their knees on the wet muddy terrain. Tears of supplication and contrition stream down the cheeks of men and women alike. Public avowals of sins and open professions of belief in the apparitions rend the air. Fervent pleas to the Lady of the carrasqueira tree ascend heavenward from all quarters.

"O my God, we are all going to die!"

"O God, forgive us our sins!"

"Mary, save us!"

"I believe! I believe!"

"Miracle! Miracle!"

But just when the tension and suspense have reached their peak and it seems that the curiously careening sun is about to obliterate everyone, it halts in its downward course and speedily reverses its zigzag path. It goes back to the heavens. There it stops moving and begins to shine again with its customary golden glow and its usual unbearable glare.

Blinded now by the sun's normal brilliancy, the people quickly lower their blinking eyes. Indescribable feelings of relief and of joy come over them as they realize that they are now out of danger and that they have just witnessed the great, long-awaited, and much publicized miracle.[5]

It is not long before the spectators at the Cova da Iria, including the atheists, the skeptics, and the liberal newspaper reporters, are excitedly exchanging their profound and reverent impressions. They soon discover that, while the description of detail imparted to one another often varies considerably, they have all witnessed the same miraculous phenomena.[6]

While this is going on, another group of persons, much smaller but no less vividly stirred, is equally busy questioning and commenting on the bizarre dance of the sun. These are the people of Alburitel who have seen the Lady's sign, notwithstanding the fact that their little mountaintop town is about twelve miles from Fátima.

Yes, the sensational miracle that the Lady from heaven announced months in advance has been witnessed at various places and by various people. And some of these, at the time they saw it, were busy with their usual occupations and quite oblivious of the promise that this celestial Visitor had made to the children of Aljustrel.

At the present moment the children and people massed in the street in front of Alburitel's grammar school have ceased their queries about the extraordinary behavior of the sun and are singing a hymn of praise and thanksgiving to the Blessed Virgin. There are many youngsters in the crowd, for when at noon startled cries and exclamations of wonder had been heard coming from the road near the school, the excitable teacher had rushed out of the building followed, of course, by her delighted pupils. And for the ten minutes during which the sun had danced and spread its changing rainbow of colors over the ground, the houses, and the weeping and wailing spectators, these children had remained in the street closely observing each new change and development. They had marveled at the lavish display of changing beams of colored light that at one moment had put the world afire in a blaze of red, and at another had dipped it in a sea of blue, and again at another had bedecked it with gold or still some other hue. And they had trembled with fear when finally the frolicking sun had begun its downward zigzag flight.

One of the Alburitel schoolboys, Inácio Lourenço Pereira,[7] a lad of nine, had found himself during the miracle near a wretched man who no longer practiced any religion. That very morning the unbeliever had spent considerable time making easy fun of the fools who let themselves be duped to the extent of traveling all the way to Fátima to see a young girl. The boy had looked at the poor creature, wondering what effect such a spectacle would have on a person of his type. To his great amazement, he had seen him transformed as though by enchantment. The man was as though petrified, standing still and rigid and staring wide-eyed at the sun. Then, as the import of what he was seeing had dawned upon him, he had begun to shake. He had trembled from head to foot like a man taken with palsy. Finally, won over by the stupendous nature of the Lady's sign, he had raised his hands heavenward and had fallen to his knees in the mud of the road, crying again and again: *Nossa Senhora! Nossa Senhora!* "Our Lady! Our Lady!"

Few of the adults had noticed this remarkable conversion, for they had been too busy crying and weeping and asking God forgiveness for their own sins in their fear that the world was about to end.

After the dance of the sun, numerous groups assemble here and there at the Cova da Iria. One of the large gatherings is huddled around a middle-aged lady, Maria do Carmo dos Santos, who comes from Arnal, a village forming part of the parish of Maceira. Word has sped through the Cova that this good woman has miraculously been cured of a serious ailment.

Here is the story of this forty-seven-year-old housewife.

Very sick for five years, Maria do Carmo had manifested all the symptoms of tuberculosis. Moreover, since the early part of 1916 she had suffered sharp and continual pain in her whole body and had experienced other discomforts which had seemed to indicate that she was afflicted with a uterine tumor. Things had gone from bad to worse and eventually she had not been able to eat or sleep.

In July, she first heard about the unusual things occurring at the Cova da Iria. Although the Cova was twenty-two miles from Arnal, she promised to walk the distance barefooted four times in the hope of obtaining her cure from the Blessed Virgin.

When August 13, the date for the first trip arrived, her husband protested. "We are poor and have not enough money to take a carriage," he said, "and your going on foot is out of the question, you would probably die on the road. So you had better resign yourself, I am not going to let you go."

That is what the good man said and meant, but his determined spouse succeeded in changing his mind and they left together at one o'clock. With his help, she hobbled along as well as she could for several long and agonizing hours. When the two of them reached Fátima, she was one mass of pain from head to foot. But, an astonishing thing, she had been there only a few minutes when she began to feel better. And not only was the return trip home much less exhausting, but she found that her appetite had improved and that she could really begin to take food.

She went again to the Cova on September 13. This time she made the trip with greater ease, and her health continued gradually to get better.

Today proved to be quite a test of her faith in Our Lady. Her husband and she had hardly left home when they ran into heavy rain. It poured all the way and when the poor woman arrived here she was soaking wet. But again she felt better, and now her pains, her coughs, the swelling of her limbs, and the other symptoms of sickness have disappeared. At this very moment she feels much stronger and also very hungry.[8]

As the people mill around, there is joy and gratitude, as well as astonishment and excitement, visible on their faces. They are happy and thankful for the marvelous things that have transpired at the Cova da Iria. There have been many exterior proofs of God's loving intervention and these have been truly astounding. The latest wonder that some people are just now discovering is the sudden and unexpected drying of their clothes. Everyone was wet through and through at the start of the dance of the sun, but now all clothes are dry.

How explain this mysterious but very welcome incident? Was it the intense heat of the falling sun that dried soaked clothes in a few brief moments? No one can say, but all are convinced that in one way or another this hitherto unheard-of phenomenon must be attributed to a special intervention of the Almighty.

But great as all these visible wonders have been, they cannot compare to the innumerable spiritual marvels that, on this day, have operated in the depths of men's souls. True apparitions are always the occasions of a tremendous outpouring of divine grace, and the ultimate aim of both the exterior graces that men call miracles and the interior graces that directly touch men's hearts and move their wills is always to bring people back to God or closer to Him.

The three little children of Aljustrel are eloquent witnesses to the fact that apparitions are accompanied by invisible though powerful grace. One of the greatest wonders of Fátima was the marvelous transformation effected in the souls of the three seers, both during and after the apparitions.

PART TWO

PART TWO

18

I Will Take Jacinta and Francisco Soon

On June 13, Our Lady had predicted that she would come and take Jacinta and Francisco to heaven soon. She claimed Francisco first. In October 1918 he came down with Spanish influenza, which developed into pneumonia. In January his health improved, but in February he suffered a relapse that was fatal. He was not surprised, for Our Lady had appeared to him and to Jacinta and had told them she would come for him soon. She had asked Jacinta if she wanted to convert more sinners. Receiving an affirmative reply, she had told her that she would go to a hospital and suffer much there.

On April 2, sensing that death was near, Francisco told his father that he would like to receive Holy Communion. The good man departed immediately for the rectory. In the meantime, Francisco began preparing for his confession and asked Jacinta and Lúcia to remind him of any sins he might have committed. A priest came later that day and heard his last confession. He returned the next morning to bring him Holy Viaticum.

As dawn broke on April 4, a smile came over the dying boy's face. He cried out to his mother: "Look, Mamma! What a beautiful light over there, by the door . . . Now, I can't see it anymore!" At ten o'clock another smile brightened his face. This smile never left him, for his heavenly Mother had fulfilled her promise and had taken him to his celestial home.

Jacinta had come down with influenza at the same time as

Francisco. Although she rallied better than he had, she never completely recovered and eventually bronchial pneumonia set in. Later, she developed pleurisy. Pus had formed in her left lung. An abscessed growth soon appeared on her left side and burst open. Our Lady appeared and spoke with Jacinta a number of times. Long before the actual events occurred, Jacinta told Lúcia: "Our Lady wants me to go to two hospitals, but it is not to be cured. It is to suffer more for love of Our Lord and for sinners."

The first hospital she went to was that of Santo Agostinho in nearby Vila Nova de Ourém. She was there during the months of July and August 1919. She was sent home toward the end of August because her condition had shown no improvement. Her long sickness with its various complications—influenza, bronchial pneumonia, purulent pleurisy, and finally tuberculosis—had reduced her almost to a skeleton and she often experienced great pain, which she generously suffered for the conversion of sinners.

Toward the end of December 1919, Our Lady appeared to her and told her a new and heavy cross lay ahead. Jacinta told her bosom friend about it: "Lúcia, Our Lady visited me again. She told me that I am going to Lisboa, to another hospital, and that I will not return to see you or my parents. She said that after much suffering I will die alone, but that I should not be afraid because she will come there to take me home." These predictions were all fulfilled.

In the middle of January 1920, Jacinta's family sent her to Lisboa for expert medical and surgical help. She left with her mother and her oldest brother, Antônio.

She went first to an orphanage on the Rua da Estrela, and her mother stayed there with her for a week. The Orfanato do Nossa Senhora dos Milagres was under the direction of a kind and loving nun, Maria da Purificação Godhino, to whom Jacinta was soon attracted and to whom she revealed many things. Among the things she disclosed was the fact that Our Lady was still appearing to her there at the orphanage.

In February, after nearly two weeks at the orphanage, Jacinta went to Dona Estefânia hospital where Dr. Eurico Lisboa had finally arranged for her to be received. The surgeon-in-chief, Dr. Leonardo de Castro Freire, declared she should be operated on. Jacinta protested, saying this was useless, since Our Lady had appeared to her and told her that she would die soon. She even had someone write to Lúcia notifying her that Our Lady had visited her and told her the day and hour of her death. But her objections were overruled, and on February 10 she was operated upon.

The operation, which consisted of the removal of two infected ribs, was successful, though it left a hole as big as a fist. The subsequent treatment of the gaping wound was extremely painful, but Jacinta never complained.

Our Lady appeared to Jacinta several times while she was in this hospital. On the seventh day after the operation, Jacinta told her beloved Mother Godhino, who had come to visit her: "O *madrinha*, Little Mother"—as everyone called her at the orphanage—"I won't complain anymore now. Our Lady came back and appeared to me and told me that she would come to get me soon. She said she would take my pains away right off. And she did."

At six o'clock on Friday, February 20, Jacinta began to feel very sick, for unexpected complications had set in and things were approaching a climax. Jacinta knew it only too well, for Our Lady had told her the day and hour of her death, and she asked to receive the Sacraments of the Anointing of the Sick and Viaticum.

Toward eight o'clock, Father Pereira dos Reis, Prior of the church dos Anjos (of the Angels), came and heard the child's confession. He refused to give her Viaticum at once, saying her condition was not critical enough and that he would return with it the next day.

Jacinta insisted, asking to be allowed to receive Holy Communion immediately, saying that she was going to die very soon. But again she was refused because it was thought she could safely wait till the next day. The child was right: there was no next day for her. She left this world serenely that very night at ten-thirty.

Not only did Jacinta die when Our Lady said she would, she also died the way Our Lady said she would, that is, alone. None of those she loved was with her at her last hour. No member of her family, not Lúcia, not even her *madrinha*, was there to comfort and console her. Only a young nurse, Aurora Gomes, was at her side when Our Lady came to get her.

Although Francisco had been interred in the Fátima parish cemetery, Jacinta was buried in the Baron of Alvaiázere's vault at Vila Nova de Ourém. But this was not to be her final resting

place. Shortly before her death, Jacinta had told Mother Godhino: "I shall return to Fátima, but only after my death." This
prediction was fulfilled in September 1935, when her remains
were transferred from Ourém to the Fátima parish cemetery at
the order of the Bishop of Leiria. She was placed in a sarcophagus
above the grave of her brother Francisco, who had been buried in
the ground.

When Jacinta died in Lisboa, her remains had been placed in a
sealed lead casket and the lower part of her body had been cov-
ered with quicklime because of the infectious nature of her illness.
Before leaving Ourém for Fátima, her lead coffin was opened and
her head and face were found to be intact. This, after fifteen years
in her tomb.

On December 21, 1949, the cause for the canonization of Jacinta and that for the canonization of Francisco were begun separately but simultaneously. By early 1951, the two causes had ad-
vanced to the point where it was decided to exhume the remains
of the two children. This was done on April 30. There was no
problem identifying Jacinta. Her features were still preserved and,
though somewhat sunken and discolored, they could easily be recognized as those of a little girl. It was now thirty years since she
had died.* As others had been buried in Francisco's grave, over his
body, it was not immediately possible to identify his remains,
which had completely disintegrated except for the full skeleton. A
new exhumation for Francisco's remains was conducted on February 14 the following year, and the process of identification was
successfully carried out on February 17.

On March 13, the remains of Francisco were taken to the basilica at the Cova da Iria. Jacinta had already been placed there in a
tomb in the left transept. Francisco was placed in a similar tomb
in the right transept.

Another important step toward the canonizations of Jacinta
and Francisco was taken on April 30, 1952, with the official com-
mencement of the processes of beatification in the diocese of
Leiria. In the July 1958 issue of *The Voice of Fátima* the Reverend Augustine Fuentes, Postulator in Rome for the two causes,

---

*It is impossible at this time to affirm with certainty that Jacinta's face is
incorrupt. If it should eventually prove not to be, this fact would not affect her
cause of sanctification.

stated that the diocesan processes for beatification were nearly completed and that theologians and cardinals of the Sacred Congregation of Rites were engaged in studying the heroicity of the virtues of Jacinta and Francisco. In 1983 The Blue Army headquarters in Washington, New Jersey, affirmed that petitions expressing a desire for the beatification of Jacinta and of Francisco are no longer requested.

Before concluding this chapter, something must be said about the apparitions of Our Lady experienced by the three children of Fátima in addition to the six that took place from May 13 to October 13, 1917. Most of those that have become public knowledge have to do with Jacinta and occurred while she was in Lisboa, both at the orphanage and at the hospital. And we have come to know about them mainly through Mother Godhino who carefully noted down the child's sayings. The good woman had sensed that many of the things that Jacinta said to her, at the orphanage and at the hospital, had been learned by her in some exceptional way. Indeed, she had candidly asked the child about the source of her information. And Jacinta had replied: "Our Lady taught me some of it and the rest I thought about myself. I like very much to think."

Many of the things Jacinta told her *madrinha* were intimately related to the messages given by Our Lady at the Cova da Iria in 1917. Here are a few examples. One day, while Jacinta was still at Aljustrel, she told her mother: "Our Lady said that sins of the flesh are the ones that take most souls to hell." Later, at the Dona Estefânia hospital, she stated that Our Lady had appeared to her there and told her that the sins which brought most souls to hell were those of the flesh, that people should avoid luxury, that they should not remain obstinately in sin, and that they should do penance.

As a result of this, Jacinta became preoccupied with sins of the flesh and with purity and spoke of them in her conversations with Mother Godhino and in her remarks to people at the hospital. "Dear *madrinha*," she told the good mother, "don't live in luxury. Flee riches. Certain styles will come that will greatly offend Our Lord . . . Many marriages are not good, do not please Our Lord, and are not acceptable to God."

The topic of war had been stressed by Our Lady on July 13,

1917. Jacinta made many statements about this subject that were far beyond her age and mental capacity. Thus, she told her dear *madrinha:* "Our Lady said that there were many wars and much strife in the world. The sins of the world are very great. Our Lady can no longer restrain the arm of her beloved Son over the world. It is necessary to do penance. If people amend their lives, Our Lord will still help the world, but, if they do not, the chastisement will follow. If people do not correct their lives, Our Lord will chastise the world as never before, and Spain will be punished first."

19

Alone

Although Our Lady had told the children on June 13, 1917, that Lúcia would soon be alone, when that time finally came she was crushed. She went as soon as she could to the niche of Cabeço and shed abundant and bitter tears.

Things moved fast. With modest offerings of money and natural produce left by people who went to the Cova da Iria, a very small and unimposing chapel was constructed close to the stump —all that was left—of the carrasqueira of the apparitions, and in place of the former rustic arch.

Crowds of pilgrims grew rapidly at that hallowed place. More and more people came on Sundays and especially on the thirteenth day of the apparition months, May through October. Frequently, these reached several thousand.

A beautiful statue of Our Lady as she appeared at the Cova, carved of Brazilian cedar and painted white and gold by o Senhor José Ferreira Thedim, one of Portugal's finest sculptors, was placed in the new chapel on May 13, 1920. This was done in spite of government opposition. Now there was a statue which could be carried through the throngs on the thirteenth of each month. It is this same statue which one still finds in the same little chapel, the *capelhina*, and it is carried around triumphantly on the anniversaries of the various apparitions. One can occasionally see a million and more people there on very special occasions.

As the months went by, it became clear that absolutely nothing

—the forbidding of gatherings and the dispatching of government troops or anything else—could stop people from coming to this spot where it seemed so easy to pray and where such great favors, both spiritual and temporal, were so abundantly dispensed. The voice of the people is the voice of God—*Vox populi, vox Dei*. The voice of God's people was not long in reaching the ears of Catholic officialdom. Various investigations were undertaken by the Church, the first one beginning as early as September 13, 1917.

The most important measure undertaken by the Church was the reestablishment of the diocese of Leiria. On July 25, 1920, José Alves Correia da Silva was consecrated Bishop of the newly restored episcopal see, and on August 5 he was officially installed in his cathedral at Leiria. Since Fátima is in that diocese and only a few miles from Leiria, the purpose of Rome in restoring that diocese was obvious. Those accepting the apparitions must have been greatly encouraged when the new Bishop, on the feast of the Assumption, ten days after his installation, solemnly consecrated his bishopric to Our Lady, the traditional sovereign of Portugal, *a Terra de Santa Maria*.

The new Bishop quickly manifested his prudent foresight. Before the year 1921 was over, he had concluded various purchases by which he acquired some thirty acres of land at the Cova da Iria. The land was bought with the donations left by the pilgrims at the Cova. Architects were soon put to work drafting plans for a simple, fitting shrine in honor of Our Lady. These plans have been revised and enlarged more than once since work on the Cova da Iria grounds first started in the summer of 1921.

Two other significant measures were taken in the fall of 1921. His Excellency authorized the celebration of Mass for the first time at the Cova da Iria, and it was said on October 13, on the open porch in front of the *capelhina*. The chapel itself was blessed that day. Thus it was clear that, whatever his personal belief might be, the new Bishop was not opposed to the apparitions.

Lúcia's continued presence at Fátima presented problems. The greatest of these was her own welfare, especially her spiritual welfare. There was the constant invasion of her home, of her private life and that of her family. But there was especially the danger of adulation—of being canonized, so to speak, before her death.

Pride is such an insidious thing, and so damaging to one's spiritual welfare.

To the Bishop, the only satisfactory solution, painful as it might be, seemed to consist in having Lúcia voluntarily isolate herself from the Cova da Iria and from everything connected with it. The plan that the Bishop worked out, and which was freely accepted by Lúcia and her mother, demanded heroism.

Lúcia would depart secretly—the date set was June 16, 1921—for a school far removed from Fátima. She would go to O Asilo de Vilar, an educational institution conducted by the Sisters of Saint Dorothy at Vilar, now a suburb of the city of O Porto. She would tell no one who she was except Mother Superior, and she would never speak to anyone of the apparitions.

To assure the secrecy requested by the Bishop, the departure took place at two o'clock in the morning. A stop was made at the Cova da Iria where she, her mother, and a friend, o Senhor Carreira, prayed for a while. Then the little group started off.

At a certain point, Lúcia turned for a last glance at the place that would always be in her heart and mind. From the little chapel of the apparitions her eyes went to the northern crest of the great hollow where she and her two cousins had been playing on May 13, 1917. There they had seen the first bright flash of light announcing Our Lady's initial appearance. Suddenly Lúcia's heartbeat quickened. At that same spot—which is today occupied by the lower steps of the basilica—was the Lady of the apparitions. Then, without speaking, the Lady disappeared. Thus were fulfilled the words spoken by the vision at the first apparition: "Afterward, I will return here a seventh time."[1]

Lúcia spent four years at O Asilo de Vilar. She was given the name of Maria das Dores, Mary Dolores, or, literally, Mary of the Sorrows. The name proved to be symbolic, for she suffered considerably at the school, especially during the first three years.

But love of Our Lady grew in her heart in the favorable atmosphere of the Asilo. It blossomed into the decision to consecrate her life to Mary by entering some religious order dedicated to her. Lúcia's first choice was the cloistered Carmelites, whose austere life offered an opportunity for prayer and sacrifice.

Told that her health was not adequate to bear up under the Carmelites' severe rule, she joined the Sisters of Saint Dorothy, who had a tradition of devotion to the Immaculate Heart of Mary. She asked to become a lay or coadjutrix sister rather than a teaching nun. She was eighteen at the time. Her postulancy began on October 2, 1925, and a year later she became a novice. The nuns called her Irmã Dores, Sister Dolores, the short form of her official name in religion, Irmã Maria das Dores, Sister Mary of the Sorrows. She continued to maintain complete secrecy about her identity, and she never inquired about Fátima from those who visited her, not even the members of her immediate family.

Due to the expulsion of the religious congregations by the Portuguese Government, the Sisters of Saint Dorothy had transferred their novitiate to the old Spanish city of Túy. This frontier city lies on the Minho River, which, in this area, divides Spain and Portugal. Irmã Dores, whom we shall continue to call Sister Lúcia, was first a postulant and then a novice at the combined provincial house and novitiate in Túy.

On October 3, 1934, the Bishop of Leiria presided at the ceremony during which Sister Lúcia made her final vows, thereby officially removing the veil of mystery that he himself had placed about her and which had been maintained with less success as time went on.

It was a relief to Sister Lúcia, after thirteen years of embarrassing and painful silence. During those long years she had known great mental suffering. At Túy, the terrible doubt concerning the reality of the apparitions that had tortured her briefly in 1917 came back to haunt her. But this time, the doubt sprang mainly from the sense of her inadequacy. She became startlingly aware of her frailty and nothingness. Was it possible that the Queen of heaven could have appeared to such a miserable creature as herself? She was absolutely sincere in this appraisal of her unworthiness. And the doubt that was founded on that belief was real and cruelly persistent. Eventually it disappeared and Sister Lúcia recovered her certainty about the apparitions.

Another interior and distressing trial had arisen from the silence that was maintained about everything concerning Fátima and the apparitions. Never hearing anything about the Cova da Iria and the events that were occurring there, Sister Lúcia occasionally found herself thinking that everything was finished at Fátima, that the Bishop of Leiria had refused to acknowledge the authenticity of the apparitions and that she personally was considered a liar and Our Lady's wishes had not been complied with. Though these thoughts caused her great sorrow, they never really disturbed the depths of her soul. "If everything is over," she said to herself, "it is because Our Lord has willed it so. For my part, I did everything that the Blessed Virgin told me to do."

Even the confessional failed to bring solace and enlightenment to her during this trying period. This was due to a misunderstanding. She felt the promise she had made to the Bishop of Leiria to conceal her identity and not talk to anyone about the apparitions extended also to her confessor. To have mentioned her doubts and anxieties would have entailed revealing who she was and speaking of the apparitions. So she said nothing.

During her novitiate, she was told that the Bishop's request for secrecy did not include her confessor. However, she continued to suffer. The novitiate chaplain was cold and distant and completely lacking in understanding of her problems. He was never able to give her a satisfactory answer. Rather than depart from the common rule and singularize herself by asking for another confessor, she preferred not to say anything.

Yet her burden was considerably lightened by Our Lord. Indeed, deprived of help from man, she turned to God for assistance and, after her unsatisfactory sessions in the confessional, she made long visits to the Blessed Sacrament. These brought her the light and peace she had sought in vain from her confessor. On the few occasions when Our Lord left her with the full weight of her cross, she still found in the Divine Presence the courage not to complain and even gladly to accept her sacrifice.

Túy was not without its valleys of consolation. While there, Sister Lúcia was favored at least twice by heavenly visits. Both apparitions relate to the message of July 13, 1917, and took place while she was a postulant. The first occurred in December 1925, not very long after she had arrived at Túy. The second followed shortly afterward, in February 1926. Both apparitions will be discussed later. These heavenly visits did much to dispel her doubts and anxieties and to strengthen her faith in the Fátima events and in her own mission in regard to them.[2]

20

Approval at Last!

Since Lúcia's departure from Aljustrel in 1921, several important things had taken place at Fátima. On October 13, 1922, Voz da Fátima, the official publication of the sanctuary of Fátima, appeared for the first time. To maintain order at the Cova da Iria, especially during the great pilgrimages, to care materially and spiritually for the sick and all others who go to the shrine, and to promote true devotion to Our Lady, an association of priests, doctors, nurses, stretcher-bearers, and zealous workers was formed. Called The Helpers of Our Lady of Fátima, Os Servitas de Nossa Senhora de Fátima, it came into existence in 1924.

With the aim of assuring the proper medical care of the sick and of facilitating the scientific examination and recording of reported physical cures, work on a first hospital was started in 1924. This marked the beginning of the construction of several buildings on the shrine grounds. Work seems to be going on there almost constantly. As late as 1982, some impressive construction was taking place next to the little chapel of the apparitions and the small open porch of the little chapel is now considerably enlarged and completely glassed in.

In 1925 the pilgrimages became regularized, and in 1926 a Medical Bureau was set up to assist the sick and examine cures that were considered miraculous.

June 26, 1927, saw His Excellency, José Correia da Silva make his first official visit to the Cova da Iria. He celebrated Mass there

that day on the occasion of the inauguration of a ten-mile Way of
the Cross. The entire event was typical of the spirit of penance
that always prevails at Fátima. Notwithstanding a leg ailment, the
Bishop, while fasting, walked the full ten miles up the mountain
road, blessing the fourteen stations and preaching at each one
himself. It took six hours, from eight a.m. to two p.m., to make
the trip from the bottom of the mountain to the Cova. The
Bishop then celebrated the Eucharist and four hundred people
who has fasted with him received Communion.

What is amazing is that all of these various steps were taken by
the Bishop before he firmly believed in the apparitions. It was not
ten years since the apparitions had taken place. Our Lady apparently felt that it was time that they be approved, for she took
occasion of the Bishop's presence at the shrine on June 26, 1927,
to perform a miracle that ended his hesitancy. She repeated for
his benefit the mysterious shower of shining globules that the
witnesses of the September 13 and October 13, 1927, apparitions
had observed at the Cova da Iria. "Then," Sister Lúcia declared to
Father Thomas McGlynn, referring to the Bishop of Leiria, "he
believed."[1]

This inexplicable phenomenon has been observed more than
once since its two occurrences in 1917. It was even photographed
on May 13, 1924, and a notarized and fully authenticated copy of
this picture was obtained by o Senhor Antônio Rebelo Martins,
Portuguese vice-consul to the United States, who happened to be
at Fátima.

It will be recalled that this phenomenon consisted of two distinct elements: a tremendous beam of light coming down from
the higher regions of the sky, with rays that widened as they
approached the earth, much as if they came from a huge heavenly
searchlight, and small shiny white balls falling in the midst of this
light. Both the widening beam of light and the glistening globules
are visible in the picture taken on May 13, 1924. It is even possible to distinguish cone-shaped shadows under the balls. Since all
these various features of this mysterious shower sensitized the pho-
tographic plate that gave us this picture, it is obvious that the
phenomenon was of an objective and material nature.[2]

Just a little over three years after this visit, the Bishop approved
the apparitions. This he did in a ceremony at the Cova da Iria on

October 13, 1930, thirteenth anniversary of the last apparition and the great miracle of the dancing sun.

In the presence of over a hundred thousand pilgrims he read a beautiful letter which ended with the declaration that Lúcia and millions of others had waited so long to hear:

> We deem well:
> 1) to declare worthy of credence the visions of the shepherds at the Cova da Iria, in the parish of Fátima of this diocese, on the thirteenth day of the months from May to October 1917;
> 2) to give official permission for the cult of Our Lady of Fátima.
>
> José, Bishop of Leiria
>
> Leiria, 13 October 1930.

The shower of shiny white balls witnessed by the Bishop during his first official visit to the Cova in 1927 undoubtedly played a part in his decision to finally approve the apparitions. But there were other factors that must have entered into that decision. One of these was the accumulated evidence of the canonical commission of investigation. Another important one surely was the readiness and generosity of the people of Portugal in accepting the Fátima message of prayer and penance and the subsequent rapid religious transformation of that country.

It is not pretended that this predominantly Catholic nation suddenly became a model of religious perfection. However, it has been the scene of a tremendous revival since 1917, the exceptional character of which can only be fully grasped by a knowledge of the deplorable state of the Church at the time of the apparitions. Indeed, the anticlerical government which had set out to destroy Fátima was itself destroyed by Fátima and the spiritual awakening that it provoked. On May 12, 1929, barely twelve years after the first heavenly manifestation at the Cova da Iria, General Carmon, the Chief of State, and Oliveira Salazar, a fervent Catholic, the President of the Council (that is, the Prime Minister), and several other members of the government made a pilgrimage to Fátima. This was a far cry from the days of the kidnapping Administrator and the government troops trying to stop people from going to the Cova. His Eminence, Manuel Cardinal Gonçalves Cerejeira, Patriarch of Lisboa, in the homily he delivered in the

presence of three hundred thousand pilgrims congregated at the
Cova for the national pilgrimage of May 13, 1942, stated that the
marvelous transformation that had taken place in Portugal during
the twenty-five years since the apparitions was due to the Blessed
Virgin and that the only Portuguese word that could describe it
was *milagre*—miracle!

21

The Attitude of Rome

The Bishop's approval of the visions was the biggest thing that had ever occurred at the Cova da Iria since the apparitions themselves. People the world over could ask for the intercession of Our Lady of Fátima, now that they had the assurance that, insofar as human prudence could determine, Our Lady had really appeared at the Cova da Iria and that in believing in the apparitions they were not being misled or deceived. That was what the Bishop had meant when he declared the visions "worthy of credence." His authentic judgment concerning the credibility of the apparitions can in no way be compared to a dogmatic definition by virtue of which the Pope proposes a statement of fact or of principle as a matter of Catholic faith which the faithful must accept. His Excellency intended simply to propose the apparitions for the instruction and edification of souls as matters of purely human faith. From the point of view of episcopal approbation the apparitions of Fátima were now on an equal footing with those of Lourdes.

It is not the policy of Rome to intervene directly and pronounce judgment concerning the authenticity of any apparition. The formal approbation of such occurrences is left to the Ordinary or Bishop of the locality where they take place. But Rome can and often does manifest its attitude toward apparitions by its actions. It does this particularly through its participation in important liturgical events, that is, in major religious celebrations that are held at the site of these apparitions. And it does it also in other ways. A number of measures emanating from Rome will be discussed later. Only two will be mentioned here.

A major event took place at Fátima on May 13, 1946. It centered around the crowning of the statue of Our Lady of Fátima as Queen of Portugal and Queen of the World. The crowning was to have taken place at the end of World War Two but was delayed until 1946 so that it could be made to coincide with the three hundredth anniversary of the consecration of Portugal to Mary Immaculate by King João IV.

His Eminence, Benedetto Cardinal Masella, who was sent from Rome for the occasion, crowned the statue as personal Legate of His Holiness, Pope Pius XII. The impressive ceremony, which also included the inauguration of bells, of a huge bronze crown, and of a luminous cross for the tower of the shrine basilica, was held at the Cova da Iria in the presence of the entire Portuguese Government and over six hundred thousand pilgrims.

Another important liturgical act whereby the Holy See indicated its mind concerning the Fátima apparitions was the closing of the Extended Holy Year at the Cova da Iria on October 13, 1951. Again, Pope Pius XII sent a Papal Legate to represent him personally at this major event. He sent His Eminence, Federico Cardinal Tedeschini. It is clear that the Pope chose the Portuguese shrine for this important act because he wished to focus attention on Our Lady and her Fátima message and because he wanted the world to know that, as he himself once stated, "the time to doubt Fátima is past."

The closing of the Extended Holy Year was the occasion of a startling revelation that showed how close Pope Pius XII was to the Immaculate Heart of Mary and how pleased the Blessed Mother was with what he had done for her Fátima message. Cardinal Tedeschini told the million people gathered at the Cova that the Supreme Pontiff had witnessed the miracle of the dancing sun four times at Rome the preceding year. Unfortunately the first new releases in the secular press of this country misrepresented the Papal Legate's statement and spoke of the Holy Father as having seen Our Lady herself. Nowhere in the Cardinal's discourse did he say such a thing. Below is the more important part of his

address, which was a sermon delivered at the shrine during the
Pontifical Mass on October 13:

> And nevertheless I tell you—but in my own name only, and I
> tell it to my new and old Portuguese friends and to the pilgrims
> united with them—an even more wonderful thing.*
> I tell you that another person has seen this miracle. He has
> seen it at a distance of years. He has seen it at Rome. The Pope,
> our own Pontiff Pius XII, has seen it.[1]
> Was this a reward? Was this a sign of sovereign divine plea-
> sure for the definition of the dogma of the Assumption? *Was
> this a heavenly testimony authenticating the connection between
> the wonders of Fátima and the center, the head of Catholic
> truth and teaching authority* [emphasis added]? It was all three
> together.
> It was four in the afternoon on October 30 and 31, and on
> November 1 of last year, 1950, and on the octave of November
> 1, the day of the definition of Mary's assumption into heaven.
> From the Vatican gardens the Holy Father turned his gaze to-
> ward the sun and there before his eyes the wonder of this valley
> and this day was renewed.
> The sun's disc was surrounded by halos. Who could gaze upon
> it? But he could! On all four days he was able to gaze upon the
> activity of the sun. Under the hand of Mary, the sun, agitated
> and entirely convulsed, was transformed into a picture of life,
> into a spectacle of heavenly movements, into a transmission of
> mute but eloquent messages to the Vicar of Christ.
> Is this not Fátima transported to the Vatican? Is this not the
> Vatican transformed into Fátima?

Just a few days after this event, on November 17, 1951, *L'Osservatore Romano*, the daily newspaper and semiofficial organ of the
Vatican, quoted verbatim the pertinent parts of Cardinal Tedeschini's sermon. *L'Osservatore Romano* even went so far as to comment: "It is not our task to formulate deductions from these
singularly analogous events [the original dance of the sun and the
one witnessed by the Pope], but intervention of the Most Blessed
Virgin is frequent in the gravest days of the history of the

---

*He had just finished describing in detail the great Fátima miracle of Octo-
ber 13, 1917, the original dance of the sun.

Church, even with intimations directed to the successor of Peter personally."

The Cardinal states explicitly that he gives this information "in my own name only." But it is inconceivable that a Cardinal Legate, representing the Pope personally, would reveal such extraordinary information unless he were absolutely sure of the facts and had the Holy Father's consent to mention them. It is equally inconceivable that *L'Osservatore Romano* would print such a story without first verifying its authenticity and assuring itself of the Pope's willingness to have it published.

The closing of the Extended Holy Year was an epochal event. His Excellency, Bishop Fulton J. Sheen was at Fátima at the time, and here are some of the comments he made concerning the significance of the ceremonies that took place there on October 12 and 13:

> On October 13, 1917, when the Blessed Virgin appeared at Fátima, it rained. The people expect it to rain as a sign of blessing. It rained on six hundred thousand people on October 12, most of whom stood all night in prayer. Only a few drops fell on the one million people on October 13, but it was enough to be a symbol of the shower of grace. Mud is not conducive to prayer; rain generally dampens spirits as well as bodies. But to the pious pilgrims, both were opportunities for sacrifice for the peace of the world.
>
> . . . Fátima is the least of the cities of the world, but out of it will come the force that will conquer Communism. The Red Square bristles with guns, and with flags dyed red with the blood of the victims of Communism. The White Square of Fátima is alive with a million handkerchiefs waving in affectionate greeting to the White Lady of Peace.
>
> Moscow has fifteen million men under arms; Fátima, on October 13, had one million faithful with rosaries. In the scales of divine justice, one has the feeling that those twisted little beads counting Aves were already the master of Stalin with his steel. *Communism was defeated on October 13, 1951, but the news has not yet leaked out* [italics added].
>
> One million penitential souls can certainly do for the world what just ten men could have done for Sodom and Gomorrah . . .
>
> Communism is a faith, and it can be conquered only by a

faith. Great nations may stop Communist aggression, but they will not stop Communism. Fátima is a flank attack on Communism through penance and sacrifice. Rain, mud, and night without sleep, and a love of Our Lady make Fátima. Most people in the world want a bed for the night; at Fátima all one wanted was a rosary. Those million of little beads on which the faithful worked during the night were more mighty than bullets in the conquest of Communism.

Stalin once asked in ridicule: "How many divisions has the Pope?" The answer was given at Fátima: "A million." Each is armed with fifteen decades of explosive love.

Stalin says he wants peace. He means a piece of China, a piece of Poland, a piece of Korea. Fátima wants peace too, but it knows that peace can come only when man has waged war against his great enemy—his selfishness, his hate, and his sin. On that dark night of October 12, hundreds of thousands of men and women were engaged in that battle against everything that was non-God, and when morning came one knew that God had won.

On October 13, 1917, when Our Lady appeared at Fátima, Communism was just beginning to gnaw into the vitals of the world. In another thirty-four years Communism will no longer be in existence. What will disappear will be a red dictator reviewing his troops in the Red Square. What will survive will be Our Lady of the Kremlin reviewing in the White Square below her troops of the Legion of Mary. And when historians look back to *the one event which turned the world upside down and brought it peace and prosperity,* they will discover it to be not a battle, but a prayer, and not a day, but *a night—the wet night of October 12—the greatest religious event of the modern world* [italics added] . . .

Fátima is like a parable. There are deep hidden mysteries in it that have not yet been sounded. But one thing is certain. No one who was among those million penitents on October 13 will doubt that Our Lady of Fátima will bring peace to the world. If other nations besides Portugal do penance, there will be no catastrophe of war.

If, however, penance is done by Portugal alone, then some kind of catastrophe may have to come briefly before peace will follow. A few all-night vigils might do much for America and the peace of the world. The future is known only to God, but what the future brings depends largely on how we spend our days and our nights.

The more they are like October 12 and 13, at Fátima, the more quickly peace will come and Russia will be converted.[2]

22

The Conversion of Russia and Peace

A most important part of the Fátima message has to do with the conversion of Russia and peace. And Rome is very much involved in that. The complete message about the conversion of Russia and peace was not given by Our Lady in 1917. It was on July 13, 1917, that she first made mention of this question and it was in these words:

> The war is going to end, but if people do not stop offending God another and worse one will begin during the reign of Pius XI. When you see a night illuminated by an unknown light, know that this is the great sign that God is giving you that He is going to punish the world for its crimes by means of war, famine, and persecution of the Church and of the Holy Father.
>
> To prevent this I shall come to ask for the consecration of Russia to my Immaculate Heart and for Communions of reparation on the first Saturdays.
>
> If they heed my requests, Russia will be converted and there will be peace. If not, she will spread her errors throughout the world, promoting wars and persecution of the Church, the good will be martyred, the Holy Father will have much to suffer, various nations will be annihilated.
>
> In the end, my Immaculate Heart will triumph. The Holy Father will consecrate Russia to me and she will be converted, and a certain period of peace will be granted to the world.
>
> In Portugal, the dogma of Faith will always be preserved.

A special message for the Pope, commonly referred to as "The Secret of 1960,"* was also given to the children on this same day. It has never been made public.

When did Our Lady return to ask for this consecration of Russia and for Communions of reparation? Though Our Lady came on two different days for each of these matters, they are very much linked.

Our Lady came first to complete her message about "the Communions of reparation on the first Saturdays." She appeared to Sister Lúcia in her convent cell on December 10, 1925, while she was a postulant at Túy in Spain. She came with the Child Jesus, Who stood beside her on a luminous cloud. She showed her Heart to the Sister and the Child Jesus said with sadness:

> Have pity on this very sweet Heart which is continually martyred because of the ingratitude of men and has no one to console it with acts of reparation.

Then Our Lady herself uttered this momentous message:

> Look, my daughter, at my Heart encircled by these thorns with which men pierce it at every moment by their blasphemies and ingratitude.
>
> Do you, at least, strive to console me, and announce:
>
> I promise to assist at the hour of death with the grace necessary for salvation all those who, with the intention of making reparation to me, will, on the first Saturday of five consecutive months, go to confession, receive Holy Communion, say five decades of the beads, and keep me company for fifteen minutes while meditating on the fifteen mysteries of the rosary.

The Child Jesus appeared again to the Sister a short time later, on February 14, 1926. He invited her to spread the devotion to the Immaculate Heart of Mary everywhere and told her not to let herself be discouraged by any difficulties that her confessors might point out, because with God's help they would easily be overcome.

Sister Lúcia profited by this heavenly visit to clarify a point concerning the First Saturday devotions. She asked Our Lord if, in the event a person could not go to confession on the first Saturday

*See Appendix A.

of the month, it would be sufficient to go during the week. Our Lord replied affirmatively, stating that it was understood that the Communion had to be received in a state of grace and in a spirit of reparation.

The Bishop of Leiria published the First Saturday devotions on September 21, 1939. In a document dated September 21, 1939, and carrying his imprimatur, he explains certain aspects of the devotions:

"The confession may be made during the eight days preceding or following the first Saturday of each month, provided that Holy Communion be received in the state of grace. Should one forget to form the intention of making reparation to the Immaculate Heart of Mary, it may be formed at the next confession, occasion to go to confession being taken at the first opportunity.

"The meditation embraces one or more mysteries; it may even include all, taken together or separately, according to individual attraction or devotion; but it is preferable to meditate on one mystery each month."[1]

The completion of Our Lady's message concerning the consecration of Russia to her Immaculate Heart was given to Sister Lúcia on December 10, 1929, while she was in the chapel of the Dorothean convent at Pontevedra, Spain, about twenty miles north of Túy. It was a Thursday night and the Sister was alone making a Holy Hour from eleven until midnight.

First she knelt at the center of the altar rail. Then she prostrated herself and recited the prayers of the angel, as she and her two cousins had done so frequently in the past. As this tired her, she rose and continued the prayers with her arms outstretched in the form of a cross. Her fidelity to the prayers taught by the angel in 1916 contains a lesson for us. It was then that she received what is often referred to as the last vision of Fátima. It might be more accurate to call it the last "public" vision and message of Fátima, for Sister Lúcia has continued to receive visits and revelations from Our Lord and Our Lady since then. But this vision portrays in picture form the entire Fátima message, and with the message about the consecration of Russia that followed it, it really constitutes an extension of the July 13, 1917, apparition.

After describing this vision, Sister Lúcia says that she was given to understand that what was shown to her was the mystery of the

Blessed Trinity. And she added the significant remark that she was also given insights into this mystery that she cannot reveal. This vision represents the three persons of the Blessed Trinity, the Immaculate Heart of Mary, the rosary, the Eucharist, and reparation (Jesus on the cross). Also, the two words Grace and Mercy that are part of the vision sum up in verbal form the whole meaning of Fátima.

It was at this point that Our Lady gave the Sister the so-called collegial form of the consecration desired by heaven. She said that the moment had arrived when "God" was asking "the Holy Father, in union with all of the bishops of the world, to make the consecration of Russia" to her Immaculate Heart. Then she told the Sister that God would save that country "by this means."

In a letter to Father José Bernardo Gonçalves, S.J., Sister Lúcia gives a little more information about the act of consecration of Russia. The letter was written at Pontevedra, Spain, but is not dated. However, it was received on May 29, 1930.[2] In it, she says that the Lord wants the Pope to make and to "command the bishops of the Catholic world to also make a solemn and public act of reparation and consecration of Russia to the Very Holy Hearts of Jesus and Mary." And the Pope must also "promise" that when the persecution is over in Russia, "he will approve and recommend the practice of the devotion of reparation [the First Saturday devotions]."

At this point, a word must be said about two important books on Fátima that were published in the early seventies.

In 1972 The Blue Army, the great worldwide and Church-approved international organization for the spreading of the Fátima message, made a major effort to acquaint the world with important information about that message which was then available to only a small number of people. This was done through an International Seminar held at Fátima in August of that year and which involved top theologians and highly qualified Fátima specialists. To bring this information to as many people as possible, the principal studies presented at the seminar were gathered together by The Blue Army and published in 1972 in a book entitled, *A Heart for All*.[3] It also contains extracts from important letters and documents emanating from Sister Lúcia, the contents of which were known to very few people. These had to do principally with the First Saturday devotions of reparation and the consecration of Russia to the Immaculate Heart.

The year 1973 saw the long-awaited publication of the complete text of Sister Lúcia's four *Memoirs*. Along with this, and almost like an extension of it, was a selection of a considerable number of the Sister's letters, most of which were answers to her confessor, the Reverend José Bernardo Gonçalves, S.J., seeking information concerning the 1917 message. There were also a few documents with information coming from the Sister. The book, entitled *Memórias e Cartas de Irmã Lúcia* (*The Memoirs and Letters of Sister Lúcia*), was published in O Porto under the direction of Dr. Antônio Maria Martins, S.J. The left-hand page of the book carries an enlarged photostatic copy of Sister Lúcia's handwritten manuscript of the four *Memoirs* that I was privileged to consult at the Bishop of Leiria's residence when I was doing research in the summer of 1950 on *The Sun Danced at Fátima* and *Fátima, Hope of the World*. The right-hand page has the edited, printed Portuguese text and also a French and English translation.[4]

When I read Sister Lúcia's letters to her confessor, I suddenly became aware in a whole new way that the conversion of Russia was not just an incidental part of the Fátima message. I was struck especially by the fact that this conversion was very much in the hand of each and every one of us, in the sense that we could all do something effective to help bring it about in the near future. When one ponders what this means, not only for the liberation of all those who are in one way or the other under the sway of Communism, but also for our country and other countries—think only of world tension and the billions spent on defense each year because of Communism—one has to become excited at the prospect of the conversion of Russia and our being able to hasten that happy event. Well, that is what Our Lady and Our Lord Himself have said in a number of communications with Sister Lúcia over the last fifty years. The Sister's letters to her confessor make this quite clear.

These same heavenly communications have also stressed the close bond between the First Saturday devotions of reparation to the Immaculate Heart of Mary and the conversion of Russia. And they reveal with a startling new starkness how much Our Lord wants devotion to the Immaculate Heart of His Mother spread throughout the world alongside devotion to His own Sacred Heart. All three of these closely linked topics constitute the very special or specific part of the Fátima message that distinguishes it from the messages of other Marian apparitions.

Although I had written two books on Fátima and felt that I was well informed about its message, I confess that I was excited by what I gleaned from these letters. They furnished new and important insights that electrified me. I saw a tremendous new hope, but only if this new information were brought to the attention of the people. I felt so strongly about this that I decided to write something about it. *Exciting Fátima News* (*Recently Revealed in Sister Lucy's letters*) was the title of this publication when it first appeared in pamphlet form in 1975 and was expanded into a book in 1979 (Assumption Publication, Worcester, Massachusetts). What follows now is taken mainly from this book.

The letter which had the greatest impact on me and that, more than any other, determined me to write *Exciting Fátima News* is one in which Our Lord is reported by Sister Lúcia as affirming that He has so fully entrusted the conversion of Russia to His Blessed Mother that it definitely will not take place until that country has been consecrated to the Immaculate Heart of Mary by the Holy Father; that He has laid down this absolute condition because He wants the whole Church to acknowledge that the conversion of Russia has been brought about through the Immaculate Heart of Mary; that this, in turn, will be used as a means to spread devotion to the Immaculate Heart throughout the world and to bring about its being honored alongside devotion to His own Sacred Heart. The letter also indirectly tells us—as do other letters—something about Sister Lúcia's present spiritual status as a mystic.

The letter was written on May 13, 1976, at Pontevedra, Spain. It was written to a priest, apparently Father José Bernardo Gonçalves, S.J., who had questioned her regarding the consecration of Russia. In the letter she tells him that she had spoken to Our Lord "intimately" about the matter and had asked Him specifically "why He did not convert Russia without the Holy Father making the consecration." And she received the reply given above which impressed me so much. It is evident that speaking "intimately" to Our Lord and receiving replies from Him implies a mystical communication, most probably a locution—a message from heaven without an accompanying vision. The letters reveal that this kind of communication has been quite frequent and this says much about the importance of the Fátima message for the Church and the world.

The most startling information imparted in this letter is that which clearly asserts that God has willed to indissolubly link the conversion of Russia with its being consecrated to the Immaculate Heart of Mary. As Sister Lúcia says elsewhere in this same letter, the salvation or conversion of Russia "has been entrusted" to the Immaculate Heart of Mary. The manner in which this consecration must be made by "the Holy Father, in union with all of the bishops of the world," is unusual, but its whole purpose is to reveal to the world, that is, to let everybody know by the publicity it will obtain, that the conversion of Russia has indeed come about through the Immaculate Heart of Mary, that it has pleased God to "entrust" that conversion to her.

This matter of the conversion of Russia being entrusted to the Immaculate Heart recalls what Our Lady said at the Cova da Iria in 1917. On July 13, she said: ". . . I want you to continue to say the beads in honor of Our Lady of the Rosary to obtain peace for the world and the end of the war, for *she alone can help you* [emphasis added]." It also recalls what Jacinta said to Lúcia during her sickness: "It will not be long before I go to heaven. You are going to stay here to make known that God wants to establish devotion to the Immaculate Heart of Mary in the world. When you are about to speak of this, don't hide yourself. Tell everybody that God grants us graces through the Immaculate Heart of Mary, that they should ask her for them, and that the Heart of Jesus wants the Immaculate Heart of Mary venerated beside His own. Tell them that they should ask the Immaculate Heart of Mary for *peace*, that *God has entrusted it to her* [emphasis added]."

All of this is like an explication, a spelling out of what was implicitly contained in the words of Our Lady when she spoke of Lúcia's mission on earth during the June 13, 1917, apparition: "Jesus wants to use you to make me known and loved. He wants to establish in the world devotion to my Immaculate Heart." The vision of Mary's Heart, vertically encircled by large thorns which pierced it on all sides, that followed Our Lady's words to Lúcia and that concluded this apparition was part of the explication of the devotion to the Immaculate Heart. The thorns that pierced the Heart were a vital part of that vision. They spoke of the sins of mankind clamoring for reparation. Indeed, in her fourth *Memoir*, Sister Lúcia states that she and her two cousins were given to understand that "this was the Immaculate Heart of Mary outraged by the sins of humanity and seeking reparation." This is why the First Saturday Communions are so important. They are Communions of reparation to the Immaculate Heart.

What Our Lady did on December 10, 1925, was give us through Sister Lúcia a formula, a definite series of acts that people would have to perform in order to satisfy heaven's wish for reparation. Most people would have been at a loss on how to go about making adequate reparation to the Immaculate Heart of Mary. So, heaven outlined an easy way of doing it. A word should be said about why the heaven-given formula included confession and Communion. The role of the confession is to remind us of our own personal sins, to provide an opportunity to reflect on them and to repent, and to strengthen us so that we won't commit them again. The role of the Communions is to further strengthen us in our struggle against sin and to help us grow in our love of God.

In a letter dated June 12, 1930, and simply addressed "Reverend Father," Sister Lúcia answered some questions the priest had asked concerning the First Saturday devotions and told him why five Saturdays of reparation were requested and not nine or seven. She said that while she was in the chapel on the night of May 30, 1930, she spoke to Our Lord about this and he "revealed" to her that the reason for five Saturdays is because there are five kinds of offenses or blasphemies committed against the Immaculate Heart, namely, blasphemies against her Immaculate Conception, her Virginity, and her divine Motherhood (refusing at the same time to acknowledge her as mother of men), attempts to instill in children indifference to, contempt of, or hatred of Mary Immaculate, and the insulting of her images.

Just how important heaven considers the First Saturday devotions of reparation is made very clear by the fact that according to the report on the collegial formula for the consecration of Russia as given by Sister Lúcia in her letter to Father Gonçalves and mentioned above, Our Lord asked that the Pope—in addition to the act of consecration itself—"promise" that when the persecution is ended in Russia "he will approve and recommend the practice of the devotion of reparation [the First Saturday devotions]."

Sister Lúcia was so convinced of the importance of the First Saturday Communions of reparation, and so frustrated at the little that was being done to promote them, that in 1946 she had made up her mind to leave the Sisters of Saint Dorothy and establish an apostolate to spread the devotion. She had actually taken steps in 1946 to leave these Sisters, and the constitutions of the new apostolate had already been approved. However, shortly afterward The Blue Army was founded. This prompted her to abandon her plans for the apostolate, because she thought that The Blue Army would be an effective means for disseminating this devotion.

This decision to abandon her religious life was a tremendously important, perhaps even traumatic one for her to have taken. It points up, as probably nothing else in her life does, how completely dedicated she is to her heavenly entrusted mission of spreading devotion to the Immaculate Heart of Mary throughout the world and how vital a part of this devotion she considers the Communions of reparation to be.

23

Obtaining the Consecration of Russia

Our Lady gave Sister Lúcia the collegial formula for the consecration of Russia on December 10, 1929. At a later date, which is not specified, the Sister was told by Our Lady "by means of an intimate communication," that is, a locution, that the desired consecration would be made but that it would be "late," so late that Russia would "have spread her errors throughout the world, provoking wars and persecutions of the Church." And she added that "the Holy Father will have much to suffer." Our Lady was merciful in not telling the Sister just how late it would be before the desired consecration would be made!

If the consecration was made as late as it was, this was not through any fault of Sister Lúcia. She was faithful to her mission and did everything she could to do whatever heaven asked of her. And God never wavered in his faithfulness to his promise. A number of Sister Lúcia's letters speak of the ever-present availability of God's mercy in regard to Russia and her conversion. They reveal Him as eager to have us put Him in a position, as it were, where he must fulfill His promise. All we have to do is obtain the consecration of Russia according to the precise demands of Our Lord and it will be converted.

God's overwhelming mercy and great desire to save Russia comes through powerfully in a letter to Father Gonçalves that Sister Lúcia wrote at Pontevedra on January 21, 1935. The letter also reveals that the Sister is deeply concerned and doing what she can to obtain the prescribed consecration of Russia. She begins by encouraging Father Gonçalves to "take steps" to get the Pope to make the desired act of consecration. Then, apparently with the intention of spurring the priest into action, she tells him that "some three years ago" Our Lord let her know that he was "quite displeased that his request had not been fulfilled." She adds that she sent the Bishop a letter telling him of this. And she also indicates that she has done everything she was supposed to do: "Up to now, Our Lord has not asked anything else of me, except prayers and sacrifices."

Apparently Our Lord's love and concern for Russia is a frequent topic of her locutions with him, for she says that in her "intimate talks" with him, "it seems he is disposed to show mercy to poor Russia, as he promised five years ago. *He wants so much to save her* [emphasis added]." In a letter written to the same priest five years later, on July 15, 1940, the Sister says: "He manifests great sorrow because he was not listened to."

Father André Richard of Paris, top Fátima expert of France, in his talk on Russia at the International Seminar held at Fátima in August 1971, said that the Bishop of Leiria wrote to Pope Pius XI in May 1937 and communicated to him the request of Our Lord concerning the consecration of Russia to the Immaculate Heart.[1] He added that Rome acknowledged receipt of the information on April 8. This was apparently the first communication Rome received concerning this matter. It was already five and a half years since Sister Lúcia had this information from Our Lady.

The outbreak of World War II on September 4, 1939, saw things move more rapidly. Sister Lúcia had been trying to get the Bishop of Leiria to approve the First Saturday devotions of reparation for quite some time prior to September 13, 1939—nine days after the start of the war—when he finally promulgated them.

Then, in an extract from the writings of Sister Lúcia (whether from a letter or from notes is not clear) dated October 22, 1940, we discover that Father José Bernardo Gonçalves and the Bishop of Gurza had sent her letters commanding her to write to the Pope. Characteristically, she communicated about this with Our Lord, spending two hours on her knees before the Blessed Sacrament exposed. And, of course, He spoke to her. He told her to pray for the Pope and to make sacrifices herself for his intention "so that his heart may not succumb from the anguish that oppresses him [because of the war]." He added that the tribulation would continue and get worse. Then, in language reminiscent of that used by Our Lady at Fátima on July 13, 1917, when she told the children what would happen if people did not heed her message, Our Lord said He would "punish the nations for their crimes, through war, hunger, and persecution of His Church," which would weigh heavily upon the Pope.

Then we discover that Our Lord in His mercy made a promise centered on the Immaculate Heart of Mary, and more specifically on consecration to that Immaculate Heart. He said that the Pope would obtain a shortening of the days of tribulation "if he takes heed of My wishes by consecrating the whole world to the Immaculate Heart of Mary, with a special mention of Russia . . ."

This particular promise is quite different from the promise of the conversion of Russia. No mention is made of the need of the bishops of the world joining the Pope in this act of consecration. Also, what is to be consecrated is not just Russia, but "the whole world . . . with a special mention of Russia."

This new promise of Our Lord reported by Sister Lúcia on October 22, 1940, is the key to several acts of consecration to the Immaculate Heart of Mary the popes made starting on October 31, 1942.

The short document from which all the above information has been gleaned ends with a notation, evidently made by Father José Bernardo Gonçalves, who copied the document, to the effect that "after that," Sister Lúcia "wrote the letter." The letter alluded to was written by the Sister at Túy on October 22, 1940, the same day the above document was written. It was addressed to "The Holy Father." The letter was never sent to Pius XII as written by the Sister on October 22. Changes were made in it and it was a copy of this modified letter, dated December 2, 1940, that the Sister eventually sent to Pius XII from Túy.

It is important to know what Sister Lúcia had originally planned to tell the Pope, so we shall begin by speaking of the things relating especially to the First Saturday devotions and the consecration of Russia to the Immaculate Heart as found in the first draft of her long letter as she herself wrote it on October 22.

The second paragraph of the letter is important, for it reveals that the request which she is about to make had already been transmitted to the Pope. It was transmitted to him "several" times, and before that to his predecessor, Pius XI. And she says that both of them received it "with the greatest benevolence."

Then the Sister goes on to relate what Our Lady had said on July 13, 1917, about the end of World War I, the prediction of another war that would begin in the reign of Pius XI and all that follows about her coming back to ask for the First Saturdays and the consecration of Russia, including that country's eventual conversion and a period of peace for the world. She mentions how they had called this a secret and had indeed kept it secret until 1926.

Next, she tells the Pope about the First Saturday devotions of reparation as Our Lady revealed them to her. She mentions telling her confessor about this and how he made "some efforts" to have Our Lady's wishes carried out. But she adds that the Bishop of Leiria "only" made this request public on September 13, 1939. She concludes this section on the First Saturdays by asking the Pope "to make public and bless this devotion for the whole world."

Finally, she speaks of the 1929 apparition, during which Our Lady told her that the time had come when God wanted the Pope, "in union with all the bishops of the world, to make the consecration of Russia to her Immaculate Heart" and that she promised to save it by this means. It will be noted that the Sister does not include here all the elements that are found in the letter she sent to Father Gonçalves, which he received on May 29, 1929, and which was mentioned in the previous chapter.

Sister Lúcia goes on to tell the Pope that she told her confessor about this request and that "he took certain means to bring it to the attention" of the Pope's predecessor, Pius XI, and to himself "in June of this year, 1940," through the Bishop of Macau. Then she adds that "it seemed" to her that Father Luis Gonzaga da Fonseca, S.J., had also presented it to him "a little later" and that he had "accepted it with great benevolence."

We learn a little more about Sister Lúcia's continuing communication with Our Lord through locutions, as she tells the Holy Father that during "several intimate communications," he has "incessantly insisted on this request."

Then she tells the Pope about the promise Our Lord has made "of late" about "shortening the days of tribulation," describing it as she did in the October 22, 1940, document quoted above. Though she does not refer to it as a "new" promise, that is definitely what it is.

There follows a short, informative paragraph. The Sister tells the Holy Father that there are times in her mystical communications with Our Lord when He "seems so grieved" at the loss of so many souls and at the persecutions—she uses the plural —the Pope will have to endure and when she herself "experiences in part the anguish of His Divine Heart," that she has "not been able to refrain" from telling the Bishop of Leiria about it in "several" private letters.

The next paragraph is also enlightening. It has to do with another promise of Our Lord. Sister Lúcia informs the Pope that Our Lord has promised a special protection for Portugal because of the consecration to the Immaculate Heart which the Portuguese bishops have made. And this protection shall be a sign or indication of the graces he would have granted to other countries if they also had been consecrated. The fact that Portugal was spared from becoming involved in World War Two has been seen as the fulfillment of Our Lord's promise. This is a powerful teaching on the great benefits to be derived from consecration to the Immaculate Heart of Mary, and this applies not only to nations, but also to religious orders, dioceses, parishes, families, and individuals.

Then the Sister makes a purely personal request, which she calls "simply an ardent desire of my poor heart," undoubtedly meaning that she is not transmitting a request made by heaven. She asks that the feast in honor of the Immaculate Heart of Mary be raised to the rank of a "principal feast" and be extended to the entire Church.

As mentioned, this letter was never sent to Pope Pius XII as written by Sister Lúcia on October 22, 1940. Important changes were made in it by other people. A copy of this modified letter, dated December 2, 1940, was sent to His Holiness from Túy by the Sister.

Two significant changes were made in the letter that was finally sent to the Pope in Sister Lúcia's name. One has to do with

Our Lady's 1929 request and the other with Our Lord's October 22, 1940, request.

The first change consisted in eliminating the clause "in union with all the bishops of the world" from the 1929 request made by Our Lady. The second consisted in adding this same clause to the October 22, 1940, request made by Our Lord.

We have found no adequate explanation for these two changes anywhere. However, it should be pointed out that Sister Lúcia states twice in her own October 24 draft of this letter that Our Lady's 1929 request "has already been transmitted several times" to the Pope (Pius XII). In fact, she affirms that it was brought to his attention by her confessor "recently, in June of this year, 1940." So, the Pope was aware of the complete text of the 1929 request, with its clause "in union with all the bishops of the world." This could explain why that clause was omitted in the December 2 letter. But it does not explain why it was added to the October 22 request as it had been received from Our Lord. Still another question is raised by the fact that Sister Lúcia sent Pope Pius XII the December 2 letter, with its changes, under her own name.

Father Joaquin Alonso, C.F.M., who was in a highly privileged position in regard to information concerning Fátima matters, has this to say of these changes and of Sister Lúcia's feelings in regard to them:

> Perhaps many people will want to know how this variance came about. We cannot develop this subject for the moment, but the correspondence of the time tells us it was because of the intervention of certain people and not the wish of Sister Lucy. (*A Heart for All*, p. 59)

The amazing thing in all this is that Pope Pius XII, notwithstanding the modified requests that were sent to him in the December 2 letter, actually fulfilled the October 22 request exactly as Our Lord gave it to Sister Lúcia. But he did not act immediately. It was almost two years later—October 31, 1942—that he made the consecration. One suspects that in the intervening time the Pope was informed of the October 22 request in the precise form in which Sister Lúcia received it from Our Lord. In fact, Father

Alonso speaks of "approaches to the Holy See from the Portuguese hierarchy" that were made during this interval:

> 1942 was the Jubilee Year of the Apparitions and also the Episcopal Jubilee of Pius XII. However, the war and its horrors overshadowed all humanity. The Pope did not seem to have decided to act on the suggestions Sister Lúcia had made, suggestions given from heaven. She, herself, deplored this, with great delicacy regarding the Holy Father. Meanwhile, the atmosphere of this double jubilee, approaches to the Holy See from the Portuguese hierarchy, publication of new books on Fátima with their startling revelations about the Immaculate Heart of Mary, all seemed to give new hope.
>
> Suddenly, like an inspiration from heaven, on the thirty-first of October 1942, Pius XII consecrated the world to the Immaculate Heart of Mary with a veiled reference, delicate but perfectly clear, to Russia . . ." (*A Heart for All*, p. 61)

Whether these "approaches to the Holy See from the Portuguese hierarchy" actually included new requests for the consecration of the world by the Pope to the Immaculate Heart of Mary with mention of Russia (but not including the participation of the bishops of the world with the Pope) is not that important, at least from a practical point of view.

The hopeful thing is that the Pope was influenced by the heavenly messages received through Sister Lúcia and did act on them. Without mentioning these messages, he did discreetly acknowledge them by making the act of consecration during the concluding ceremonies commemorating the twenty-fifth anniversary of the Fátima apparitions. The consecration was an integral part of these ceremonies. As we wrote in *Fátima, Hope of the World*:

"The consecration itself was preceded by a message to the Portuguese nation and the entire program was delivered by the Holy Father in the Portuguese language. Though it was meant in a special way for Portugal, it was broadcast to the entire world by the Vatican radio. It was truly the crowning event of the jubilee celebrations. His Eminence, the Cardinal Patriarch of Lisbon, all the Portuguese bishops, and many ecclesiastical and civil dignitaries gathered in the cathedral, which had been equipped with loudspeakers, to listen to the Pope deliver his message and pronounce the act of consecration" (p. 122).

The Pope complied with another request made by Sister Lúcia, namely, that "the feast in honor of the Immaculate Heart of Mary be extended to the whole world as one of the principal feasts of the Church." The December 2 letter repeated this request in the same terms in which Sister Lúcia had expressed it in her October 24 draft of the letter. She made no claim to have received this request from heaven but represented it as "simply an ardent desire of my poor heart."

On May 8, 1944, the Holy See established the Feast of the Immaculate Heart of Mary as a universal feast for the whole Church and gave it the important liturgical rank (since suppressed) of Double of the Second Class. The date chosen for its celebration, August 22, was not without significance. At that time, this was the octave day of the Assumption, Our Lady's most important feast.[2]

Our Lord promised that if the Pope consecrated the world to the Immaculate Heart of Mary, with a special mention of Russia, the end of the war would be hastened. His promise was fulfilled.

A few months after Pius XII had consecrated Russia to the Immaculate Heart, Our Lord spoke about what He had done to Sister Lúcia and expressed His pleasure with the act of consecration. Father Alonso quotes from one of the Sister's letters, which, he says, was written at "the beginning of 1943":

> God has already shown me his satisfaction with the act, "although incomplete according to His wish," performed by the Holy Father and by several bishops. He promises in return to put a stop to the war soon; the conversion of Russia is not for now.[3]

When Sister Lúcia says that the October 31, 1942, consecration of Russia was "incomplete according to His wish," she is referring to the first wish, which was expressed by Our Lady in 1929. Indeed, the October 31, 1942, consecration was complete according to the second and different wish expressed by Our Lord on October 22, 1940. Because the October 31, 1942, consecration was complete, Our Lord honored the promise he attached to its fulfillment and he accelerated the end of the war. That was the only promise connected with the October 31, 1942, consecration of Russia. The promise of the conversion of Russia and a period of peace for the world was attached to the 1929 request and its more involved stipulation.

The war did not come to a quick end after the October 31, 1942, consecration. The German surrender was signed on May 7, 1945, and the Japanese surrender on September 2, 1945. However, a first step toward victory did come quite soon with the Italian unconditional surrender on September 3, 1943.

It should be noted that expressions of time in prophetic messages normally present a problem. The person receiving the message usually experiences a sense of urgency and feels that the prediction will take place sooner than actually happens.

This is the second promise regarding a public act of consecration to the Immaculate Heart of Mary that has been fulfilled. The first had to do with the consecration of Portugal and its "special protection." This should enlighten and encourage us concerning the promised conversion of Russia and the ensuing period of peace.

The October 31, 1942, consecration was only the first in a whole series of public acts performed by Pope Pius XII as a result of the Fátima event.

On December 8, 1942, he personally consecrated his own diocese of Rome to the Immaculate Heart of Mary. He did this during a ceremony in Saint Peter's Basilica that was attended by many cardinals, archbishops, and bishops, and thousands of others.

In his encyclical *Auspicia Quaedam*, issued on May 1, 1948, he asked for the consecration of dioceses, parishes, and families to the Immaculate Heart of Mary:

> Some years ago, as all will remember, while the last war was still in its fury, when human beings showed themselves uncertain and inadequate to face that terrible conflagration, we addressed our fervent prayers to the all-merciful Redeemer, invoking the powerful patronage of the Immaculate Heart of Mary.
>
> And even as our predecessor of immortal memory, Leo XIII, at the dawn of the twentieth century, saw fit to consecrate the whole human race to the Most Sacred Heart of Jesus, so we have likewise, in the role of representative of the whole human family which He redeemed, desired to dedicate it in turn to the Immaculate Heart of the Virgin Mary.

It is our wish, consequently, that wherever the opportunity presents itself this consecration be made in the various dioceses as well as in each of the parishes and families. And we are confident that abundant blessings and favors from heaven will surge forth from this private and public consecration.

In 1952, on July 7, Feast of Saints Cyril and Methodius, apostles of the Slavs, Pius XII issued the apostolic letter *Sacro Vergente Ano*. In this document he again consecrated Russia to the Immaculate Heart of Mary. The earlier consecration of October 31, 1942, had contained a somewhat veiled allusion to Russia:

Give peace to those peoples separated from us by error and discord, particularly those who profess a special devotion to you, where there was no house that did not display your venerated icon (today perhaps hidden and kept in reserve for better days); bring them back to the one fold of Christ, under the one true Shepherd.

The July 7, 1952, consecration, however, was explicit in regard to Russia: "We entrust and consecrate in a very special way to the Immaculate Heart of Mary all the peoples of Russia . . ."

In the apostolic letter, the Pope states that some of those who sent him letters congratulating him for the definition of the Dogma of the Assumption, "pleaded with insistence that [he] consecrate the entire Russian people to the Immaculate Heart of Mary." He adds: "This request greatly pleased us . . ." He was pleased because he knew that the Holy Spirit works in the Church at the grass roots level as it does at the top and that listening to the voice of the faithful helps him in his discernment as he seeks God's will in guiding the Church.

Finally, on October 11, 1954, the same Pope issued the encyclical *Ad Caeli Reginam*, in which he said:

. . . We, by our apostolic power, decree and institute the Feast of Mary as Queen to be celebrated throughout the entire world every year on May 31. And likewise we command that on that same day there be renewed the consecration of the human race to the Immaculate Heart of the Blessed Virgin Mary. Upon this there is founded a great hope that there may arise an era of happiness that will rejoice in the triumph of religion and in Christian peace.

Two things should be noted. This "command" for the renewal of the consecration was issued to all bishops, since encyclicals are always addressed specifically to them. This is precisely what was asked of the Pope in 1929 in regard to the consecration of Russia. He is to "command" all the bishops of the world to join with him in making that consecration. Also, when Pius XII says that the blessings he expects from this renewal of the consecration are "the triumph of religion" and "Christian peace," one sees a close resemblance to the blessings which Our Lady said would flow from the consecration of Russia by the Pope in union with the bishops. These are the conversion of Russia and a period of peace for the world.

Pope Paul VI made two significant public acts in which he manifested his positive attitude toward Fátima, Sister Lúcia, and the consecration of Russia to the Immaculate Heart of Mary. On November 21, 1964, at the end of the third session of the Second Vatican Council, in the presence of all the bishops and fathers of the council gathered in Saint Peter's Basilica, he proclaimed Mary the Mother of the Church and renewed the October 31, 1942, consecration of the world to the Immaculate Heart of Mary, with special mention of Russia, and he made specific reference to Fátima. At first, many wondered if this were not sufficient to satisfy the request made by Our Lady in 1929, but now it is generally agreed that the passive presence of the bishops as the Pope alone made the act of consecration was not an adequate compliance with heaven's specific demands in the matter. The bishops must join the Pope in making the consecration; they must actively take part in making the act of consecration, although they need not necessarily do this in the same physical place with the Pope.

On May 13, 1967, Paul VI came to the shrine of Fátima and took part in the fiftieth-anniversary celebration of the apparitions. At one moment during the open-air ceremony held on the basilica platform in the presence of two million people, he invited Sister Lúcia to stand beside him and together they faced the enthusiastic crowd.

On this same occasion, he promulgated the exhortation *Signum Magnum*, in which he asked the members of the Church to renew their personal consecration "to the Immaculate Heart of the Holy Mother of the Church."

Three things stand out from the facts examined in this chapter. God has remained faithful to what he sought to obtain through Our Lady on July 13, 1917, and December 10, 1929. He has frequently spoken to Sister Lúcia of these designs of love and mercy and has encouraged her to take the means to see they are fulfilled. Sister Lúcia has faithfully pursued her mission and done what she could. Finally, the popes have not been lacking in good will nor in courage concerning what heaven has sought from them. However, none of these early acts of consecration of Russia or of the world and Russia have been fully in keeping with the specific request of heaven made on December 10, 1929. One important element has always been missing: the active participation of the bishops of the world in the act of consecration.

24

May 13, 1982

Obtaining the active participation of the bishops of the world in a public act of consecration to the Immaculate Heart of Mary evidently presented a problem. The major one, it would seem, is the fact that the Church does not impose belief in apparitions on any of its members. A Catholic is not obliged to accept the fact that an apparition took place, nor must he or she accept the message reported as having been imparted during an apparition. It is significant that in approving the Fátima apparitions, the Bishop of Leiria did not even mention the message. The short document he issued on October 13, 1930, only states that he deems "the visions of the shepherds at the Cova da Iria worthy of credence" and that he gives "official permission for the cult of Our Lady of Fátima." So we could not expect the Pope to oblige the bishops of the world to actively join him in the act of consecration simply because Our Lady had requested this at Fátima.

But God will not be thwarted in his plans. To overcome the problem just mentioned, he did several things. First, he inspired The Blue Army to make an important decision on December 10, 1974, at Pontevedra, Spain, in the very Dorothean convent where Our Lady had given Sister Lúcia the formula of consecration which requested the active participation of the bishops of the world along with the Pope. The decision was made at a high-level meeting and had to do with making a public effort to obtain the desired act of consecration. All previous efforts had been of a private nature and had been kept secret. It was decided to approach the Pope personally through a Cardinal and ask that he make the consecration with the bishops of the world in 1975. And it was also decided to seek grass-roots support by telling people of the plan and asking them to send letters in support of the petition.[1] Joseph Cardinal Slipyj, who had spent eighteen years in the prison camps of Siberia, presented the petition to the Pope in May 1975.

Through the Cardinal, The Blue Army sought two things: 1) that the Pope solemnly consecrate the world, with all the bishops of the world, to the Sacred Heart of Jesus on June 6, Feast of the Sacred Heart; 2) that he solemnly consecrate Russia, with all the bishops of the world, to the Immaculate Heart of Mary on June 7, Feast of the Immaculate Heart.

The Holy Father was not approached early enough to allow the two acts of consecration to be made on the requested dates. However, by June 6, over half a million letters from all over the world arrived at the Vatican in support of the petition presented to the Pope by Cardinal Slipyj.

The Blue Army, encouraged by the Cardinal, submitted another petition to the Holy Father, asking him to make the same double consecration to both Hearts, with the bishops, on Sunday, November 23, Feast of Christ the King, of that same year, 1975. By that time the petition to the Holy Father had been supported by two million letters from all over the world. However, as we know, the consecration was not made. It is very likely that Paul VI did not have enough time to undertake and conclude the considerable preliminary work that would be required before he could make the kind of solemn and public consecration of Russia with all the bishops of the world that Our Lady requested.

A year after their first meeting, on December 10, 1975, the same Pontevedra Committee of Fátima apostolate leaders from all over the world met again to evaluate what had taken place and to determine what steps to take for the future. Noting that most of the two million petitions had come from the United States, the Committee resolved to intensify solicitation of petitions to the Holy See for the collegial consecration of Russia to the Immaculate Heart. It believed more petitions were needed from other countries all over the world, since, according to Our Lady's request, the act of consecration was to involve the bishops of all the world. Also, this effort to obtain petitions from many countries all over the world would have the effect of making the whole Church aware of the consecration and why it was being made.

Eventually, it was suggested that people send their petitions to their local Bishop so that he might know their personal feelings on this important issue. Knowledge by bishops that a large number of people in their respective dioceses are solidly behind a project speaks powerfully to them and has an influence on their decisions and actions. "The voice of the people is the voice of God" is an old axiom to which they are sensitive, as is the Holy Father himself. The Holy Spirit speaks to the Church through the laity as well as through the hierarchy.

Not only did God inspire The Blue Army to make a supreme public effort to obtain the collegial consecration of Russia to the Immaculate Heart, but only a few years after that, He provided a Pope whose background had disposed him to make the desired act of consecration. The election of John Paul II in 1978 raised hopes that the consecration might not be too far off. As was stated in the 1979 edition of our book *Exciting Fátima News:*

> We should be greatly encouraged in this new worldwide effort for petitions by the new Pope God has given to His Church. Not only has John Paul II repeatedly brought Mary into his public addresses, beginning with the very first one he made on the balcony of Saint Peter's immediately after his election, but his visit to the shrine of Our Lady of Guadalupe in Mexico is a worldwide witness to his own personal attitude toward Marian apparitions. Also, not without significance is the fact that he comes from a country with extraordinary love for the mother of God and where a Marian shrine, that of Częstochowa, has played such an important role in the nurturing and promotion of that love.
>
> Even more significant and encouraging is the fact that the Polish hierarchy, at a time when Pope John Paul II was a part of it, openly manifested its approval of public acts of consecration to Mary by making such acts itself and by once publicly asking His Holiness, Paul VI, to make the collegial consecration requested by Our Lady of Fátima. No hierarchy in the world has shown itself more open to diocesan, national, and worldwide consecrations to Mary than the Polish hierarchy.

It would appear that now is the time that God has chosen for the consecration. We have to learn to read the signs of the times, and it seems more than a mere coincidence that The Blue Army should have been inspired to make a public move (we saw that several highly confidential, not to say secret moves were made unsuccessfully in the past), a publicized and organized effort to obtain the consecration just before God gave His Church its first Polish Pope. The fact that our present Pope is Polish is more unusual than the fact he is non-Italian. And everyone agrees that his election was clearly the work of the Holy Spirit.

Grace builds on nature, because in God's plan they were always meant to go together and function as one. God uses and works human qualities and circumstances into His plans for His Church. Who could be more open and sensitive to the need for this consecration than a Pope who had lived under Communism and under the very shadow of Communism's terrifying power and might, a Pope who had been in such a high position in the Polish hierarchy that he had to work directly with high-ranking Communists? We can be sure that he has acquired a convincing knowledge of the Communist threat to the Church and to the world that only personal experience can give. And he also has that same special convincing knowledge of Mary's protection and power that comes from personally witnessing what she did for the Catholic Church in his own country. There is probably no country in the world where the faith is so strong and vibrant today.

A third factor that God used—but certainly did not provoke—was the shooting of Pope John Paul II at Saint Peter's Square in Rome on May 13, 1981. That he was only wounded and not killed (he was shot three times at close range by a trained assassin), the Pope attributes to the special protection of Our Lady of Fátima, on the anniversary of whose first apparition to the three little shepherds the incident occurred. It was eventually reported that had it taken five more minutes to reach the hospital—it actually took some twenty-five minutes—the Pope would have bled to death. Likewise, had one of the bullets come only a fraction of an inch closer to some vital organ, this also would have caused his death. As the Pope himself expressed it during his Wednesday audience nearly five months after the shooting:

And again I have become indebted to the Blessed Virgin and to all the Patron Saints. Could I forget that the event in Saint

Peter's Square took place on the day and at the hour when the first appearance of the Mother of Christ to the poor little peasants has been remembered for over sixty years at Fátima in Portugal? For, *in everything that happened to me on that very day* [emphasis added], I felt that extraordinary motherly protection and care, which turned out to be stronger than the deadly bullet.[2]

The Pope's long convalescence in the hospital seems to have been used by God to help bring about the collegial consecration of Russia. John M. Haffert, in the November–December 1981 issue of *Soul*, the official publication of The Blue Army in the United States and Canada, shared the following "inside" information. He said that when he was in Rome on September 2, 1981, he saw the Pope in the hospital and received his blessing. Shortly before that, Sister Mary Ludovica, secretary of The Blue Army of Italy, received a message from the Policlinico Gemelli stating that the Holy Father wanted "the Fátima documents." She brought him a copy of the book mentioned above, *Memorias e Cartas de Irmã Lúcia (The Memoirs and Letters of Sister Lúcia)*. Then, on September 1, Sister Ludovica was summoned by the Pope and received a message which sent her "packing" (sic) to Fátima the same week to see its retired Bishop, John P. Venancio. Mr. Haffert apparently received all this information directly from Sister Ludovica, for he said: "She could not share with me what the Pope had told her, but over and over she said: 'It is good news! It is good news!' "[3]

Subsequent events seem to indicate that her mission had to do with the collegial consecration of Russia to the Immaculate Heart. Indeed, in April 1982 a letter dealing with this consecration was sent by Pope John Paul II, through his Secretary of State, Agostino Cardinal Casaroli, to all the bishops of the world.

Before discussing this letter, mention must be made of one last factor that only recently came to light and that seems to have a bearing on this letter and its content. The May–June 1983 issue of *Soul*, in an article entitled "Was the Collegial Consecration of Russia Complete?" carried this statement: "Pope John Paul II *did personally experience a prodigy* [emphasis in text] last year after the attempt on his life. We await permission to publish this news." The context in which this statement appears implies that this prodigy had an effect on the act of consecration about which the Pope wrote in the letter.

The English version of the letter that Cardinal Casaroli sent to the American bishops was dated April 19, 1982. The main thrust of it is the collegial act of consecration, which it says the Pope is planning to make at Fátima on the occasion of his visit there "on May 13 next."

In the opening sentence of the first paragraph, it is stated that Pope John Paul II had received letters from "many bishops" and "a number of episcopal conferences, . . . recalling the message of Fátima and asking him to renew, by *collegial* act [emphasis added], the consecration to the Immaculate Heart of Mary made by Pope Pius XII on October 31, 1942, and on July 7, 1952," copies of which were enclosed.

In the second paragraph, the letter recalls the reference Pope Paul VI made on November 21, 1964, to the act of consecration to the Immaculate Heart made by Pius XII on October 31, 1942, and reference is made likewise to the fact that John Paul II "explicitly referred to both of the above-mentioned acts" on the Solemnities of Pentecost and of the Immaculate Conception of 1981.

In the all-important third paragraph, the bishops are advised that during his visit to Fátima on May 13, 1982, when he will thank the Blessed Virgin for saving his life when he was attacked on May 13 of 1981, the Pope "also intends, *in spiritual union with all the bishops of the world* [emphasis added], to renew the two acts whereby Pope Pius XII entrusted the world to the Immaculate Heart of Mary."

When one reflects on the key words of the letter, which we emphasized and certainly were chosen with the greatest care, and especially on the contents of the two acts of consecration made by Pope Pius XII, copies of which were included with the letter so that the bishops could refresh their memories and know exactly what the Pope intended to do, there can be no doubt that he wanted to comply with the precise request Our Lady made at Pontevedra on June 13, 1929. Also, the Pope had undoubtedly received enough letters to lead him to hope that a sufficient number of bishops of the world would respond favorably to his invitation to join him on May 13 in his act of consecration. I asked one

Bishop if he had understood the letter he had received from the Pope through Cardinal Casaroli to be making such a request to him. He replied unhesitatingly that he had understood it to be doing that.

The opening paragraph of the April 19 letter is a fine tribute to the great effort made by The Blue Army to get people to send petitions to the Holy Father and to their bishops. These letters assuredly played an important role in getting "many bishops and a number of episcopal conferences" to send letters to the Pope asking him to make the collegial consecration. The Conference of American Bishops on the occasion of their November 1981 general meeting sent a petition to Rome asking the Pope to make such an act.[4]

Pope John Paul II participated in the vigil of prayer that is held traditionally at the Cova da Iria on the eve of the anniversaries of the six Fátima apparitions. On May 13, he presided at the liturgy that followed the procession in which the original statue of Our Lady of Fátima (which had been placed in the little chapel of the apparitions on May 13, 1920) was carried through the grounds from that chapel to the steps of the basilica. There, the Eucharist was celebrated before more than a million people, including an impressive number of concelebrating priests and bishops, and Sister Lúcia. The Pope had requested her presence and she came from Saint Joseph's Carmel in Coimbra. On March 25, 1948, the Sister had left the Sisters of Saint Dorothy to join the more austere cloistered order of the Carmelite nuns. This was her third visit to Fátima since she had left home in 1921 for the school in Vilar. Her first visit was in 1946, on the occasion of the crowning of Our Lady of Fátima as Queen of Portugal and Queen of the World on May 13. The second visit was in 1967, when Pope Paul VI came to Fátima to participate in the fiftieth anniversary of the apparitions. On that day in 1967, from the platform on the basilica stairs, His Holiness presented Bishop John P. Venancio of Fátima, who stood at his right, and Sister Lúcia, who was on his left, to the immense crowd that packed and overflowed the vast esplanade.

On May 13, 1982, Sister Lúcia was on the platform with Pope John Paul II for the morning Mass and the blessing of the sick that immediately followed it. The Pope delivered a remarkable homily of great theological significance, an important section of which had to do with consecration to Mary during which he explicitly recalled what Pius XII had done: "He consecrated the human race and especially the peoples of Russia to the Immaculate Heart of Mary."[5] This part of his homily was obviously a preparation for his own act of consecration to the Immaculate Heart, which took place at the end of the Mass. Below is the entire act of consecration announced by the Pope at the end of the Mass. Those parts that we have emphasized with italics make it clear that he intended his act to be collegial and that Russia was alluded to in a special, though discreet, way:

1. "We have recourse to your protection, holy Mother of God."
As I utter the words of this antiphon with which the Church of Christ has prayed for centuries, I find myself today in this place chosen by you, O Mother, and by you particularly loved.
I am here, united with all the pastors of the Church in that particular bond whereby we constitute a body and a college, just as Christ desired the apostles to be in union with Peter.
In the bond of this union, I utter the words of the present act, in which I wish to include once more the hopes and anxieties of the Church in the modern world.
Forty years ago and again ten years later your servant Pope Pius XII, having before his eyes the painful experience of the human family, entrusted and consecrated to your Immaculate Heart *the whole world, especially the peoples for which you had particular love and solicitude.*
This world of individuals and nations I too have before my eyes today as *I renew the entrusting and consecration carried out by my predecessor in the See of Peter*: the world of the second millennium that is drawing to a close, the modern world, our world today.
The Church, mindful of the Lord's words: "Go . . . and make disciples of all the nations . . . And know that I am with you always, to the end of time" [Matthew 28:19–20], renewed, at the Second Vatican Council, her awareness of her mission in this world.
And therefore, O Mother of individuals and peoples, you who "know all their sufferings and their hopes," you who have a mother's awareness of all the struggles between good and evil, between light and darkness, which afflict the modern world, accept the cry which we, as though moved by the Holy Spirit, address

directly to your Heart. Embrace with the love of a mother and handmaid this human world of ours, which we entrust and consecrate to you, for we are full of disquiet for the earthly and eternal destiny of individuals and peoples.

In a special way we entrust and consecrate to you those individuals and nations which particularly need to be entrusted and consecrated.

"We have recourse to your protection, holy Mother of God. Reject not the prayers we send up to you in our necessities."

Reject them not!

Accept our humble trust—and our act of entrusting!

2. "For God so loved the world that He gave His only Son, that whoever believes in Him may not be lost but have eternal life" [John 3:16].

It was precisely by reason of this love that the Son of God consecrated Himself for all mankind: "And for their sake I consecrate Myself, so that they too may be consecrated in truth" [John 17:19].

By reason of that consecration the disciples of all ages are called to spend themselves for the salvation of the world and to supplement Christ's afflictions for the sake of His body, that is, the Church [cf. 2 Corinthians 12:15, Colossians 1:24].

Before you, Mother of Christ, before your Immaculate Heart, I today, together with the whole Church, unite myself with our Redeemer in this His consecration for the world and for people, in which only His Divine Heart has the power to obtain pardon and to secure reparation.

The power of this consecration lasts for all time and embraces all individuals, peoples, and nations. It overcomes every evil that the spirit of darkness is able to awaken and has in fact awakened in our time and in the heart of man and in his history.

The Church, the mystical body of Christ, unites herself through the service of Peter's successor to this consecration by our Redeemer.

Oh, how deeply we feel the need for consecration on the part of humanity and of the world—our modern world—in union with Christ Himself! The redeeming work of Christ, in fact, must be shared in by the world by means of the Church.

Oh, how pained we are by all the things in the Church and in each one of us that are opposed to holiness and consecration! How pained we are that the invitation to repentance, to conversion, to prayer, has not met with the acceptance that it should have received!

How pained we are that many share so coldly in Christ's work of redemption, that "what is lacking in Christ's afflictions" is so insufficiently completed in our flesh!

And so, blessed be all those souls who obey the call of eternal love! Blessed be all those who, day after day, with undiminished generosity accept your invitation, O Mother, to do what your Jesus tells them [cf. John 2:5] and give the Church and the world a serene testimony of lives inspired by the Gospel.

Above all, blessed be you, the handmaid of the Lord, who in the fullest way obey the divine call!

Hail to you, who are wholly united to the redeeming consecration of your Son!

Mother of the Church, enlighten the people of God along the paths of faith, of hope and love! Help us to live with the whole truth of the consecration of Christ for the entire human family of the modern world.

3. In entrusting to you, O Mother, the world, all individuals and peoples, we also entrust to you the consecration itself, for the world's sake placing it in your motherly Heart.

O Immaculate Heart, help us to conquer the menace of evil, which so easily takes root in the hearts of the people of today and whose immeasurable effects already weigh down upon our modern world and seem to block the paths toward the future.

From famine and war, deliver us.

From nuclear war, from incalculable self-destruction, from every kind of war, deliver us.

From sins against the life of man from its very beginning, deliver us.

From hatred and from the demeaning of the dignity of the children of God, deliver us.

From every kind of injustice in the life of society, both national and international, deliver us.

From readiness to trample on the commandments of God, deliver us.

From attempts to stifle in human hearts the very truth of God, deliver us.

From sins against the Holy Spirit, deliver us, deliver us.

Accept, O Mother of Christ, this cry laden with the sufferings of all individual human beings, laden with the sufferings of whole societies.

May the infinite power of merciful love be revealed once more in the history of the world. May it put a stop to evil, transform consciences. May the light of hope be revealed to all in your Immaculate Heart . . .[6]

The importance Pope John Paul II attaches to the collegial consecration can be seen from the fact that on June 28, 1982, he spoke to the Sacred College of Cardinals in Rome and invited them to join him collegially, as he repeated the last paragraph of the act of consecration he had pronounced at Fátima:

This year, in a special way, after the attempt on my life, which by coincidence occurred on the anniversary of the apparition of the Virgin at Fátima, my conversation with Mary has been, I should say, uninterrupted. I have repeatedly entrusted to her the destiny of all peoples. *I ask you to be united with me, all together, in this consecration to the Virgin,* who must enliven and sanctify even our daily toil. *Together, we humbly collaborate* in this great intention, which I expressed in my prayer to Our Lady: "May the infinite power of merciful love be revealed once more in the history of the world. May it put a stop to evil, transform consciences. May the light of hope be revealed to all in your Immaculate Heart . . ." (emphasis added)

What the Pope wanted to do and hoped to do at Fátima on May 13 was to consecrate collegially, in union with all the bishops, the world and Russia to the Immaculate Heart of Mary. The clearest indication that Russia was included is the fact that three times he made direct mention of the two acts of consecration previously pronounced by Pius XII. He did this in his letter to the bishops on April 19 and even included copies of those two acts. The apostolic letter of July 7, 1952, containing one of the acts, made explicit mention of Russia. In his homily at the Mass on May 13, he again alluded to those two documents and mentioned the peoples of Russia. Then in the actual act of consecration at the conclusion of the May 13 Mass, he again alluded to those documents, mentioning there that in the acts he made "forty years ago and again ten years later your servant Pope Pius XII . . . entrusted and consecrated to your Immaculate Heart the whole world, especially the peoples for which you had particular love and solicitude."

One of the bishops who was with the Holy Father just after the consecration told John Haffert that a fellow Bishop congratulated the Pope on the act of consecration of the world, and the Pope added, ". . . and of Russia," emphasizing his remark with an emphatic gesture of the hand.

So, there is every indication that what the Pope wanted to do and hoped to do at Fátima on May 13, 1982, was to comply with heaven's wishes as expressed to Sister Lúcia. But were those wishes completely complied with? Some thought that they were, and some thought that they were not.

We now have what can be considered an authoritative answer. It came from a meeting that took place between Sister Lúcia and a high-ranking churchman, the important part of which was given in an article which appeared in the May–June 1983 issue of *Soul*. According to that article, what the Pope did on May 13, 1982, was "the first and most important phase of the consecration of Russia." There is a "second" and "final phase of this collegial act of consecration" that has not yet been accomplished: "There still remains one very important act to be accomplished which was impossible of achievement on last May 13. It still remains for the Holy Father to designate a specific day for the consecration of Russia to the Immaculate Heart when bishops, in their own cathedrals throughout the world, will join in this solemn and public act of consecration" (pp. 7–8).

It must be remembered, as was stated earlier, that the conversion of Russia "has been entrusted" to the Immaculate Heart of Mary, and Our Lord wants the whole world to know that the conversion of that country has been brought about through the Immaculate Heart of Mary. The collegial act of consecration of the Pope and bishops is to be a great sign to the world that Russia's conversion has come about through the Immaculate Heart, since that conversion simply will not occur until the collegial act has been performed. Now, the sign will be more manifest and more surely brought to the attention of the entire world by the fact that bishops throughout the world make the act solemnly and publicly in their respective cathedrals.

The worldwide acknowledgment of the role of the Immaculate Heart of Mary in bringing about the conversion of Russia will in turn help spread devotion to the Immaculate Heart of Mary throughout the world and bring about its being honored alongside devotion to the Sacred Heart. This is the ultimate purpose of the collegial act of consecration and, indeed, of the Fátima apparitions. We are moving toward the era of the two Hearts, the Sacred Heart and the Immaculate Heart.

The Pope has shown us the way. By the act of consecration he made at Fátima, he has indicated his personal belief in Fátima and in the value of consecration to the Immaculate Heart of Mary. Now the Church at large, each and every man and woman, needs to comply with the requests made at Fátima in 1917. We are all members of the one Body of Christ, we and the peoples of Russia and the other countries under her sway. What Saint Paul said of himself applies to us: "In my own body, I do what I can to complete what was still to be undergone by Christ for the sake of His body, the Church" (Colossians 1:24).

Our Lady asked specifically for the consecration of Russia to her Immaculate Heart. She did not make an explicit request for the consecration of each individual to her Heart, but that request was implied in her appearance on October 13, 1917, as Our Lady of Mount Carmel and her holding the brown scapular in her hand, for the wearing of the brown scapular of Mount Carmel is a form of consecration to Mary. And the Church has officially recommended the scapular devotion and individual consecration to the Immaculate Heart of Mary. We recall again this quotation from Pope Pius XII's encyclical *Auspicia Quaedam*, issued on May 1, 1948:

> It is our wish . . . that, wherever the opportunity presents itself, this consecration [to the Immaculate Heart of Mary] be made in the various dioceses as well as in each of the parishes and families. And we are confident that abundant blessings and favors from heaven will surge forth from the private and public consecration.

Worthy of note is the manner in which the hierarchy of Ireland responded to what the Pope did at Fátima on May 13. We quote from *Soul* magazine, July–August 1982:

> At the instruction of the Cardinal and the bishops, in every diocese in Ireland, every parish was consecrated to the Immaculate Heart of Mary at all the Masses on the Sunday following May

13, just a few days after the action of the Pope together with all the bishops of the world.

Furthermore, two large seminars were arranged in two different centers of Ireland, on devotion to the Immaculate Heart of Mary . . .

Equally worthy of note is what had taken place more than ten years earlier in Poland regarding public consecration to the Immaculate Heart of Mary. In October 1971, on the day following the beatification of the heroic Polish Franciscan Maximilian Kolbe, the Polish pilgrims were granted a special papal audience. During that audience, the Primate of Poland, Stefan Cardinal Wyszynski, speaking in the name of the Church in Poland, asked Paul VI to make a collegial act of consecration of the world and Russia to the Immaculate Heart of Mary. This request to the Pope had been prepared by a national act of consecration to Mary which was made by the entire Polish hierarchy assembled at the great Polish Marian shrine of Częstochowa. This was followed the next Sunday by a consecration of every parish in the country.

In the wake of what Pope John Paul II did at Fátima on May 13, 1982, The Blue Army is attempting to get bishops to consecrate their dioceses to the Immaculate Heart and is also asking them to urge pastors to consecrate their parishes to the Immaculate Heart. The initial response to this effort has been encouraging.

Reparation, prayer [rosary], sacrifice, and the Eucharist, which are the other most important elements of the Fátima message, are all incorporated in the First Saturday devotions so strongly recommended by Our Lady and Our Lord. As another follow-up to what the Pope did at Fátima on May 13, 1982, The Blue Army is seeking to get people to practice the First Saturday devotions.

There is a personal dimension to the Fátima First Saturday devotions to the Immaculate Heart: a rich personal reward, the promise of the grace of a happy death. However, the First Saturday devotions to the Immaculate Heart have also a strong social dimension to them, and it was this social dimension that was first brought to our attention by Our Lady at Fátima on July 13, 1917. She presented both these Communions of reparations and the consecration of Russia to her Immaculate Heart as antidotes to the social evils of war, famine, persecution of the Church, and atheistic Communism. She said that these evils were the products of man's sinfulness and that they would continue to befall the world if people did not heed her message and turn back to God. As means that would help to bring men to repentance and conversion—and to avoid the chastisement she had announced as otherwise inevitable—she held forth the consecration of Russia to her Immaculate Heart and these First Saturday Communions of reparation.

First Saturday Communions of reparation are clearly presented by Our Lady on July 13, 1917, in a social context and as a means of social welfare or blessings—peace, religious freedom, etc. One has the feeling that most people have seen in these Communions only their personal aspect. It is time that we awaken to the important social dimension that Our Lady—and this means Our Lord also—attributed to them. We must make of these First Saturday devotions a continuing monthly practice, beyond the first "five." We must go to confession, Communion, recite the rosary, keep Our Lady company for fifteen minutes, while meditating on the mysteries (one, several, or all, as we prefer), and do all this in a spirit of reparation to the Immaculate Heart of Mary. We must do this every month and encourage our relatives and friends to do the same. And we must continually remind ourselves that we are doing this for love of neighbor, to bring men and the world—including Russia—back to God, and that in so doing we are doing one of the most important things we can to bring about the conversion of Russia to the Immaculate Heart and to hasten peace.

The numerous heavenly communications that Sister Lúcia has received since 1917 have imparted to her a great sense of urgency in regard to the spreading of the First Saturday Communions of reparation. One of the things that must have impressed on Sister Lúcia the importance of working to spread the First Saturday Communions of reparation was the fact that heaven itself, through Our Lady, specified on June 13, 1929, that one of the conditions for the conversion of Russia was that the Pope must "promise that at the conclusion of the persecution [once Russia is converted], he will approve and recommend the practice of the devotion of reparation [the First Saturday Communions]."

Although devotion to the Immaculate Heart of Mary as presented at Fátima is characterized by a strong accent on atone-

ment, this should not detract our attention from the fact that
Mary's love appears there in its traditional aspects of mercy and
grace. The Mary that is revealed at Fátima through her dealings
with the children and through her messages for Russia and the
world is the Mother of Mercy and of Grace, the Mother whom
the Church has honored and prayed to for centuries in the Hail
Holy Queen and the Memorare. The love of Mary that comes
through at Fátima in everything that she did and said, is the tender, merciful love proclaimed by Saint Bernard of Clairvaux and
so many others before and after him. It is the concerned, compas-
sionate love of the Cana wedding feast. It is the forgiving love
that poured out of her Heart for us at the foot of the cross. It is
the love that goes to the weak and the needy, that bends over the
wounded and the suffering, that consoles and lifts up.

Since in all her apparitions Mary comes to us as God's messenger, the bottom line on the Fátima apparitions is how much God
loves us and how much He pursues us in His overwhelming love
for us. At Fátima, He showed Himself so clearly to be the Good
Shepherd Who does not want a single one of His little ones to be
lost and Who, should one of them wander away, leaves all the
others on the hillside and goes in search of the stray (Matthew
18:12–14). It would be interesting to know exactly how many
times since 1917 Our Lord and Our Lady have spoken to Sister
Lúcia and through her pursued the lost sheep of Russia. Each
and every one of us is now being asked to participate in the final
stage of this pursuit by our practice of the First Saturday devotions and by our efforts to get others to do likewise.

But there is more than the conversion of Russia at stake: peace
for the world and the avoidance of a nuclear holocaust. Never before has the world been faced with such a challenge. Dare we not
do something about it? Or shall we go merrily along our way, like
the people at the time of Noah and the flood?

On May 13, 1982, Pope John Paul II brought us a step closer to
the conversion of Russia and the period of peace that will follow.
Another important step remains to be taken, "the final phase" of
the collegial consecration of Russia to the Immaculate Heart. As
we helped to bring about the "first phase" of that consecration, so
we can and must hasten its "final phase."

In June 1938, on the occasion of a book sent to her by the author, Canon José Galamba de Oliveira, Sister Lúcia wrote a letter to the Bishop of Leiria in which she said:

> . . . Most Reverend Bishop, Jacinta was greatly impressed by certain things revealed in the secret, and with her great love for the Holy Father and for sinners, she often said, "Poor Holy Father!" "I am so sorry for sinners!"
>
> And now I add: If she were living at this time, when these things are so near realization, how much more would she not be impressed! If the world only appreciated the moment of grace that is still conceded to it and did penance! . . .

What Sister Lúcia wrote as she sensed the approach of World War Two applies to us today who live under the constant threat of an atomic war. Will the world only appreciate the moment of grace that is still conceded to it and do penance?

Appendix A

THE SECRET OF 1960

The July 13, 1917, apparition is the one that contained the most startling parts of the Fátima message. There are three parts of this particular apparition that were not made known in 1917. All three parts were referred to by the children as secrets. The first part has to do with the vision of hell. The second part, that Sister Lúcia refers to as the Immaculate Heart of Mary part of the secret, includes the following related elements: the prediction of World War Two, the punishment of the world by means of war, famine, and persecution of the Church and the Pope, the consecration of Russia to the Immaculate Heart, the Communions of reparation, the conversion of Russia and peace for the world.

The first two parts of the July secret were incorporated by Sister Lúcia in *Memoir III* (completed in November 1937) and also in *Memoir IV* (completed on August 31, 1941),[1] which were turned over to the Bishop of Leiria, who had explicitly requested them. But the Bishop did not immediately release the text of these two parts of the secret to the general public. It was Cardinal Schuster of Milano who first revealed their content during the Lenten season of 1942.[2] It was the revealing of these two parts of the secret twenty-five years after the children had received them from Our Lady that electrified the Catholic world and suddenly sparked a new era of interest in the Fátima event.

In *Memoir III*, in which these first two parts of the July secret were first revealed, Sister Lúcia has this interesting comment:

> It might be, Most Reverend Bishop, that some will think that I should have revealed all these things some time ago because, in their opinion, they would have had twice as much value a few years ago.
>
> This would be true if God had wanted to present me to the world as a prophetess, but I think that in 1917, instead of commanding me to keep silent, an order that was confirmed by His representatives, He would have ordered me to speak.
>
> I believe then, Most Reverend Bishop, that God only wanted to use me to recall to the world the necessity of avoiding sin and of making reparation to the offended Godhead by prayer and penance.[3]

In 1947, the Sister gave substantially the same reply to Father McGlynn when he inquired why Our Lady's warning of World War Two as a punishment for sin had not been published until after the punishment had begun. She told him that people had been advised as early as 1917 of the part of the Fátima message that they needed to know, that is, that they should amend their lives and stop offending God, Who was already greatly offended.[4]

The third part of the July 13 secret, the so-called "1960 Secret" has still to this day not been made public. It has had quite an interesting history, the highlights only of which we shall attempt to give.

It was sometime between December 25, 1943, and January 9, 1944, that Sister Lúcia finally put this third part of the secret in writing and it was only on June 17, 1944, that the single sheet of paper on which it was inscribed reached the Bishop of Leiria. It was in a sealed envelope. Later the Bishop of Leiria put it in a larger sealed envelope on which he wrote: "This envelope with its contents shall be entrusted to His Eminence, Cardinal Manuel, Patriarch of Lisboa, after my death. Leiria, December 8, 1945, José, Bishop of Leiria."[5] Sister Lúcia is the one who suggested to him that he do this.

Bishop José Alves Correia da Silva could have acquainted himself and the world with the contents of the secret even before Sister Lúcia put it in writing, but he persistently refused to do this, saying that he did not feel he was called "to interfere" and that if God wanted the secret to be revealed, then "he would have said so specifically."[6]

Eventually, it was agreed between the Bishop of Leiria and Sister Lúcia that the secret would definitely be opened and communicated to the world either at her death or in 1960, whichever came first. In May 1955, Alfredo Cardinal Ottaviani asked the Sister why the secret could not be revealed before 1960 and she replied: "Because then it will appear clearer." The Cardinal said that this answer led him to think that "the message had a prophetic tone."

The Bishop of Leiria would have liked to pass the sealed secret to the Cardinal Patriarch even before his death. He approached the Cardinal concerning this, but the Cardinal refused to accept it. So the famous document remained in Leiria until shortly before the death of the Bishop, which occurred on December 4, 1957.

Early in 1957, the Sacred Congregation for the Doctrine of the Faith asked the authorities at Leiria to send it a photocopy of all of Sister Lúcia's writings. Rather than risk exposing the secret by having it copied, the Bishop sent the original document to the Papal Nuncio in Lisboa. This occurred in the last part of March 1957. The Nuncio faithfully transmitted the document to the Sacred Congregation. This was during the pontificate of Pius XII, who governed the Church until his death on October 9, 1958. Father Alonso, who is the source of all this information, does not think that Pius XII read the secret.

Pope John XXIII, who succeeded Pius XII and governed the Church until his death on June 3, 1963, definitely read the secret in 1960 and "probably in the early days of the year." Cardinal Ottaviani has stated that in 1960 the secret, still sealed, was taken from the Sacred Congregation to the Pope, who opened and read it and later told the Cardinal that, although the message was written in Portuguese, he had understood it all. The Pope then passed the document to the Cardinal, who was present, and allowed him to read it. John XXIII put the secret in another envelope, sealed it, and sent it to the secret archives of the Vatican.

Father Alonso's book on this secret of Fátima was published in 1976 when Paul VI was Pope. He says that nothing can be affirmed with certainty regarding Paul VI's having read the secret, yet he thinks there is "the very greatest probability," "*la más alta probabilidad*," that he actually did so. He also quotes Cardinal

Ottaviani as saying that, having read the secret himself, he can affirm that all the things which circulate about the secret "are fantasy."[7] The wildest rumors have indeed circulated.

What do we know with certainty about the secret of 1960? We know that it is short. It was written on one sheet of paper in Portuguese. Sister Lúcia has told us that, and so has Cardinal Ottaviani, who has read it. The Cardinal has also let us know that it contains a message for the Pope. We also know that the Pope decided in his wisdom not to reveal its contents to the world.

Let us recall what Sister Lúcia said to the Bishop of Leiria in *Memoir III* in answer to those who had criticized her for not having made known in 1917 the first two parts of the secret and what she told Father McGlynn when he asked her why Our Lady's warning of World War Two as a punishment for sin had not been published until after the war had already begun. What she said in those two circumstances can be said to apply to the Pope's decision not to reveal the 1960 secret. We have known since 1917 the part of the Fátima message that needs to be known by everyone, namely, that we should amend our lives and stop offending God, Who is already greatly offended. This is what we need to do to hasten the conversion of Russia and bring about the period of peace that will eliminate the threat of atomic war.

Appendix B

1. "And from that hour the disciple took her to his own home" (John 19:27).

These are the concluding words of the Gospel in today's liturgy at Fátima. The disciple's name was John. It was he, John, the son of Zebedee, the apostle and evangelist, who heard from the cross the words of Christ: "Behold your mother." But first Christ had said to His mother: "Woman, behold your son."

This was a wonderful testament.

As He left this world, Christ gave to His mother a man, a human being, to be like a son for her: John. He entrusted him to her. And as a consequence of this giving and entrusting, Mary became the mother of John. The mother of God became the mother of man.

From that hour John "took her to his own home" and became the earthly guardian of the mother of his Master; for sons have the right and duty to care for their mother. John became by Christ's will the son of the mother of God. And in John every human being became her child.

*This is the Vatican's translation of the Portuguese-language homily. It is taken from *Origins*, NC Documentary Service, Publication Number ISSN 0093-609X, May 27, 1982, Vol. 12: No. 2.

2. The words "he took her to his own home" can be taken in the literal sense as referring to the place where he lived.

Mary's motherhood in our regard is manifested in a particular way in the places where she meets us: her dwelling places; places in which a special presence of the mother is felt.

There are many such dwelling places. They are of all kinds: from a special corner in the home or little wayside shrines built in her honor. However, in certain places the mother's presence is felt in a particularly vivid way. These places sometimes radiate their light over a great distance and draw people from afar. Their radiance may extend over a diocese, a whole nation, or at times over several countries and even continents. These places are the Marian sanctuaries or shrines.

In all these places that unique testament of the crucified Lord is wonderfully actualized. In them man feels that he is entrusted and confided to Mary; he goes there in order to be with her, as with his mother; he opens his heart to her and speaks to her about everything. He "takes her to his own home," that is to say, he brings her into all his problems, which at times are difficult—his own problems and those of others. The problems of the family, of societies, of nations, and of the whole of humanity.

3. Is this not the case with the shrine at Lourdes in France? Is this not the case with Jasna Gora in Poland, my own country's shrine, which this year is celebrating its six hundredth anniversary?

There too, as in so many other shrines of Mary throughout the world, the words of today's liturgy seem to resound with a particularly authentic force: "You are the splendid boast of our people" (Judith 15:9), and also: "When your people were being oppressed . . . you averted our disaster, walking uprightly before our God" (Judith 13:20).

At Fátima these words resound as one particular echo of the experiences not only of the Portuguese nation, but also of so many other countries and peoples on this earth. Indeed, they echo the experience of modern mankind as a whole, the whole of the human family.

4. And so I come here today because on this very day last year, in Saint Peter's Square in Rome, the attempt on the Pope's life

was made in mysterious coincidence with the anniversary of the first apparition at Fátima, which occurred May 13, 1917.

I seemed to recognize in the coincidence of the dates a special call to come to this place. And so today I am here. I have come in order to thank Divine Providence in this place which the mother of God seems to have chosen in a particular way. *"Misericordiae domini, quia non sumus consumpti"*—"The favors of the Lord are not exhausted, His mercies are not spent" (Lamentations 3:22), I repeat once more with the prophet.

I have come especially in order to confess here the glory of God Himself:

"Blessed be the Lord God, the creator of heaven and earth," I say in the words of today's liturgy (Judith 13:18).

And to the Creator of heaven and earth I also raise that special hymn of glory which is she herself, the immaculate mother of the Incarnate Word:

"Blessed are you daughter, by the Most High God, above all the women on earth . . . your deed of hope will never be forgotten by those who tell of the might of God. May God make this redound to your everlasting honor" (Judith 13:18–20).

At the basis of this song of praise, which the Church lifts up with joy here as in so many other places on the earth, is the incomparable choice of a daughter of the human race to be the mother of God.

And therefore let God above all be praised: Father, Son, and Holy Spirit.

May blessing and veneration be given to Mary, the model of the Church, as the "dwelling place of the most holy Trinity."

5. From the time when Jesus, dying on the cross, said to John: "Behold your mother," from the time when "the disciple took her to his own home," the mystery of the spiritual motherhood of Mary has been actualized boundlessly in history.

Motherhood means caring for the life of the child. Since Mary is the mother of us all, her care for the life of man is universal. The care of a mother embraces her child totally. Mary's motherhood has its beginning in her motherly care for Christ. In Christ, at the foot of the cross, she accepted John, and in John she accepted all of us totally.

Mary embraces us all with special solicitude in the Holy Spirit.

For as we profess in our creed, He is the "giver of life," it is He Who gives the fullness of life, open toward eternity.

Mary's spiritual motherhood is therefore a sharing in the power of the Holy Spirit, of "the giver of life." It is the humble service of she who says of herself: "Behold, I am the handmaid of the Lord" (Luke 1:38).

In the light of the mystery of Mary's spiritual motherhood, let us seek to understand the extraordinary message which began May 13, 1917, to resound throughout the world from Fátima, continuing for five months until October 13 of the same year.

6. The Church has always taught and continues to proclaim that God's revelation was brought to completion in Jesus Christ, Who is the fullness of that revelation, and that "no new public revelation is to be expected before the glorious manifestation of Our Lord" (Constitution on Divine Revelation, 4). The Church evaluates and judges private revelations by the criterion of conformity with that single public revelation.

If the Church has accepted the message of Fátima, it is above all because that message contains a truth and a call whose basic content is the truth and the call of the Gospel itself.

"Reform your lives, and believe in the Gospel" (Mark 1:15). These are the first words that the Messiah addressed to humanity. The message of Fátima is in its basic nucleus a call to conversion and repentance, as in the Gospel. This call was uttered at the beginning of the twentieth century, and it was thus addressed particularly to this present century. The Lady of the message seems to have read with special insight the "signs of the time," the signs of our time.

The call to repentance is a motherly one, and at the same time it is strong and decisive. The love that "rejoices in the truth" (cf. 1 Corinthians 13:6) is capable of being clear-cut and firm. The call to repentance is linked, as always, with a call to prayer. In harmony with the tradition of many centuries the Lady of the message indicates the rosary, which can rightly be defined as "Mary's prayer," the prayer in which she feels particularly united with us.

She herself prays with us. The rosary prayer embraces the problems of the Church, of the See of Saint Peter, the problems of the whole world. In it we also remember sinners, that they may be converted and saved, and the souls in purgatory.

The words of the message were addressed to children aged from seven to ten. Children, like Bernadette of Lourdes, are particularly privileged in these apparitions of the mother of God.

Hence the fact that also her language is simple, within the limits of their understanding. The children of Fátima became partners in dialogue with the Lady of the message and collaborators with her. One of them is still living.

7. When Jesus on the cross said: "Woman, behold your son" (John 19:26), in a new way He opened his mother's heart, the Immaculate Heart, and revealed to it the new dimensions and extent of the love to which she was called in the Holy Spirit by the power of the sacrifice of the cross.

In the words of Fátima we seem to find this dimension of motherly love, whose range covers the whole of man's path toward God: the path that leads through this world and that goes, through purgatory, beyond this world. The solicitude of the mother of the Saviour is solicitude for the work of salvation, the work of her Son. It is solicitude for the salvation, the eternal salvation of all.

Now that sixty-five years have passed since that May 13, 1917, it is difficult to fail to notice how the range of this salvific love of the mother embraces in a particular way our century.

·In the light of a mother's love we understand the whole message of the Lady of Fátima. The greatest obstacle to man's journey toward God is sin, perseverance in sin and, finally, denial of God—the deliberate blotting out of God from the world of human thought, the detachment from Him of the whole of man's earthly activity, the rejection of God by man.

In reality, the eternal salvation of man is only in God. Man's rejection of God, if it becomes definitive, leads logically to God's rejection of man (cf. Matthew 7:23, 10:33), to damnation.

Can the mother who, with all the force of the love that she fosters in the Holy Spirit, desires everyone's salvation keep silence on what undermines the very basis of their salvation? No, she cannot.

And so, while the message of Our Lady of Fátima is a motherly one, it is also strong and decisive. It sounds severe. It sounds like

John the Baptist speaking on the banks of the Jordan. It invites to repentance. It gives a warning. It calls to prayer. It recommends the rosary.

The message is addressed to every human being. The love of the Saviour's mother reaches every place touched by the work of salvation. Her care extends to every individual of our time and to all the societies, nations, and people—societies menaced by apostasy, threatened by moral degradation. The collapse of morality involves the collapse of societies.

8. On the cross Christ said: "Woman, behold your son." With these words he opened in a new way His mother's heart. A little later, the Roman soldier's spear pierced the side of the Crucified One. That pierced Heart became a sign of the redemption achieved through the death of the Lamb of God.

The Immaculate Heart of Mary, opened with the words "Woman, behold your son," is spiritually united with the Heart of her Son opened by the soldier's spear. Mary's Heart was opened by the same love for man and for the world with which Christ loved man and the world, offering Himself for them on the cross, until the soldier's spear struck that blow.

Consecrating the world to the Immaculate Heart of Mary means drawing near, through the mother's intercession, to the very fountain of life that sprang from Golgotha. This fountain pours forth unceasingly redemption and grace. In it reparation is made continually for the sins of the world. It is a ceaseless source of new life and holiness.

Consecrating the world to the Immaculate Heart of the mother means returning beneath the cross of the Son. It means consecrating this world to the pierced Heart of the Saviour, bringing it back to the very source of its redemption. Redemption is always greater than man's sin and the "sin of the world." The power of the redemption is infinitely superior to the whole range of evil in man and the world.

The Heart of the mother is aware of this, more than any other heart in the whole universe, visible and invisible.

And so she calls us.

She not only calls us to be converted, she calls us to accept her motherly help to return to the source of redemption.

9. Consecrating ourselves to Mary means accepting her help to

offer ourselves and the whole of mankind to Him who is holy, infinitely holy; it means accepting her help—by having recourse to her motherly heart, which beneath the cross was opened to love for every human being, for the whole world—in order to offer the world, the individual human being, mankind as a whole, and all the nations to Him Who is infinitely holy. God's holiness showed itself in the redemption of man, of the world, of the whole of mankind, and of the nations, a redemption brought about through the sacrifice of the cross. "I consecrate Myself for their sakes," Jesus said (John 17:19).

By the power of the redemption the world and man have been consecrated. They have been consecrated to Him Who is infinitely holy. They have been offered and entrusted to love itself, merciful love.

The mother of Christ calls us, invites us to join with the Church of the living God in the consecration of the world in this act of confiding by which the world, mankind as a whole, the nations, and each individual person are presented to the eternal Father with the power of the redemption won by Christ. They are offered in the Heart of the Redeemer, which was pierced on the cross.

The mother of the Redeemer calls us, invites us, and helps us to join in this consecration, this act of confiding the world. By joining in it we shall be as close as possible to the Heart of Jesus pierced on the cross.

10. The appeal of the Lady of the message of Fátima is so deeply rooted in the Gospel and the whole of tradition that the Church feels that the message imposes a commitment on her.

She has responded through the servant of God, Pius XII (whose episcopal ordination took place precisely on May 13, 1917). *He consecrated the human race and especially the peoples of Russia to the Immaculate Heart of Mary* [emphasis added]. Was not that consecration his response to the evangelical eloquence of the call of Fátima?

In its Dogmatic Constitution on the Church and its Pastoral Constitution on the Church in the Modern World, the Second Vatican Council amply illustrated the reasons for the link between the Church and the world of today. Furthermore, its teaching on Mary's special place in the mystery of Christ and the

Church bore mature fruit in Paul VI's action in calling Mary mother of the Church and thus indicating more profoundly the nature of her union with the Church and of her care for the world, for mankind, for each human being, and for all the nations: What characterizes them is her motherhood.

This brought a further deepening of understanding of the meaning of the act of consecrating that the Church is called upon to perform with the help of the Heart of Christ's mother and ours.

11. Today John Paul II, successor of Peter, continuator of the work of Pius, John, and Paul, and particular heir of the Second Vatican Council, presents himself before the mother of the Son of God in her shrine at Fátima. In what way does he come?

He presents himself, reading again with trepidation the motherly call to penance, to conversion, the ardent appeal of the Heart of Mary that resounded at Fátima sixty-five years ago. Yes, he reads it again with trepidation in his heart, because he sees how many people and societies—how many Christians—have gone in the opposite direction to the one indicated in the message of Fátima. Sin has thus made itself firmly at home in the world, and denial of God has become widespread in the ideologies, ideas, and plans of human beings.

But for this very reason the evangelical call to repentance and conversion, uttered in the mother's message, remains ever relevant. It is still more relevant than it was sixty-five years ago. It is still more urgent. And so it is to be the subject of next year's synod of bishops, for which we are already preparing.

The successor of Peter presents himself here also as a witness to the immensity of human suffering, a witness to the almost apocalyptic menaces looming over the nations and mankind as a whole. He is trying to embrace these sufferings with his own weak human heart as he places himself before the mystery of the Heart of the mother, the Immaculate Heart of Mary.

In the name of these sufferings and with awareness of the evil that is spreading throughout the world and menacing the individual human being, the nations, and mankind as a whole, Peter's successor presents himself here with greater faith in the redemption of the world, in the saving love that is always stronger, always more powerful than any evil.

My heart is oppressed when I see the sin of the world and the whole range of menaces gathering like a dark cloud over mankind, but it also rejoices with hope as I once more do what has been done by my predecessors when they consecrated the world to the Heart of the mother, when they consecrated especially to that Heart those peoples which particularly need to be consecrated. Doing this means consecrating the world to Him Who is infinite holiness. This holiness means redemption. It means a love more powerful than evil. No "sin of the world" can ever overcome this love.

Once more this act is being done. Mary's appeal is not just for once. Her appeal must be taken up by generation after generation in accordance with the ever-new "signs of the times." It must be unceasingly returned to. It must ever be taken up anew.

12. The author of the Apocalypse wrote: "I also saw a new Jerusalem, the holy city, coming down out of heaven from God, beautiful as a bride prepared to meet her husband. I heard a loud voice from the throne cry out: 'This is God's dwelling among men. He shall dwell with them, and they shall be His people, and He shall be their God Who is always with them'" (Revelation 21:2–3).

This is the faith by which the Church lives.

This is the faith with which the people of God makes its journey.

"The dwelling of God is with men" on earth even now.

In that dwelling is the Heart of the bride and mother, Mary, a Heart adorned with the jewel of her Immaculate Conception. The Heart of the bride and mother which was opened beneath the cross by the word of her Son to a great new love for man and the world. The Heart of the bride and mother which is aware of all the sufferings of individuals and societies on earth.

The people of God is a pilgrim along the ways of this world in an eschatological direction. It is making its pilgrimage toward the eternal Jerusalem, toward "the dwelling of God with men."

There God will "wipe away every tear from their eyes, and there shall be no more death or mourning, crying out or pain, for the former world has passed away" (Revelation 21:4).

But at present "the former world" is still in existence. It constitutes the temporal setting of our pilgrimage.

For that reason we look toward "the One who sat on the

throne [and] said . . . 'See, I make all things new!'" (cf. Revelation 21:5).

And together with the evangelist and apostle we try to see with the eyes of faith "the new heaven and the new earth"; for the first heaven and the first earth have passed away.

But "the first heaven and the first earth" still exist about us and within us. We cannot ignore it. But this enables us to recognize what an immense grace was granted to us human beings when in the midst of our pilgrimage there shone forth on the horizon of the faith of our times this "great sign in the sky, a woman" (cf. Revelation 12:1).

Yes, truly we can repeat: "Blessed are you, daughter, by the Most High God above all the women on earth . . . Walking uprightly before our God . . . you averted our disaster."

Truly, indeed, you are blessed.

Yes, here and throughout the Church, in the heart of every individual and in the world as a whole, may you be blessed, O Mary, our sweet mother.

Notes

1 AN ANGEL TO PREPARE THE WAY

1. Lúcia thinks this is the date. "I can't give the exact dates with certainty," she says, "because at that time I did not yet know how to count the years, nor the months, nor even the days of the week" (*Memoir IV*, pp. 57–58). The page numbers refer to Lúcia's original handwritten text that the author was privileged to consult in 1950.

2. Lúcia de Jesús was born on March 22, 1907, to Antônio and Maria Rosa dos Santos. She was the last of seven children. One child died at birth so that there were five girls and one boy living at the time of the apparitions.

3. Francisco was born on June 11, 1908, and Jacinta on March 11, 1910. Olímpia, their mother, first married José Fernandes Rosa in 1888. She lived with José seven and a half years and two sons, Antônio and Manuel, were born to that union. A year and a half after the death of her first husband Olímpia married Manuel Pedro Marto. Seven children came from this second marriage. They are, in the order of their birth: José, Teresa, Florinda, Teresa (a second Teresa, the first having died), João, Francisco, and Jacinta. (P. João M. de Marchi, I.M.C., *Era uma senhora mais brilhante que o sol*, third ed., Cova da Iria: Edição do Seminário das Missões de Nossa Senhora da Fátima, p. 33, note 1)

When the author met Olímpia and Manuel Pedro Marto in July 1950, they appeared in good health. She was eighty-one years old, and he, seventy-eight.

4. In her *Memoirs*, Lúcia refers to this opening in the boulders as a "cave" or "grotto" (*lapa*, v.g., *Memoir IV*, p. 62), which led everyone

to mistake a real cave, ten or twelve feet deep less than a hundred yards away, for this niche. When in 1946 she visited Fátima for the first time since her departure in 1921 Lúcia identified the niche as the exact place of this apparition.

5. *Depois de repetir isto três vezes*, literally: "After repeating this three times" (Sister Lúcia, *Memoir IV*, p. 59).

6. *Estam atentos* (Sister Lúcia, *Memoir IV*, p. 59). The literal translation, "are attentive," is somewhat awkward, but we prefer to follow it. We have adopted the rule of adhering as much as possible to a literal translation of all important conversations and events recorded by Sister Lúcia in her four *Memoirs*. We shall also quote Lúcia's *Memoirs* in Portuguese exactly as she wrote them, for example, in the present case she used the old form *estam* instead of the newer form *estão*.

7. *Os Coraçoẽs de Jesús e Maria têm sobre vós desígnios de misericórdia* (Sister Lúcia, *Memoir IV*, pp. 60–61).

8. *De tudo que podereis, oferecei um sacrifício em acto de reparação pelos pecados com que Ele é ofendido e de súplica pela conversão dos pecadores.* Literally: "With everything that you can, offer a sacrifice as an act of reparation for the sins by which He is offended and of supplication for the conversion of sinners" (Sister Lúcia, *Memoir IV*, p. 61).

9. Sister Lúcia has explicitly affirmed that she and her two cousins had the impression that the Angel of Portugal and the Angel of Peace were the same individual. (C. Barthas, *Il était trois petits Enfants*, third ed., Toulouse: Fátima-Éditions, 1947, p. 46, note 2) Saint Michael, the archangel, is the guardian angel of Portugal.

10. . . . *trazendo na mão um caliz e, sobre ele, uma hóstia, da qual caíam dentro do caliz algumas gotas de sangue* (Sister Lúcia, *Memoir IV*, p. 62).

11. *E pelos méritos infinitos do seu Santíssimo Coração, e do Coração Imaculado de Maria*; literally: "And by the infinite merits of His Most Holy Heart and of the Immaculate Heart of Mary" (Sister Lúcia, *Memoir IV*, p. 62).

12. Lúcia felt the host on her tongue and believes that she really received Holy Communion from the hands of the angel. (See C. Barthas, *Il était trois*, p. 48.)

13. This entire description of the children's subjective state during and after the apparitions of the angel (including the rather startling words "annihilated" and "annihilation") is based upon Sister Lúcia's *Memoirs*. (*aniquilava quasi por completo*, and *aniquilamento* in *Memoir IV*, pp. 63–64)

2   A LADY ALL OF LIGHT

1. Lúcia usually refers to the apparition as *a Senhora,* "the Lady," or *Nossa Senhora,* "Our Lady," but this does not imply that she appeared old. Lúcia's mother, in her testimony during the canonical inquiry of 1923, says that Lúcia told her that she had seen "a little woman" *uma mulherzinha* (*Interrogatórios oficiais de Manuel Pedro Marto, Olímpia de Jesús,* etc., 1923). On October 11, 1917, describing the Lady's age to the ecclesiastical investigator Dr. Formigão, Lúcia said: "She appears to be about fifteen years old," *Parece ter uns quinze anos* (De Marchi, *Era uma Senhora,* p. 150). During the 1924 canonical inquiry she declared that the Lady "appeared young, maybe from eighteen to twenty-two years old" *com aparéncias de nova, talvez de dezóito a vinte e dois anos* (*Interrogatório oficial de Lúcia de Jesús,* 1924, p. 2), and in early February 1947, Sister Lúcia told Father Thomas McGlynn, O.P., that the Lady appeared to be "perhaps seventeen" (*Vision of Fátima,* Boston: Little, Brown & Company, 1948, p. 94). It is interesting to note here that caution which always characterizes Lúcia's answers: the Lady appears to be "about" fifteen, "maybe" from eighteen to twenty-two, "perhaps" seventeen.

2. In our description of the Lady's facial expression we have attempted to conciliate two different statements made by Lúcia at different moments of her life. On September 27, 1917, she was questioned by Dr. Formigão: "Did she smile at times, or appear sad?" To which Lúcia replied: "She never smiled or appeared sad, but was always serious." Francisco was also questioned on the same day by the same priest: "Has she wept at times or smiled?" His reply was similar to Lúcia's: "Neither one or the other. She is always serious." (For the Portuguese texts of both these quotations see De Marchi, pp. 141 and 144.) In early February 1947, Father McGlynn interviewed Sister Lúcia and asked her: "What was Our Lady's expression?" She replied: "Pleasing but sad; sweet but sad." *Agradável mas triste; doce mas triste.* (*Vision of Fátima,* p. 68)

3. Questioned by Father McGlynn about the cloud upon which all early authors said that the Lady rested her feet, Sister Lúcia replied: "The people spoke of a cloud but I saw none. Our Lady's feet rested lightly on the tops of the leaves" (*Vision of Fátima,* p. 64).

4. Some will find this description of the Lady quite unusual, not to say queer. Yet it is Lúcia's own description as taken, verbatim in several instances, from her *Memoirs* and from the answers she gave to ecclesiastical visitors. The new material not found in the older accounts was taken from the first interview between Father McGlynn and Sister Lúcia as related in chapter seven of his book *Vision of Fátima.*

5. *Depois voltarei ainda aquí uma sétima vez* (Sister Lúcia, *Memoir IV*, p. 67). This seventh visit has taken place. It occurred on June 16, 1921, the day Lúcia left Aljustrel for the school conducted by the Sisters of Saint Dorothy at Vilar, which is now a suburb of O Porto. On departing from home, Lúcia paid a last visit to the Cova da Iria and saw Our Lady standing at the spot now occupied by the lower steps of the basilica. The author received this information directly from a very reliable person who in turn obtained it directly from Sister Lúcia in 1946.

6. *muitos terços* (Sister Lúcia, *Memoir IV*, p. 67). In the canonical inquiry of 1924 Lúcia declared that Our Lady affirmed Francisco must say "the" beads—*o terço*—(*Interrogatório oficial de Lúcia*, p. 3). However, that the correct version is "many" beads can be gleaned from another interesting passage of *Memoir IV*. Indeed, on page 12 of this important document Sister Lúcia says: "Later we told Francisco all that Our Lady had said. And he, manifesting his satisfaction in the promise to go to heaven, crossed his hands upon his breast and said: 'O Our Lady, I will say as many beads as you want.' And from that time on he adopted the practice of withdrawing from us as though going on a walk. If we called him and asked him what he was going to do, he would raise his arm and show us the rosary. If we told him to come and play, and pray afterward with us, he would reply: 'I will say it afterward too. Don't you remember that Our Lady said I would have to say many beads?'"

7. *Estará no purgatório até ao fim do mundo* (Sister Lúcia, *Memoir IV*, p. 68). In the canonical inquiry of 1924 Lúcia simply stated that Our Lady replied Amelia "was in purgatory" *estava no purgatório* (*Interrogatório oficial de Lúcia*, p. 2). This question of Amelia's stay in purgatory has created considerable discussion. Questioned in February 1946 by the Reverend H. Jongen, S.M.M., author of an excellent book on Fátima, Lúcia affirmed categorically that Our Lady did say that Amelia would stay in purgatory until the end of the world. She reaffirmed the same thing to Father Thomas McGlynn in 1947, and when he declared that this troubled many people she replied that she did not think it very remarkable, since one could go to hell for all eternity for missing Mass on Sunday (*Vision of Fátima*, p. 98).

It is important to note that Amelia was no child at the time of her death. Lúcia says it seems to her she was "between eighteen and twenty" (*Memoir IV*, p. 68). Also, it should be remembered that Our Lady's statement does not preclude the possibility of Amelia's stay in purgatory being shortened by the prayers of friends and relatives. It simply implies that the condition of her soul at the time of her death was such as to merit that severe punishment, that is, remaining in purgatory until the end of time. Many souls have merited a long period of punishment in purgatory which was shortened by the charitable assistance of persons still on earth.

In the nineteenth Italian edition of his book *Le Meraviglie di Fátima* (Roma: Edizione Paoline, 1967), p. 21, note 5, Father Luis Gonzaga da Fonseca, S.J., says that Amelia, who was a friend of Lúcia's, "had been tempted" in the same way that Saint Maria Goretti had, but that "she had not had the courage of the saint" who had resisted her would-be seducer and had been cruelly stabbed to death by him. He adds that Amelia had "died shortly afterward" and "had barely had time to make a hurried confession."

8. This request is one of the so-called "secrets" which the children felt interiorly inspired not to reveal and which they did actually conceal at the time of the apparitions (the July secret is the only one which Our Lady expressly forbade them to reveal to the people). For this reason it is not found in the early books on Fátima. It was first made known when Sister Lúcia wrote her *Memoirs* at the demand of her Bishop, the Bishop of Leiria.

9. *fazendo-nos ver a nós mesmos em Deus, que era essa luz, mais claramente que nos vemos no melhor dos espelhos* (Sister Lúcia, *Memoir IV*, p. 68). The comparison with the *Dominus Vobiscum* of the Mass is also Lúcia's.

10. This description of the Lady's departure is an accurate account combined from Lúcia's *Memoirs* and from Lúcia's and Francisco's answers during the inquiry conducted on October 13, 1917, by the ecclesiastical investigator, Dr. Formigão. In *Memoir IV*, p. 69, Sister Lúcia says: "The light that surrounded her seemed to be opening a path among the dense stars, which is the reason why we sometimes said we saw heaven open up."

3 THE LADY WAS SO PRETTY!

1. Lúcia relates this incident in the 1924 canonical investigation (*Interrogatório oficial de Lúcia*, p. 3). According to her the man used the conditional tense in referring to the eating of the vetches: *veio um homen dizer . . . que os chícaros estariam comidos.*

2. Lúcia has affirmed that she and her two cousins were convinced from the very first apparition that the Lady from heaven was the Blessed Virgin.

3. There is some question as to whether Francisco saw Our Lady at the start of the apparition.

Manuel Pedro Marto in his testimony during the 1923 canonical inquiry states that Francisco told his mother on the night of May 13, 1917, that "he had also seen the Lady, though he had not seen her from the beginning." It is not certain that Manuel Pedro heard Francisco make this statement himself, though it is very probable that he did. (*Interrogatórios oficiais de Manuel Pedro*, etc.)

Manuel's wife, Olímpia, gives considerable information concerning this topic in her testimony during the same canonical inquiry of 1923. "At the beginning of the apparition," she reports, "when Lúcia said that she saw Our Lady, Francisco, not seeing anything, advised his cousin to throw a stone at her. Lúcia said to the Lady: 'How is it that you are Our Lady from heaven and Francisco can't see you?' Indeed, the Lady had already said that she was from heaven. Our Lady replied to Lúcia: 'Tell him to say his rosary and he will see me.' The boy declared [these canonical inquiries are written in the third person] that he put his hand in his vest pocket where he had his Mass rosary (*as contas da Missa*) and started to recite it. When he had said six or seven *Ave Marias* he saw the Lady and could not pray anymore. After he had started to see her, he noticed that the sheep were beginning to go into a wheat patch located in the lowest part of the Cova da Iria and he said that he was going to chase them out. He was on the point of leaving when Lúcia said to him: 'Francisco don't go, because Our Lady said that the flock is not eating the wheat.' He then remarked: 'You mean that the sheep are already in the wheat and are not eating it.' And he turned back. The mother asked him: 'After Our Lady left, did the sheep eat the wheat?' He answered: 'Ah, if I had let them, they would have eaten all of it.' "

Memoir IV (concluded on December 8, 1941), which contains Sister Lúcia's last and most detailed account of the apparitions, makes no mention of the fact related by Olímpia.

In the 1924 canonical inquiry Lúcia does describe the incident (worked into our text) of the sheep straying into the vetches and of their not eating them. But she says nothing of Francisco's asking her to throw a stone at Our Lady and of his preoccupation concerning the sheep during the apparition. However, questioned about these facts by Canon Barthas, Sister Lúcia, in a letter dated February 24, 1947, answered: "Francisco saw our Lady from the first moment . . . During the apparition we never so much as thought that the sheep existed" (*Il était trois*, p. 55, footnote 12 *bis*).

The value of Lúcia's testimony is naturally very strong. From a critical point of view, it seems difficult to admit a lapse in Lúcia's memory, both in 1924 and in 1947. Indeed, Francisco's not having seen the Lady, etc., are things too important for Lúcia to have forgotten, had they really occurred. Also, it must be remembered that Lúcia has a truly remarkable memory and enjoys a certain measure of divine protection when imparting the story of Fátima, though this last cannot be stressed too much lest we make her infallible. On the other hand, it must be admitted that the sworn testimony of a God-fearing person like Olímpia Marto carries some probability. That probability is considerably strengthened by an analysis of the facts themselves. Throwing a stone to prove the presence of a lady (in the hypothesis that he had no idea it was the Blessed Virgin—having seen and heard nothing) is exactly what one would expect of a mountain lad. Then, the fact that Francisco can see the lady only after saying a part of the beads fits perfectly with the message of the June apparition in which Our Lady affirms he must say "many beads" if he wants to go to heaven.

4 JACINTA TALKS

1. This entire conversation between the mother and her child is from Olímpia's own testimony concerning the May 13 apparition as related in the 1923 canonical inquiry. To her report of this conversation a Senhora Marto adds this very interesting comment: "Seeing that the children continued to say the beads every day, either when they went out with the flock or at home, the parents [the report, as usual, is in the third person] resolved that they too would recite the beads every day in common with all the family. And if on any particular day, for some extraordinary reason, they omitted this practice, the child would become sad and say with evident grief: 'Dear Mamma, I have already said the beads but you haven't said them yet'" (*Interrogatórios oficiais de Manuel Pedro*, etc.). The father says that after Our Lady appeared Francisco too became an ardent apostle of the rosary within the family (De Marchi, p. 37).

Olímpia's testimony concerning the June 13 apparition throws additional light on Francisco's and Jacinta's devotion to the rosary. She says: "No change for the better was noticed in the youngsters after the apparitions. There was one new thing they did and that was recite the beads . . . They asked permission to recite the beads and they said them each day and they also always said them at night. Notwithstanding this, it was not rare for them to recite the beads two or three times while they were with the flock" (*Interrogatórios oficiais de Manuel Pedro*, etc.).

2. Olímpia attached enough importance to it (or was it only a woman's natural inclination for gossip?) to speak about it to the neighbors first thing next morning—as shall be seen.

3. Father De Marchi quotes Manuel Pedro as saying: "From the beginning, I practically admitted that what the children said was true . . . Yes, I believed immediately." E, logo de caminho, quase fiquei a fazer juizo que era verdade o que as crianças diziam . . . Sim, logo acreditei (*Era uma senhora*, p. 64).

5 AT THE RECTORY

1. The pastor's 1919 report reveals how conscientious he was in investigating the apparitions. He states that he sent for Maria Rosa and Lúcia in May as soon as he heard of the first apparition, that is to say, "about fifteen days after" it occurred (p. 10). He questioned the same two "immediately after the thirteenth of June" (p. 5), "on the fourteenth of July" (p. 6), "on the fifteenth of September" (p. 11), and "on the sixteenth of the current month of October" (p. 13). In August he says that he questioned Lúcia on August 21, which was two days after the unexpected apparition at os Valinhos (p. 10). He affirms that he questioned Jacinta "various times" (p. 16), and that he also questioned Francisco "a few times and in diverse occasions" (p. 18).

2. Fátima had formerly possessed a priory and the pastor was still called "the Prior" or more literally "Mr. Prior," for the Portuguese people use the word *o Senhor*, Mr., before the various religious titles, for example, *o Senhor Padre*, Mr. Father, *o Senhor Bispo*, Mr. Bishop.

6 A HEART PIERCED WITH THORNS

1. *O terço*, the third part of the rosary, that is, "the beads." Our Lady always used this expression in each of her six apparitions when requesting the rosary. The only time she used the word "rosary" is when she referred to Our Lady of the Rosary. The documents testify to this and Sister Lúcia explicitly confirmed it in one of her interviews with Father McGlynn (*Vision of Fátima*, p. 92).

2. According to *Memoir IV*, in which Sister Lúcia gives a complete account of Our Lady's words during each of the six apparitions, Our Lady used the expression "every day" five times in requesting the recitation of the beads, that is, in May, June, July, August, and October (pp. 69, 71, 72, 77, and 81). According to this same document Our Lady said in September: "Continue to say the beads in order to obtain the cessation of the war" (p. 80).

Jacinta bears witness to the same fact. Dr. Formigão asked Jacinta on September 27, 1917: "What was it that Our Lady recommended to Lúcia with greatest insistence?" The child answered: "She requested that we say the beads every day" *Mandou que rezássemos o terço todos os dias*. On October 13, 1917, he questioned her again: "What did Our Lady say?" And she replied: "She told us to say the beads every day—*todos os dias* . . ." (De Marchi, pp. 142 and 179)

3. *Aprendam* (Sister Lúcia, *Memoir IV*, p. 70). This is the third person of the plural, which would indicate that Our Lady wants the three children to learn to read.

4. *Sim, a Jacinta e o Francisco levo-os em breve, mas tu ficas cá mais algum tempo* (Sister Lúcia, *Memoir IV*, p. 71).

5. The promise contained in the last two sentences: "To those . . .", is not found in Sister Lúcia's *Memoirs* and undoubtedly for that reason is not found in many books on Fátima. However, the promise is authentic. In 1928 Sister Lúcia wrote a letter to her confessor in which she stated that Our Lady declared during the second apparition: "He wants to establish in the world devotion to my Immaculate Heart. To those who embrace it, I promise salvation. These souls will be loved by God like flowers placed by me to adorn His throne." Requested, on February 4, 1946, by Father Jongen, to explain why she did not mention this promise in the later reports she made of this apparition (her *Memoirs* were started some eight years after the letter to her confessor), she answered: "When I wrote those later reports, I did not think of it." (This information was given by Father Jongen in an article which originally appeared in the magazine *Médiatrice et Reine* published by the Montfortin Fathers of Louvain, Belgium.)

6. This is the description of the thorns given to Father McGlynn by Sister Lúcia (*Vision of Fátima*, pp. 104–5).

7. Many other details of this description, in addition to those of the thorns, are taken from Father McGlynn's book, *Vision of Fátima*.

8. This difference in the experiences of the bystanders is one of the very curious but undeniable facts of the Fátima apparitions. At Lourdes there was nothing of this nature. The spectators did not witness extraordinary phenomena as they did at the Cova da Iria. Witnesses who testified in the canonical process speak of the underground thunder (Da Fonseca, *Le Meraviglie di Fátima*, p. 28). Maria Carreira's report of this can be found in the 1923 canonical inquiry (*Interrogatórios oficiais de Manuel Pedro*, etc.).

9. This description of the bent branches is a literal translation of Maria Carreira's own testimony of the event as recorded in the 1923 canonical inquiry: *Antes da apparição, viu os grelos da azinheira* [another name commonly used as synonymous of *carrasqueira*] *vicosos é muito direitos. Depois da apparição os grelos estavam como que inclinados, n'uma rodazinha em cima, para o nascente como se os vestidos os tivessem tombado n'essa direcção* (*Interrogatórios oficiais de Manuel Pedro*, etc.).

We do not believe that Maria Carreira's sworn testimony, which was confirmed under oath by her husband, who was also present at the apparition, is destroyed by what Sister Lúcia has declared in recent years. Indeed, questioned by Father McGlynn about the above facts, the Sister replied: "The leaves did not bend" (*Vision of Fátima*, p. 67). It seems legitimate to assume that Lúcia was too absorbed in the Lady during the apparition, and too much under her spell immediately after it, to notice or pay much attention to such things as bent branches.

10. *essa luz tão grande, que é Deus?* These are Francisco's very words as reported by Sister Lúcia in *Memoir IV*, p. 16.

11. *Foi, e eu viu n'essa luz que nos meteu no peito* (Sister Lúcia, *Memoir IV*, p. 16).

7 A LAST MINUTE CHANGE OF MIND

1. Lúcia mentions this strong interior impulse in her *Memoirs*, but she makes no statement at all concerning her mental attitude at the time. It would seem that the doubt was not dispelled at this precise moment, but only later as a result of the apparition itself.

8 HELL, WAR, AND THE IMMACULATE HEART OF MARY

1. Father De Marchi claims that Lúcia's mother did go to the Cova and that she went with her sister-in-law, Olímpia Marto (*Era uma Senhora*, pp. 88–94). But this contradicts statements found in the 1923 canonical inquiry. In his testimony, Manuel Pedro says: "On the thirteenth of July, the parents [he and his wife] also went to the Cova da Iria, the children having gone on ahead. An individual from the parish, named Mathias, a barber, seeing the father of the children, called him to the azinheira where his wife already was." Manuel Pedro makes no mention of Maria Rosa being with his wife. Then, Maria Rosa in her own testimony gives this information: "Lúcia's mother did not go because o Senhor Prior advised her not to go." Finally Maria Rosa's testimony for the October 13 apparition confirms that given above for the July 13 one: "On the thirteenth of October the mother went to the place of the apparitions—*ao local*—for the first time, in spite of o Senhor Prior's recommendation to the contrary" (*Interrogatórios oficiais de Manuel Pedro*, etc.).

2. *porque só ela lhes poderá valer* (Sister Lúcia, *Memoir IV*, p. 72).

3. Maria Carreira gave this information in the 1923 canonical inquiry (*Interrogatórios oficiais de Manuel Pedro*, etc.). Our Lady's promise has been fulfilled. João and his mother became caretakers of the little chapel of the apparitions (*a capelinha das aparições*) built at the very spot of the apparitions. They earned their living in this way. In 1948 the author actually met João at the *capelinha* while he was performing his duties there. It was through him that he met his mother, who was also at the shrine at that moment. A widow in her late seventies, her memory of the apparitions was still precise. However, "Maria da capelinha," as she was commonly and very appropriately called, died

recently. This is truly a great loss, for she had become a historic figure in the story of Fátima. João continues his functions and performs them in a very modest and edifying way. When the author tried to photograph him in 1950, he rose from where he was sitting and disappeared into one of the lower rooms of the hospital behind the *capelinha*.

4. *pecados cometidos contra o Imaculado Coração de Maria* (Sister Lúcia, *Memoir IV*, p. 73).

5. *Esta vista foi um momento, e graças á nossa boa Mãe do céu, que antes nos tinha prevenido com a promessa de nos levar para o céu (na primeira apparição); se assim não fosse, creio que teríamos morrido de susto e pavor* (Sister Lúcia, *Memoir III*, p. 2). Both *Memoir III* and *IV* treat of this important vision of hell and the following prophecy concerning World War Two and Russia, but only *Memoir III* has the above detail.

6. *no reinado de Pio XI* (Sister Lúcia, *Memoir IV*, p. 74).

7. *virei*, the future tense (Sister Lúcia, *Memoir IV*, p. 75).

8. *virei pedir a consagração da Rússia* (Sister Lúcia, *Memoir IV*, p. 75).

9. *a Comunhão reparadora nos primeiros sábados* (Sister Lúcia, *Memoir IV*, p. 75).

10. Our Lady used the plural *perseguições*, "persecutions," both here and a few lines above (Sister Lúcia, *Memoir IV*, pp. 74 and 75).

11. *várias nações serão aniquiladas* (Sister Lúcia, *Memoir IV*, p. 75).

12. *Por fim* (Sister Lúcia, *Memoir IV*, p. 75).

13. *algum tempo de paz* (Sister Lúcia, *Memoir IV*, p. 75).

14. *Em Portugal se conservará sempre o dogma da Fé* (Sister Lúcia, *Memoir IV*, p. 75). *Memoir III* does not carry this phrase, which undoubtedly explains why some books do not mention it.

15. At some time in 1917, possibly during this or some later apparition, Our Lady said that the prediction of war as punishment for sin was not to be made known until 1927. This information was given to Father McGlynn by Sister Lúcia. "She [Sister Lúcia] explained that Our Lady had told her in 1917 that this part of the Secret was not to be revealed until 1927. The threat of punishment was part of the Secret" (*Vision of Fátima*, p. 90).

16. This interdecade prayer has been the object of considerable controversy. First of all, all authors do not place it with the July apparition. Yet Lúcia places it there in the 1924 canonical inquiry (*Interrogatório oficial de Lúcia*, p. 5) and in *Memoir IV* (p. 75).

Then the text itself of the prayer has led to much confusion. In the 1924 canonical inquiry the text reads as follows: *O' meu Jesus, perdoai-nos, livrai-nos do fogo do inferno e levai as alminhas todas para o céu, principalmente aquelas que mais precisarem.* In *Memoir IV* the text is absolutely identical. The word that has caused the trouble is "*alminhas.*" In Portugal the word commonly indicates the souls in purgatory. The result was that the original text was changed and a new one, in favor of the souls in purgatory, was adopted and used extensively. The modified clause read: "Deliver the souls in purgatory, especially the most abandoned."

But this interpretation is certainly erroneous. First, it is interesting to note that Lúcia herself, as early as September 27, 1917, when questioned by Dr. Formigão concerning this prayer, used the word *almas* (souls) and not *alminhas.* Here are her words as reported by the Doctor: *O' meu Jesus, perdoai-nos, livrai-nos do fogo do inferno, levai as almas todas para o céu, especialmente as que mais precisarem* (De Marchi, p. 145). Then we have a letter which she wrote on December 17, 1939, and in which she clarifies the meaning of the ambiguous expression *as que mais precisarem* "those most in need." Indeed, strictly speaking, this clause could well apply to the souls in purgatory. But the Sister insists that its true meaning is "those in greatest danger of eternal damnation," *as que se encontram em maior perigo de condenação eterna.* In this same letter she gives two reasons for this interpretation: first, the "intimate understanding which Our Lady's words infuse" in the soul that receives them: and then the fact that the salvation of sinners seemed to be the "total sorrow and preoccupation of her Immaculate Heart." In fact, the prayer was taught to the children during the same apparition in which Our Lady showed them the flaming sea of hell and revealed that devotion to her Immaculate Heart was a specially efficacious means for obtaining the salvation of sinners. (For Sister Lúcia's December 17, 1939, letter see *Francisco, O Pastorinho de Nossa Senhora,* by Fernando Leite, S.J., Braga: Edição do "Mensageiro do Coração de Jesus," 1946, p. 47, note 1.) This same interpretation of the last part of the interdecade prayer is also given by Sister Lúcia in *Memoir III,* p. 4.

For confirmatory evidence on this matter, the reader can consult Mc-Glynn, *Vision of Fátima,* p. 94; Da Fonseca, *Le Miraviglie di Fátima,* p. 36, note 2, and *Nossa Senhora da Fátima,* p. 59, note 1; Barthas, *Il était trois,* p. 88, note 7; and De Marchi, *Era uma Senhora,* p. 76, note 1.

There is no longer any reason for doubting the real meaning of this rosary prayer. It is interesting to note that in its correct form it summarizes the essence of the Fátima message: repentance for sins; resolve of a life worthy of heaven consequent to the fear of hell; and concern for the salvation of others, especially of sinners in grave danger of eternal damnation.

17. There is still a part of the July 13 secret which has not yet been made public. The vision of hell and the prophecy given above were only released by the Bishop of Leiria on the occasion of the twenty-fifth anniversary of the apparitions.

18. In the 1923 canonical inquiry Maria Carreira stated that she heard "the same buzz when they talked and the same mounting of a rocket at the end." In his testimony Manuel Pedro affirmed that "it was very hot and immediately after the weather turned cool" (*Interrogatórios oficiais de Manuel Pedro*, etc.). In a more recent report made to Father De Marchi, Manuel Pedro gave much more detailed information about what he observed during the July 13 apparition. At the start of the apparition he saw "a sort of little grayish cloud floating over the azinheira tree"; he noticed "the sun cloud up" and "a breeze so cool that it was refreshing"; he heard "a noise, a buzzing sound (*uma zoada*) similar to that of a horsefly in an empty jug," though he did not detect any words; and when the Lady departed he heard "a big clap of thunder" and the rustic arch with its two lanterns "trembled as though there had been an earthquake." All of these signs were for him "a great proof of the miracle," *uma grande aprovação do milagre*, "a great proof" (De Marchi, pp. 90 and 93).

9   STRANGE HAPPENINGS

1. This extraordinary incident is related by Sister Lúcia in *Memoir III*, pp. 8–9.

2. Sister Lúcia, *Memoir III*, p. 9.

3. This incident is also related by Lúcia (Leite, *Francisco*, p. 49). It will be recalled that in the vision of hell the children saw fallen angels "in the terrifying and loathsome forms of horrible, unknown animals" that were "transparent and black or bronze-colored, like live embers." It does not seem possible to explain the above incident as a dream, for Lúcia and Jacinta find Francisco on his knees. The events involving Jacinta are also described by Sister Lúcia in such a way as to preclude the possibility of their being simple dreams. In the first case, Jacinta was sitting on the edge of the well, and in the second, she rose from a prostrate position on the ground where she had been reciting the angel's prayers.

These three incidents that Lúcia has deemed worthy of noting and passing on to us have been related here because they would seem to indicate that the Cova apparitions were amplified, as it were, for each of the seers individually. At least, such was the case for Francisco and

Jacinta, and it can legitimately be supposed that in this respect Lúcia was not less favored than her two cousins. Unfortunately, our information concerning Lúcia is incomplete, since she speaks least about herself in her *Memoirs*.

11   UNLUCKY THIRTEENTH

1. Today there is a road that goes by the Marto home, but in the 1923 canonical inquiry Manuel Pedro affirms: "As the road was not made, the carriage was parked at a crossroad" (*Interrogatórios oficiais de Manuel Pedro*, etc.).

2. Antônio dos Santos' religious status is one of the vague points of the Fátima story that the author has attempted to clarify. In July 1948, during the author's first visit to Fátima, Olímpia Marto told him that her brother, Antônio dos Santos, had always attended Mass faithfully on Sundays and holy days. And in July 1950, in the course of the author's second Fátima visit, Maria dos Anjos and Teresa, two of Antônio's daughters, informed him that their wine-loving father had fulfilled his Easter duties regularly each year, with the exception of one. Concerning his death and the reception of the Last Sacraments, the author received the following information from the same two daughters. Antônio dos Santos' last sickness did not last long. At the final moment the priest was sought but did not have time to arrive before Antônio died. He was on his way and was actually passing by the Marto home, which is at a distance of a hundred yards or so from the dos Santos residence, when Antônio passed away. His death occurred at the end of July 1919. However, the good man did go to confession and received Holy Communion at the beginning of that month, on the occasion of a nearby religious celebration.

12   THE PEOPLE ARE NOT LEFT FORGOTTEN

1. The multiplicity of these "signs" (*signaes*), as the Portuguese people called them, and the diversity in the experiences of those who witnessed them are two of the extraordinary things of the Fátima apparitions. To allow the reader to form a personal judgment from original sources we shall now quote five persons who testified under oath during the 1923 canonical inquiry concerning these August 13 "signs."

Manuel Pedro Marto: "At the Cova da Iria, after talking with various persons, he heard perfectly a clap of thunder (*um estrondo*), followed by dust and thick fog (*poeira e nevoeiro*). The people fled. Almost all the people removed their hats, called to Our Lady, and were very pleased, saying that, though it was true that the children had been kidnapped, Our Lady had manifested herself. He also saw a luminous globe roaming among the clouds (*uma espécie de globo luminoso girando nas nuvens*). There seemed to be a mist (*uma névoa*) around the carrasqueira tree, after the clap of thunder."

Olímpia Marto: "On the road to the Cova da Iria, where she was headed for, Jacinta's mother learned that the Administrator had taken the children to Ourém. She then turned back and went to tell what had happened to her sister-in-law, Lúcia's mother . . . In her sister-in-law's house, when they heard the people cry out, she said: 'What is going on there?' Lúcia's mother looked at the sun and said: 'The sun is different.' The people came and told how they had seen signs in the sun and in the sky (*signaes no sol e no céu*)."

Maria Rosa: "Then that evening many people came and tried to comfort her [Maria Rosa, because of the kidnapping], saying that they believed more now because this was the first day on which the signs appeared." (Signs had appeared before, but evidently these people—and possibly Maria Rosa herself—were not aware of it.)

Maria Carreira: "A noise (*um rumor*) was heard at the foot of the azinheira tree [of the apparitions] which caused such great fear among the people that they all seemed to be crazy (*doidos*), emitting great cries and thinking that they were going to die. Little by little the people started to go away. This witness did not see anything extraordinary." (Maria Carreira in a relatively recent report incorporated in Father De Marchi's book, states that after the noise or clap of thunder she saw a flash of lightning [*relâmpago*] and "a small cloud, very pretty, very white, very light [*uma nuvenzinha, muito linda, muito branquinha, muito leve*] that hovered a few minutes over the carrasqueira tree and then rose toward the sky and disappeared in the air." She also affirms seeing a "strange thing" [*coisa estranha*], the people's faces and clothes shone "with all the colors of the rainbow" [*com todas as cores do arco-iris*], etc. This recent report of Maria Carreira can be found in Father De Marchi's *Era uma Senhora*, pp. 111–12. Maria Carreira's two reports of the August 13 apparition do not concur, but as the good woman was at the Cova five times on the thirteenth of the month when signs were witnessed, it is understandable that she should confuse dates and even certain details of what she experienced on these occasions. As shall be seen shortly, Lúcia's sisters, Teresa and Maria, seem to have confused dates concerning "falling flowers" that they claim to have seen on August 13.)

José Alves (a resident of Moita, which is about a mile from the Cova da Iria): "José Alves went there on the thirteenth of almost all the months after May and never saw anything. He only heard people telling others that they had seen things in the sky (*que viam coisas no céu*).

He did not hear the clap of thunder (*o estrondo*) in August. He heard say many times that a small cloud of smoke (*fumosinho*) appeared." (For all these sworn reports see *Interrogatórios oficiais de Manuel Pedro*, etc.)

2. Most books and pamphlets written thus far in the English language do not mention this important phenomenon. However, the best sources do describe it. Da Fonseca's *Le Meraviglie di Fátima* mentions it: *Presto tuttavia si* [the people] *fermarono, osservando le nubi che ad un tratto apparvero colorate dei brillanti colori dell'arcobaleno, tanto che 'le foglie degli alberi sembravano fiori'. A tale spettacolo molti, dicendo che era miracolo della Madonna, si misero a pregare* (p. 40). His Portuguese *Nossa Senhora da Fátima* carries the same text on page 65. Father De Marchi quotes the descriptions of two eyewitnesses, Maria Carreira (already cited in abbreviated and incomplete form), and Manuel Gonçalves Júnior (pp. 112 and 148, respectively). According to Father McGlynn, Lúcia's sister Teresa, in August, saw "colored light like a rainbow on the ground," and her sister Maria dos Anjos on the same occasion saw "clouds around the sun reflecting different colors on the people" (*Vision of Fátima*, pp. 44 and 49). They both also mention seeing "falling flowers" in August. This is the first time we have heard of these "flowers" in August. We believe that Teresa and Maria are confusing August with September. Their appraisal of the small numbers present at the apparitions preceding that of October are also at variance with all books and with the explicit testimony of Sister Lúcia and other witnesses considered most reliable. Father McGlynn quotes Sister Lúcia as saying to him: "In June there was only a group, not a crowd; at the other apparitions the whole place was full of people, lined up from the Cova to Aljustrel. From the third apparition on there were tremendous crowds. It was hard to make one's way through them" (*Vision of Fátima*, p. 97). In the 1924 canonical inquiry Lúcia says that one of the arguments used by the Tinsmith to try and entice them to go to the Cova in his carriage was that in this way "they would be unmolested by the people" (*livres do povo*) (*Interrogatório oficial de Lúcia*, p. 6). And in the 1923 canonical inquiry Maria Rosa states that when Lúcia returned with the flock on August 13 [around ten o'clock] "the house was already filled with people"; and Maria Carreira affirms: "In August many people came" (*Interrogatórios oficiais de Manuel Pedro*, etc.).

3. The facts concerning the infuriated mob and Manuel Pedro's efforts to pacify it are taken from reports by Maria Carreira and Manuel Pedro Marto (De Marchi, *Era uma Senhora*, p. 112).

4. Here is an extract from a letter written by an "eyewitness" and

quoted by Da Fonseca: "I and some friends had started off soon for the town of Fátima . . . Shortly afterward some men came. They were very pleased, saying that Our Lady had appeared. I went with great haste to the place of the apparitions. The roads were already filled with people who were commenting on the prodigious fact (*o assombroso facto*). All were unanimous in affirming that they had heard a clap of thunder (*um trovão*) and had seen near the carrasqueira a flash of lightning and a very beautiful cloud (*uma nuvem formosíssima*) which rose in the air and disappeared in a short while. In a word, all had been satisfied . . ." (Portuguese ed., pp. 64–65). This report is strikingly similar to that of Manuel Pedro Marto quoted above.

5. Notwithstanding the tone of this letter, which was actually published, all authors agree that the pastor did not believe in the apparitions. If the letter is read carefully, it will be found that it does not contain one single explicit affirmation of belief in the reality of the apparitions. It was carefully worded, because of the explosive nature of the situation, so as not to indicate his disbelief.

The letter has been translated literally and in its entirety (except for a few lines) from the Portuguese text, which can be found in *Fátima à prova* (Leiria: Gráfica, 1946), pp. 52–54, by Canon José Galamba de Oliveira, and in De Marchi, p. 112, footnote 1.

13   PRISON AND BOILING OIL

1. In the 1923 canonical inquiry Lúcia's mother affirms that Jacinta's brothers went by bicycle to Vila Nova de Ourém to find out what was happening. They saw the children playing on the veranda of the Administrator's house and learned that they were being well treated (*Interrogatórios oficiais de Manuel Pedro*, etc.).

2. Those are Lúcia's own words: *ele dizia-me com imensa paz e alegria* (*Memoir IV*, p. 20).

3. Most, if not all books, place this scene before the ordeal of the boiling oil. But this does not seem to be in accordance with Lúcia's *Memoirs*, for she writes: "When, after having separated us [the only separation recorded is the one that occurred when they were taken individually to be dipped in boiling oil], they brought us together in a room of the jail, saying that in a short while they were coming to get us in order to fry us, Jacinta withdrew to a window that opens on the cattle market" (Canon José Galamba de Oliveira, *Jacinta*, Leiria: Gráfica, 1946, p. 109).

The prison in which the children were placed was located at that time in the town hall (*os Paços do Concelho*). All the interviews with the Administrator (except those that occurred in his own residence), including the affair of the boiling oil just described, took place in this same building. Today the Vila Nova de Ourém prison is in another location. (De Oliveira, *Jacinta*, p. 109, note 1)

4. I met the Administrator, o Senhor Artur de Oliveira Santos, at Vila Nova de Ourém on Sunday, July 30, 1950. By way of self-introduction he said: "I am a Christian but don't go to Mass or confession." With him and another man, member of the actual district administration, I visited the town hall where the three children of Fátima had suffered so much. The Tinsmith pointed out his old office where he had questioned the children (and their parents too, on August 11). But he would not admit having put the seers in prison. Indeed, he always quickly diverted the conversation whenever the topic of the prison was mentioned. However, the government agent, seeing my interest in the matter, took me alone and showed the room—directly across the hall from the Tinsmith's old office—which was used as a prison in 1917.

While in his old office, which is still being used by the actual district administration, the Tinsmith pointed to a recent copy of an Ourém newspaper which was on a desk. On the front page it carried a short article he had written. The article was signed *João de Ourém*, "John of Ourém."

By the man's face, which carried a two-day beard, his shabby suit, and neglected-looking house, for which he felt obliged to apologize, I gathered that he was not very prosperous.

I took several pictures of the Tinsmith, both in black-and-white and in color. He asked me to send him some of the pictures and gave me a Lisboa address for that purpose. What he does in Lisboa, I do not know. I talked with him for about thirty minutes. In the course of this time, he rode with me in a taxi from the town hall to his own home, the same home where the children slept and ate when he kidnapped them. I did not go into his house, but he entered it and returned with two pictures that he showed me. When he talked, it was with an affected air of grandeur, and I could not help feeling sorry for the poor fellow, who seems to live in the past, when he was really somebody. People told me that I was extremely fortunate in finding the man so friendly and communicative, because as a rule he absolutely refuses to talk of the Fátima events to anyone, and he refuses with equal firmness to pose for pictures. Incidentally, he said that he was known all over the world "and in Russia too."

On November 5, 1962, *The North American Voice of Fátima* published an article, "The Sad Story of Arturo dos Santos," which stated that "he died a lonely and embittered man on June 17, 1955, without the Sacraments, without Christian burial." May God rest his soul.

14 THE HEAVENLY LADY WON'T BE DENIED

1. The pastor, in his 1919 report (p. 10), and Manuel Pedro, Olímpia, Maria Rosa, and Maria Carreira, in the 1923 canonical inquiry, all explicitly mention August 19 as the date of this apparition. Maria dos Anjos, Lúcia's oldest sister, gave this same date to Father McGlynn (*Vision of Fátima*, p. 49), and Teresa told me in July 1950 that she saw colored lights on August 19 as well as August 13. However, Lúcia has always claimed that this apparition occurred on the same day that she returned from her captivity at Ourém. See the 1924 canonical inquiry, *Interrogatório oficial de Lúcia*, p. 7, and *Memoir IV*, p. 20, and especially p. 76, where she says: "It could be that I am the one who is mistaken, but I still think (*conservo a idéia*) that it was on the same day on which we returned from Vila Nova de Ourém."

2. This text is slightly different from the one that appeared in the book when it was first printed. It is one of the most important of several changes that have been made at the suggestion of Fátima specialists who have been kind enough to write the author. This present change was occasioned by a letter from Father Luis Gonzaga da Fonseca, to whom we had sent a copy of the book. Our original text read: "If they had not taken you to the town [*aldeia*, popular designation for Vila Nova de Ourém] the miracle would have been more grandiose."

This original text was adopted because it is found in both Da Fonseca (Portuguese ed., p. 78; Italian ed., p. 46) and De Marchi (p. 127). We had attempted to find the source of this text, but without success. The only bit of historical evidence that we had encountered had been a confusing statement by Jacinta. On November 2, 1917, questioned by Dr. Formigão concerning Our Lady's August message, the child replied: "She said that if they had not taken us to Ourém, Saint Joseph would have come with the Child Jesus to give peace to the world. And Our Lady of the Rosary would have come with two little angels, one on each side" (De Marchi, *Era uma Senhora*, p. 191). As Father Da Fonseca remarked in his letter: "[Jacinta's reply] is not clear and one cannot tell whether she is speaking of the missed apparition (August 13) or the last one [October 13]." Indeed, on October 13, Saint Joseph and the Child Jesus did appear near the sun and both blessed the world. But Our Lady was never accompanied by angels on that day.

Father Da Fonseca explains that he had based himself originally on some document which he no longer recalls. But since then he consulted the pastor's report of 1919 and found the following text, which he considers the true one: ". . . if they had not taken you to the town [Vila Nova de Ourém] the miracle would be better known" *se nao tivessem abalado contigo para à aldeia* [Vila Nova de Ourém] *o milagre seria mais conhecido*. This statement was made by Lúcia to her pastor and incorporated by him in the report mentioned above. We also consulted this report but must confess that this important detail escaped our attention. We are very grateful to Father Da Fonseca for this information, which would seem to explain the mysterious silence that shrouded Fátima from 1917 to World War Two.

3. *Com São José viria o Menino Jesus dar a bencão ao mundo (Interrogatório oficial de Lúcia,* p. 8). In this text Lúcia definitely says "bless the world" and not "give peace to the world," as so many books have it.

4. *Nosso Senhor viria dar a paz ao mundo (Interrogatório oficial de Lúcia,* p. 8). It is here that Lúcia—at least in the 1924 canonical inquiry—uses the expression "give peace to the world." According to Maria Rosa, Lúcia said that Our Lady told her "the soldiers would return from the war" *haviam de vir da guerra (Interrogatórios oficiais de Manuel Pedro,* etc.).

The three last statements, which we have incorporated into this part of Our Lady's August 19 message and which follow the words "In the last month, I will perform a miracle so that all may believe," are not found anywhere in Sister Lúcia's *Memoirs*. However, there is serious reason to believe they are authentic, since they are found in early and highly reliable documents, as we have indicated in this footnote and in the two preceding ones.

A fourth statement, "Our Lady of the Rosary and Our Lady of Sorrows will also come," was carried in the first editions of this book but has been eliminated in the present one because we have not been able to track down its source.

5. These biers (*andores*) seem to allude to small biers that were used in certain regions of Portugal, including Fátima, for the purpose of "collecting and carrying offerings in money and natural produce, with which the faithful contribute to the expenses of feast days" (Da Fonseca, *Nossa Senhora da Fátima,* p. 79, footnote 1).

In *Memoir IV,* p. 77, Sister Lúcia states: "The money on the biers is for the feast of Our Lady of the Rosary and that which remains is to help toward a chapel which should be ordered built." As Lúcia's statements in the pastor's 1919 report and in the 1924 canonical inquiry do not mention using the remainder of the money for the construction of a chapel, it would seem that she has confused facts, attributing this detail to the August 19 apparition, whereas in reality it belongs with the September 13 one. Indeed, Maria Carreira, in her report during the 1923 canonical inquiry, says: ". . . Our Lady said [on August 19] that two biers should be made and that they should be carried to Our Lady of the Rosary at the church [this undoubtedly alludes to the statue of Our Lady of Joy, *Nossa Senhora dos Prazeres*, called Our Lady of the Rosary by the people and located in the parish church]. Many people were sorry that the money was not applied to making something at the spot of the apparitions and they told Lúcia to request authorization to build a little chapel (*uma ermida*) at that place. The Lady granted that authorization on September 13, but with the stipulation that half of the existing money be given to Our Lady of the Rosary of Fátima" (*Interrogatórios oficiais de Manuel Pedro*, etc.). And Lúcia herself, reporting on the September 13 apparition in the 1924 canonical inquiry affirms: "At the request of Maria do Rosário [Carreira] I asked if she wanted a little chapel [*capelinha*] built there and she requested that a little chapel be built there in honor of Our Lady of the Rosary" (*Interrogatório oficial de Lúcia*, pp. 8–9). Maria Carreira's and Lúcia's statements concerning the September 13 apparition make it clear that on August 19 Our Lady could not have mentioned using part of the money on the biers for a chapel.

6. In the 1924 canonical inquiry Lúcia always uses the expression "within a year," *dentro dum ano*, whereas in *Memoir IV*, written in 1941, she says "within the year," *durante o ano*.

7. We are fortunate in having Maria Rosa's own account of this important event in the 1923 canonical inquiry: "The mother took the branch and noticed that it smelled very nice (*notou che cheirava muito bem*). The smell could not be compared with any other smell. She was an unbeliever but was slightly shaken and became slightly more convinced (*Ella era descrente e ficou um pouco quebrada, um pouco mais convencida*)" (*Interrogatórios oficiais de Manuel Pedro*, etc.).

We have it, then, on Maria Rosa's own admission, that this incident of the odoriferous branch produced in her soul the first hesitant beginnings of belief in the apparitions. As shall be seen, a similar incident occurred on October 13 to somewhat strengthen this incipient faith. However, it was only several years later that firm belief in the apparitions came to the good woman.

The details of this branch episode have been taken from reports of it made by Maria dos Anjos (De Marchi, pp. 128–29, and McGlynn, pp. 49–50).

8. This information about Lúcia's godmother's experience was given to Father McGlynn by Maria dos Anjos (*Vision of Fátima*, pp. 50–51).

1. These last two dramatic paragraphs are taken almost verbatim from *Memoir IV*, pp. 78–79. Other excellent witnesses have also insisted on the very gripping spectacle presented by the multitude at the Cova on September 13.

2. Da Fonseca mentions these extraordinary phenomena (*Nossa Senhora da Fátima*, pp. 85 and 91), and so does De Marchi (p. 137).

3. *Em Outubro virá tambem Nosso Senhor, Nossa Senhora das Dôres, e do Carmo, S. José com o Menino Jesus para abençoarem o mundo* (Sister Lúcia, *Memoir IV*, p. 80).

4. We have included in this reply information not usually found in accounts of this apparition. It was taken from the interrogatories made by Dr. Formigão on September 27 and October 11, 1917.

On September 27 he asked Lúcia: "What did the Lady say should be done with the money that the people place at the foot of the Cova da Iria holm oak?" She replied: "She said that we should place it on two biers. Jacinta and I and two other girls are to carry one, and Francisco and three other boys, the other, to the parish church. One part of this money should be used for the cult and feast of the Lady of the Rosary and the other part to help build a new chapel."

Then on October 11 he questioned her again about this in the presence of four accredited witnesses: "You told me a few days ago that Our Lady wanted the money offered by the people taken to the parish church on two biers. How are they to acquire the biers and when should they be taken to the church?" Lúcia answered: "The biers are to be purchased with the money offered and should be carried during the festivities in honor of the Lady of the Rosary." (Translations by the author from De Marchi's Portuguese text, pp. 145 and 149.)

5. Manuel Pedro Marto gave the following testimony in the 1923 canonical inquiry: "He stood at a little distance from the children. He saw nothing and heard nothing, but heard that some people had seen extraordinary things in the atmosphere (*na atmosphera*)."

In the same inquiry, Olímpia Marto reports that she went to the Cova da Iria on September 13 with her sister-in-law. But as already stated above, Maria Rosa affirms—always in this same inquiry—that she was told by the pastor not to go to the Cova da Iria and that the only time she went was in October (because she feared the children might be put to death). Here is Olímpia's testimony as reported in this 1923 inquiry: ". . . They stayed on the slope of the hill: not wanting to be seen, they did not go to the foot of the tree. When the people shouted that they saw signs, they did not understand what they said, but they thought they saw a small cloud of smoke rise through the crowd at the foot of the tree of the apparitions (*paraceu-lhes vêr um fumosinho subir do meio do povo ao pé da azinheira*)" (*Interrogatórios oficiais de Manuel Pedro*, etc.).

6. All facts relating to Father Quaresma and his clerical friend used in this chapter are strictly historical and are taken from a long letter which the former, who eventually became Vicar General of the Leiria diocese, wrote. For the text of the letter see De Marchi, pp. 135–36, and Da Fonseca, *Nossa Senhora da Fátima*, pp. 88–89.

7. A fact that deserves to be emphasized is the difference in the experiences of the various spectators. Some people saw certain prodigies, while others did not see them. Some observed certain phenomena for a long while, whereas others only witnessed them for a short duration of time.

What about this diversity? Does it not destroy the value of these people's testimony? No. On the contrary, it increases it. The very diversity of the experiences reported is the best argument there is in favor of their objectivity. It completely refutes the theory circulated by the anticlericals according to which all these extraordinary phenomena were the result of collective hallucination. Indeed, if these prodigies that the spectators claimed to have observed were purely subjective, the imaginary product of mob suggestion, then why was it that only some and not everyone observed them? Especially, how explain that some of those who witnessed nothing or next to nothing were among the most anxious and therefore among the best-disposed subjectively to see everything. Father Quaresma mentions a pious woman standing near him who cried bitterly because she was not fortunate enough to see anything. Also, the mysterious shower of shiny globules was actually photographed when it occurred again at a later date.

The fact is, the Lady from heaven judged her message so important that she did not wait until October 13 to give concrete proof of her presence at the Cova da Iria.

16   THE LAST VISIT OVER THE CARRASQUEIRA TREE

1. See Maria Rosa's testimony concerning the October apparition in the 1923 canonical inquiry (*Interrogatórios oficiais de Manuel Pedro*, etc.).

2. Dr. Almeida Garret of the University of Coimbra, who was present at the Cova on this day, estimated the crowd at over a hundred thousand (De Marchi, p. 160).

3. . . . *levada por um movimento interior* (Sister Lúcia, *Memoir IV*, p. 81).

4. This incident of the priest is told by Maria Carreira (De Marchi, pp. 161–62).

5. According to Maria Rosa's testimony in the 1923 canonical inquiry: ". . . she noticed the same odor of the Valinhos branch when her daughter said: 'She is already here!' (*notou o mesmo cheiro do raminho dos Valinhos, quando a filha disse: 'Já cá está!'*)" (*Interrogatórios oficiais de Manuel Pedro*, etc.).

The simple fact that Maria Rosa reported these "odor" incidents in the canonical inquiry (p. 156, note 7) shows what an impression they made upon her. Yet, they did not generate full faith in the apparitions. Even the miracle of the dancing sun, which she admits witnessing (in the same canonical inquiry she says she "saw the sun move back and down three times," *viu o sol trez vezez a desandar e a descer*), did not completely convince her.

During a conversation we had with her in July 1950, Maria dos Anjos confirmed all these facts concerning her mother. She affirmed that her mother had been very much impressed by the two aroma episodes and that on October 13 she smelled the fragrant odor during the whole apparition, from the time Lúcia cried that the Lady was coming to the moment she shouted that she was leaving.

Maria dos Anjos also told us that her mother continued to have returning doubts concerning the apparitions even after October 13. When asked to explain her mother's lack of firm belief after all this evidence, she replied that her mother did not think her family was worthy of such a great favor as visits from the Blessed Virgin. Neither Maria dos Anjos nor her younger sister, Teresa, could give the author any definite answer as to when their mother had definitely and permanently believed in the apparitions. But in 1948 Olímpia Marto told him that Maria Rosa had come to believe in the apparitions a few years before she died, in 1942. Olímpia's own slowness in fully accepting the apparitions seems also to have been due in great part to her humility and the feeling that her family was not worthy of heavenly visits. It must be remembered that the wine-loving Antônio Marto was her brother.

6. These facts about the nudging and sighing are told by Olímpia Marto in the 1923 canonical inquiry. She places them during the October 13 apparition (*Interrogatórios oficiais de Manuel Pedro*, etc.).

7. Here are Lúcia's words as reported in *Memoir IV*, p. 81: *Que continuem sempre a rezar o terço todos os dias.*

8. *A guerra vai acabar e os militares voltarão em breve para suas casas.* These are the words used by Sister Lúcia in *Memoir IV*, p. 81. However, in other documents, as in the 1924 canonical inquiry, Lúcia reports Our Lady's prophecy differently. Jacinta's version of this prediction also dif-

fers from the one above. The divergency in these various reports has caused considerable discussion. In their relation of the October 13 apparition, both De Marchi (p. 165) and Da Fonseca (Portuguese, p. 116) adopt the above report of *Memoir IV*, p. 81, as we have done. This question is studied at some length by De Marchi (pp. 183–89, especially pp. 188 and 189).

9. Sister Lúcia has stressed this important fact in these words: "The words of this apparition which engraved themselves most in my memory —*que mais se me gravaram no coração*—were the request of our most holy heavenly Mother: 'People must not offend Our Lord anymore, for He is already greatly offended'" (Da Fonseca, *Nossa Senhora da Fátima*, p. 117, note 1). This fact is not astonishing, since these words indicate the ultimate purpose for which Our Lady came: to lead her erring children of the earth back to God and the observance of His commandments.

17   THE SUN DANCES

1. "Saint Joseph and the Child Jesus seemed to be blessing the world with gestures that they were making with their hand in the form of a cross" (Sister Lúcia, *Memoir IV*, p. 82).

2. Apparently Lúcia did not clearly see Our Lord bless the people. On October 13, 1917, she said to Dr. Formigão: "Our Lord also appeared blessing the people . . ." But on October 19, when asked directly by the priest if she saw Our Lord bless the people, she answered: "I did not, but Our Lady had said that Our Lord would come and bless the people" (De Marchi, pp. 176 and 186).

The reason for this vagueness is given by Lúcia in the 1924 canonical inquiry at the point where she explains why she only "had an idea" that the "man" with the Child Jesus was Saint Joseph: "There was such a great glare that we could not see at will (*Estava un resplendor tão grande que não nos deixava ver à vontade*)." Yet, in this same document she says unhesitatingly: "Our Lord was making various signs of the cross (*Nosso Senhor fazia varias cruzes*)" (*Interrogatório oficial de Lúcia*, p. 10).

3. There is a lack of definiteness and precision that runs all through the seers' description of the scenes observed in the sky beside the sun. This is due to the fact that the vision was one of light similar to the visions of the Lady over the carrasqueira tree. When asked to give details of this series of apparitions or tableaux beside the sun, Sister Lúcia replied to Father McGlynn, her interrogator: "The changes which took place were all changes of light. I can't explain" (*Vision of Fátima*, p. 96).

The apparition of Our Lady of Mount Carmel is the most controverted of this series that took place near the sun. When asked by Dr. Formigão on October 13, 1917: "What do you mean by that—Our Lady appeared in two ways (*dos dois naipes*)?" Lúcia replied: "The Lady appeared dressed as the Lady of Sorrows but without the sword in her heart, and she appeared dressed I don't know exactly how (*não sei bem como*) but it seems to me that it was the Lady of Carmel." A little later in the same questioning period Dr. Formigão reverted to this topic and asked: "Why did you say that the Lady, one of these times, appeared to you to be dressed as the Lady of Carmel?" And Lúcia answered: "Because she had some things hanging from her hand (*Porque tinha umas coisas penduradas na mão*)" (De Marchi, pp. 176 and 177). Lúcia describes this tableau in practically the same terms in the 1924 canonical inquiry: "It seems to me that I saw still another figure that appeared to be Our Lady of Carmel, because she had something hanging in her right hand (*porque tinha qualquer cousa pendurada na mão direita*)" (*Interrogatório oficial de Lúcia*, p. 10).

4. Some witnesses mention "all the colors of the rainbow" in a general way, but the only colors that the author has ever seen explicitly mentioned are red, violet, blue, yellow, gray, and white.

5. Bishop Fulton J. Sheen saw in the falling sun (filled with atomic energy) which suddenly stopped in its downward flight, as it seemed on the point of crushing the people at the Cova da Iria, a possible symbol of Our Lady's intervention to halt the fall of atomic bombs at a moment when it appears they are about to destroy the world. (See the magazine *Soul*, March–April 1950, pp. 3–4, "The Vision in the Heavens," by Bishop Fulton J. Sheen, D.D., published by Ave Maria Institute, Washington, New Jersey.)

6. It is the author's opinion, one arrived at after close scrutiny of numerous eyewitness reports, that those who saw the miracle, whether at the Cova da Iria or at other places miles away from the Cova, all actually contemplated or experienced the same phenomena. But, because of varying capacities in their powers of observation and especially of remembering, and also because of the very nature of the miracle, which easily lent itself to various descriptions or interpretations, the witnesses described the dancing sun in such different ways that one is at first led to believe that they did not all see or experience exactly the same thing, that there were objective differences in what the different people observed. Though the author does not think that there were any objective differences, it is certain that there were many quantitative differences in the experiences of the various spectators. Some saw more of the miracle than others: some witnessed all of it, others more or less numerous parts of it. Father McGlynn even reports that one woman did

not see the sun at all, the only extraordinary thing remarked by her being the sudden stopping of the rain (*Vision of Fátima*, p. 185). But, on the other hand, we have numerous newspaper accounts written by reporters who were present at the Cova da Iria at the time of the miracle. Some of their reports, even those published by the liberal papers, go into considerable detail in describing the great miracle. In fact, the author has borrowed considerably from these newspaper reports in his own description of the miracle of the sun. We also have excellent pictures that appeared in Portuguese publications at the time of the apparitions. Such are the pictures that figure in this book and that show the people at the Cova da Iria looking at the miracle of the sun on October 13, 1917. They are photostatic copies of pictures that appeared in the magazine *Ilustração Portugueza*, for October 29, 1917. The author expresses his gratitude here to the newspaper *O Século* for allowing him to reprint them.

In regard to the differences in the amount of the miracle experienced by different people, this can be explained by differences in the spiritual needs of these same persons, or by the varied dispositions of their hearts.

The above remarks would seem to apply also to all of the miraculous (beyond the ordinary laws of nature) phenomena observed by the bystanders during any of the various apparitions, for example, to the globe of light that seemed to serve as the Lady's heavenly chariot, and to the shower of petals or luminous globules that melted into nothingness on reaching the earth, etc.

Father C. C. Martindale, S.J., has a detailed discussion of the dance of the sun in his book "*The Message of Fátima*" (London: Burns, Oates & Washbourne, Ltd., 1950). This book was published in the United States under the title of *The Meaning of Fátima* (New York: P. J. Kenedy & Sons, 1951).

7. He later became a priest and went as a missionary to India. The facts related here are based on a report that Father Pereira made in a letter written at the request of His Excellency Antônio M. Teixeira, who at that time was Bishop of Meliapor. Both Father Da Fonseca (Portuguese, pp. 125–27) and Father De Marchi (pp. 173–74) quote extracts from the letter. Moreover, Father De Marchi states that he personally verified the report by questioning several persons from Alburitel, among whom was the schoolteacher alluded to in the text, D. Delfina Pereira Lopes (p. 173). And the author, in July 1950, spoke with Father Pereira's brother Joaquim, also a priest, who had recently returned to Leiria from India. He too had seen the miracle of the sun at Alburitel and remembered well the play of colors, red, pink, and yellow, on the houses. He recalled especially a certain yellow. He saw

the sun shake and zigzag toward the earth. People thought it was the end of the world and prepared for death by asking forgiveness for their sins. When it was over, they were all convinced they had witnessed a miracle.

8. This woman's cure was complete and permanent. The description of her ailment and its gradual cure as described in the text is historically accurate (Da Fonseca, Italian, pp. 71–72).

19 ALONE

1. The author received this information in 1950 from Canon José Galamba de Oliveira, who obtained it directly from Sister Lúcia herself in 1946. The Sister gave this information in reply to the question whether Our Lady had really said: "Afterward, I will return here a seventh time." (Early accounts of the apparitions did not carry this statement.) She assured the Canon that Our Lady had said these words and then went on to tell where the seventh apparition had occurred, etc., as related above.

2. Antero de Figueiredo, in his excellent book *Fátima-Graças-Segrêdos-Mistérios*, asserts that doubts involving the apparitions began to assail Lúcia while she was at O Asilo de Vilar and that they later recurred during her postulancy and novitiate at Túy. He says that at both places she suffered considerably because of her erroneous belief that she could not reveal who she really was or mention the Fátima apparitions to her confessor (Fourteenth ed., Lisboa: Livraria Bertrand, 1945, pp. 125–41).

20 APPROVAL AT LAST!

1. *Vision of Fátima* (Boston: Little, Brown & Company, 1948), p. 97.

2. *Fátima, Merveille Inouie,* by Canon C. Barthas and Father L. G. da Fonseca, S.J. (new ed., 1943, pp. 237–38), and *More About Fátima and the Immaculate Heart of Mary,* by the Reverend V. Montes de Oca, C.S. Sp. (Baltimore: Newman Bookshop, 1947, pp. 32 and 46; the book also carries a copy of the May 13, 1924, photo, opposite p. 65), which is a translation of *Le Prodige Inouï de Fátima,* by the Reverend J. da Cruz, C.S. Sp. (who writes under the pen name of J. Castelbranco).

21 THE ATTITUDE OF ROME

1. The European Pilgrim Virgin statue was in a chapel close to the Vatican at the time the Pope witnessed the renewed Fátima miracle of the sun.

2. "The Conversion of Islam and Russia," by the Most Reverend Fulton J. Sheen, D.D., *The Scapular,* January–February 1952, pp. 9–11.

22 THE CONVERSION OF RUSSIA AND PEACE

1. The Most Reverend Finbar Ryan, O.P., *Our Lady of Fátima* (Dublin: Browne and Noland, Ltd., 1948), pp. 178–79.

2. This information concerning the lack of a date on the letter and when it was received is from Father Joaquin Maria Alonso, C.F.M., in *A Heart for All* (Washington, N.J.: AMI Press), p. 47.

3. *A Heart for All* was published by AMI Press, Washington, New Jersey. It was also published in French, German, Portuguese, Spanish, and Italian. *The Immaculate Heart of Mary in the Apparitions of Fátima* is the translation of the title in all foreign-language editions. It appears as a subtitle in the English-language edition.

4. Since Father Martins' book appeared, Sister Lúcia's complete *Memoirs* have been published, but without the letters and documents of his work, in at least three languages, Spanish (1974), Portuguese (Second ed., May 1977), and English. The English text has been published by two sources. The Blue Army book entitled *Lúcia Speaks* (Washington, N.J.: AMI Press), in addition to the complete text of the four *Memoirs*, has other interesting material, including a considerable number of letters of Lúcia to her confessor, Father José Bernardo Gonçalves, S.J., that bear the message of Fátima. The other English text, *Fátima in Lucia's Own Words*, has only the four *Memoirs*. It was edited by Father Louis Konder, S.V.D. (Fátima: Postulation Center).

23 OBTAINING THE CONSECRATION OF RUSSIA

1. See *A Heart for All*, p. 103. According to the text printed in this edition of the book, the Bishop transmitted to the Pope "the desire of Our Lord for a public and solemn act of reparation and for the consecration of Russia to the Most Holy Hearts of Jesus and Mary, in order to approve and to recommend the practice of the reparative devotion [of the first Saturday of the month]."

2. The octave of the Assumption has now been suppressed. Also, the Feast of the Immaculate Heart of Mary has been reduced in rank to an Optional Memorial and it is presently celebrated on the Saturday after the Feast of the Sacred Heart of Jesus.

3. *A Heart for All*, p. 62.

24 MAY 13, 1982

1. The Blue Army's decision for a public grass-roots campaign for the collegial consecration had been preceded by the efforts of another Marian organization, Maximilian Kolbe's Knights of the Immaculata, which initiated a campaign for signatures from its headquarters in Marytown, Libertyville, Illinois.

2. Reported in the Vatican newspaper, *L'Osservatore Romano*, October 12, 1981.

3. The article is entitled "Was Russian Behind Attempt on Pope's Life?" and is found on page 3. Mr. Haffert has been the driving force behind The Blue Army and the person mainly responsible for its many marvelous achievements. His recent book, *Dear Bishop!—Memoirs of the Author Concerning the History of The Blue Army*, was published in 1982 by AMI International Press, Washington, New Jersey.

4. This was the second manifestation that the American bishops had made within a relatively short time of their love and awareness of the importance of the mother of Jesus in God's plan for the salvation of mankind. On November 21, 1973, the National Conference of Catholic Bishops had issued a comprehensive and lengthy Pastoral Letter entitled *Behold Your Mother—Woman of Faith*.

5. This rather long homily is so important that it is reproduced in its entirety in Appendix B.

6. The last three paragraphs of the Pope's talk were a prayer to Our Lady that "the hostilities that now divide two great countries in the waters of the South Atlantic may cease" and that "my projected pastoral visit to Great Britain may be happily accomplished."

APPENDIX A

1. The two accounts are identical except for the fact that *Memoir III* does not have the phrase "In Portugal, the dogma of Faith will always be preserved."

2. We saw that the First Saturday Communions of reparation were published before this by the Bishop of Leiria in September 1939.

3. *Memoir III*, p. 12.

4. See *Vision of Fátima*, pp. 90–91.

5. All the circumstances of the writing of this part of the secret, starting with Sister Lúcia's pleurisy in early June 1943, are told in great detail by the late Mariologist and Fátima expert, Joaquin Maria Alonso, in *La Verdad Sobre el Secreto de Fátima* (Madrid: Publicaciones Claretianas, 1976), pp. 29–36.

6. See April Oursler Armstrong and Martin F. Armstrong, Jr., *Fátima: Pilgrimage to Peace* (Garden City, N.Y.: Hanover House, 1954), pp. 104–5.

7. *La Verdad*, pp. 36–44.

ABOUT THE AUTHOR

Father Joseph Pelletier is the author of two authoritative books on the Fátima apparitions, *The Sun Danced at Fátima* (1951) and *Fátima, Hope of the World* (1954).

A native of Winchendon, Massachusetts, Father Pelletier graduated from Assumption College in 1932. After a year at the Assumption novitiate he went to Rome to pursue his theological studies. He received a licentiate in Sacred Theology from the Pontifical Institute Angelicum and then returned to his alma mater. He obtained a master's degree in Sociology from Boston College in 1947. He served as Dean of Men at Assumption College from 1948 to 1953.

Since retiring from teaching in 1974, he has devoted his time to writing and research on religious subjects.